World War II
Primary Sources

12/01

World War II
Primary Sources

Barbara C. Bigelow
Edited by Christine Slovey

REF
940.53
BIG

AN IMPRINT OF THE GALE GROUP

DETROIT · SAN FRANCISCO · LONDON
BOSTON · WOODBRIDGE, CT

Barbara C. Bigelow

Staff

Christine Slovey, *U•X•L Editor*
Carol DeKane Nagel, *U•X•L Managing Editor*
Tom Romig, *U•X•L Publisher*

Rita Wimberley, *Senior Buyer*
Dorothy Maki, *Manufacturing Manager*
Evi Seoud, *Assistant Production Manager*
Mary Beth Trimper, *Production Director*

Margaret A. Chamberlain, *Permissions Specialist*

Eric Johnson and Martha Schiebold, *Cover Art Directors*
Pamela A.E. Galbreath, *Page Art Director*
Cynthia Baldwin, *Product Design Manager*
Barbara J. Yarrow, *Graphic Services Supervisor*

Linda Mahoney, LM Design, *Typesetting*

Laura Exner, XNR Productions, Inc., *Cartographer*

Front cover photographs reproduced by permission of Corbis and Corbis/Dean Wong.

Library of Congress Cataloging-in-Publication Data

World War II: primary sources / [compiled by] Barbara C. Bigelow ; Christine Slovey, editor.

p.   cm.

Includes bibliographical references and index.

Summary: Presents fifteen excerpts from primary sources related to World War II, including speeches, diary entries, newspaper accounts, novels, poems, and memoirs.

ISBN 0-7876-3896-X

1. World War, 1939-1945 Sources Juvenile literature.   [1. World War, 1939-1945 Sources.] I. Bigelow, Barbara C. II. Slovey, Christine. III.Title: World War 2. IV. Title: World War Two.

D743.7.W68   1999
940.53-dc21

99-36179
CIP

This publication is a creative work copyrighted by U•X•L and fully protected by all applicable copyright laws, as well as by misappropriation, trade secret, unfair competition, and other applicable laws. The author and editors of this work have added value to the underlying factual material herein through one or more of the following: unique and original selection, coordination, expression, arrangement, and classification of the information. All rights to this publication will be vigorously defended.

Copyright © 2000   U•X•L, an imprint of The Gale Group

All rights reserved, including the right of reproduction in whole or in part in any form.

Printed in the United States of America

10 9 8 7 6 5 4 3

Contents

Advisory Board ix

Reader's Guide xi

Timeline xv

Words to Know xxxiii

Winston Churchill
*(Reproduced by permission of
the Library of Congress)*

Primary Sources

Intensification 1

  Winston Churchill 5

    "Blood, Toil, Tears, and Sweat" 10

    "Be Ye Men of Valour" 11

    "Their Finest Hour" 13

    Winston Churchill (box) 14

  Winston Churchill and Franklin D. Roosevelt . . . 21

    Franklin D. Roosevelt (box) 24

    The Atlantic Charter 26

A young Japanese American girl awaits relocation.
(Courtesy of the National Archives and Records Administration)

Adolf Hitler 31
"Hitler's Order of the Day to the German
Troops on the Eastern Front" 34
Adolf Hitler (box). 35
Joseph Stalin (box) 38

Herbert A. Werner 43
*Iron Coffins: A Personal Account of the
German U-Boat Battles of World War II* 48

Franklin D. Roosevelt 59
"A Date Which Will Live in Infamy" 62
Hideki Tojo (box). 66

Home Front 69

Catherine "Renee" Young Pike 71
*Since You Went Away: World War II
Letters from American Women
on the Home Front* 74

Jerry Stanley 85
*I Am an American: A True Story
of Japanese Internment* 89

The Human Cost 97

Ruth Minsky Sender 101
The Cage 105
Ruth Minsky Sender (box) 109

Harry S. Truman 117
Comments on the Manhattan Project
from *Memoirs by Harry S. Truman*
Volume 1: *Year of Decisions* 120
Harry S. Truman (box) 122

Rodney Barker 129
*The Hiroshima Maidens: A Story of Courage,
Compassion, and Survival* 133

Ernie Pyle 143
"Notes from a Battered Country" 147
"The Death of Captain Waskow" 147
Ernie Pyle (box) 149
"I Thought It Was the End" 151

"Waiting for Tomorrow" 152
"On Victory in Europe" 155

World War II Nurses 159
No Time for Fear: Voices of American
Military Nurses in World War II 161

Breakthrough 171

Veterans of D-Day 173
Voices of D-Day: The Story of the Allied
Invasion Told By Those Who Were There 177

Stephen E. Ambrose 187
Citizen Soldiers: The U.S. Army from
the Normandy Beaches to the Bulge
to the Surrender of Germany 188

E. B. Sledge 197
E. B. Sledge (box) 198
With the Old Breed at Peleliu and Okinawa 199

Harry S. Truman 211
Truman's Statement on the
German Surrender. 214
Truman's Statement on the
Japanese Surrender 215
Douglas MacArthur (box) 218

Text Credits xxxiii

Index xxxv

Advisory Board

Special thanks are due to U•X•L's World War II Reference Library advisors for their invaluable comments and suggestions:

- Sidney Bolkosky, Professor of History, University of Michigan-Dearborn, Dearborn, Michigan

- Sara Brooke, Director of Libraries, The Ellis School, Pittsburgh, Pennsylvania

- Jacquelyn Divers, Librarian, Roanoke County Schools, Roanoke, Virginia

- Elaine Ezell, Library Media Specialist, Bowling Green Junior High School, Bowling Green, Ohio

- Melvin Small, Department of History, Wayne State University, Detroit, Michigan

Reader's Guide

Between 1939 and 1945 a war was fought among all the major powers of the world. It was a war that affected a vast percentage of the world's population. More people died during World War II than had died in any previous war. From the soldiers on the front lines to the citizens on the home front, *World War II: Primary Sources* tells the story of the war in the words of the people who lived it.

While all aspects of a war of this scale could not be covered completely in one volume, every effort has been made to offer a variety of World War II experiences. Sixteen full or excerpted documents include speeches from world leaders, such as Winston Churchill's "Blood, Toil, Tears, and Sweat" speech and Franklin D. Roosevelt's "Day of Infamy" speech. The soldiers' view of the war is presented in excerpts from such works as Stephen Ambrose's *Citizen Soldiers* and Ernie Pyle's dispatches from the front lines of the war, while such pieces as *Since You Went Away: World War II Letters from American Women on the Home Front* and *The Hiroshima Maidens: A Story of Courage, Compassion, and Survival* relate civilians' war experiences.

Format

The excerpts in *World War II: Primary Sources* are divided into four chapters. Each of the chapters focuses on a specific theme. "Intensification" examines events leading up to the war and the escalation of the conflict into a world war. "Home Front" relates experiences of Americans on the home front during the war. "The Human Cost" looks at the human toll of the war, from the horror of the Holocaust to soldiers' experiences. "Breakthrough" examines major turning points that led to the Allied victory and the conclusion of the war. Every chapter opens with a historical overview, followed by two to five document excerpts.

Each excerpt has seven sections:

- **Introductory material** places the document and its author in historical context.

- **Things to remember while reading** offers important background information about the featured text.

- **Excerpt** presents the document in its original spelling and format.

- **What happened next...** discusses the impact of the document and/or relevant historical events following the date of the document.

- **Did you know...** provides interesting facts about the document and its author.

- **For More Information** offers resources for further study of the document and its author.

- **Sources** presents citations to material used to compile the entry.

Additional Features

The chapters contain numerous sidebar boxes, some focusing on the author of the featured document, others highlighting interesting, related information. More than seventy black-and-white photos and maps illustrate the text. Each excerpt is accompanied by a glossary running in the margin alongside the reprinted document that defines terms, people, and ideas mentioned in the text. The volume begins with a timeline of events and a "Words to Know" section. It concludes with a subject index so students can easily find the people, places, and events discussed throughout *World War II: Primary Sources.*

Comments and Suggestions

We welcome your comments on *World War II: Primary Sources* and suggestions for other topics in history to consider. Please write. Editors, *World War II: Primary Sources,* U•X•L, 27500 Drake Rd., Farmington Hills, Michigan 48331-3535; call toll-free: 1-800-877-4253; fax to (248) 414-5043; or send e-mail via http://www.galegroup.com.

Timeline

1919: Germany signs the Treaty of Versailles, officially ending World War I. The treaty takes land away from Germany, severely limits the size of its armed forces, and requires Germany to pay reparations and admit guilt for causing the war.

1919: Adolf Hitler joins the tiny German Workers' Party in Munich. The party soon changes its name to the National Socialist German Workers' Party (NSDAP), called the Nazi Party for short.

1922: Benito Mussolini and his Fascist Party march on Rome, the capital of Italy, and Mussolini is named premier of Italy.

1908
Model T Ford is introduced

1914
World War I begins; it ends in 1918

1920
The League of Nations is formed

| 1905 | 1910 | 1915 | 1920 |

Franklin D. Roosevelt.
(Reproduced by permission of the Library of Congress)

1923: Hyperinflation hits Germany; its currency becomes worthless, causing severe economic distress.

1924: Benito Mussolini becomes dictator of Italy.

1926: Hirohito becomes emperor of Japan, giving his reign the name Showa ("enlightened peace").

1932: Franklin D. Roosevelt begins the first of four terms as president of the United States.

1933: Adolf Hitler becomes chancellor (head of the government) of Germany on January 30. Within a few months he and his National Socialist German Workers' Party have taken control of the German government.

1933: Dachau, the first permanent concentration camp, is opened in a suburb of Munich in March. Ten thousand opponents of Nazis, especially communists, are arrested and sent to newly established concentration camps.

1934: Upon the death of German president Paul von Hindenburg, the office of chancellor (head of government) is combined with president. Adolf Hitler is now the führer (leader) of the Third Reich (Empire) with absolute powers.

1935: March 16, Germany announces the reintroduction of the military draft and a major expansion of its army, violating the Treaty of Versailles.

1935: Germany passes the Nuremberg laws, which define Jews in racial terms, strip them of German citizenship, and ban marriages between Jews and non-Jews.

1936: Germany and Italy enter into agreements that establish a political and military alliance between the two countries called the "Rome-Berlin Axis."

1938: Europe is at the brink of war as Adolf Hitler makes territorial demands on Czechoslovakia. At a conference

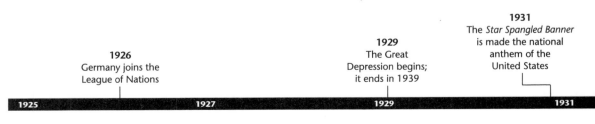

1926
Germany joins the League of Nations

1929
The Great Depression begins; it ends in 1939

1931
The *Star Spangled Banner* is made the national anthem of the United States

| 1925 | 1927 | 1929 | 1931 |

in Munich in September, leaders of France and Britain agree to grant Germany a section of Czechoslovakia with a large German-speaking population.

1939: Adolf Hitler violates the Munich agreement by taking over the remainder of Czechoslovakia by March.

1939: August 23, Germany and the Soviet Union sign the Nazi-Soviet Pact. The two countries promise not to attack each other and secretly agree to divide Poland after Germany conquers it.

1939: World War II officially begins. Germany invades Poland on September 1. Britain and France declare war on Germany two days later.

1940: April 10, Germany invades Norway and Denmark. Denmark soon surrenders, but fighting continues in Norway, aided by British and French forces.

1940: Winston Churchill becomes prime minister of Great Britain on May 10.

1940: Germany invades the Netherlands, Belgium, Luxembourg, and France on May 10.

1940: German forces take Paris on June 14. France signs an armistice with Germany on June 22.

1940: Italy invades Egypt on September 14.

1940: Germany, Japan, and Italy sign a military alliance called the Tripartite Pact.

1941: Germany sends troops to North Africa to help Italy with its invasion in North Africa.

1941: U.S. Congress passes the Lend-Lease Act, which immediately provides large amounts of war aid to Britain and later to the Soviet Union and others.

1941: The HMS *Hood* is sunk by the German battleship *Bismark* on May 24. Only three members of the fourteen-hundred-member crew survive.

The HMS *Hood*.
(Reproduced by permission of AP/Wide World Photos)

1933
U.S. President Franklin D. Roosevelt begins the New Deal Program

1936
The Olympic Games are held in Berlin, Germany

1938
World War II begins

1939
Television broadcasting is introduced at the World's fair in New York

1933 1935 1937 1939

Woman working on an assembly line of a factory producing goods for the war effort. *(Courtesy of the National Archives and Records Administration)*

1941: May 27, the British Royal Navy tracks down the German battleship *Bismark*. After repeated attacks, the *Bismarck* is sunk. More than two thousand German sailors on board die.

1941: June 22, Germany invades the Soviet Union in an offensive called Operation Barbarossa and quickly takes control of much of the country.

1941: After pressure from the Japanese government, the Vichy French government (the French government working with the Nazis) allows Japan to establish bases in the southern part of French Indochina (Vietnam).

1941: July, the United States bans trade with Japan.

1941: Winston Churchill and Franklin D. Roosevelt meet aboard a warship off the coast of Newfoundland in August and issue the Atlantic Charter, in which they agree to promote peace and democracy around the world.

1941: Japan bombs the U.S. naval base at Pearl Harbor in Hawaii on December 7.

1941: The United States and Britain declare war on Japan on December 8.

1941: Japan's allies, Germany and Italy, declare war on the United States on December 11.

1941: Japan attacks British-controlled Hong Kong. British troops surrender on December 25.

1942: Rationing begins in the United States.

1942: Franklin D. Roosevelt signs Executive Order 9066, directing all Japanese Americans living on the West Coast of the United States to report to internment camps.

1942: Germany launches its "Final Solution" against the Jews of Europe; gassing of prisoners in the Auschwitz concentration camp begins.

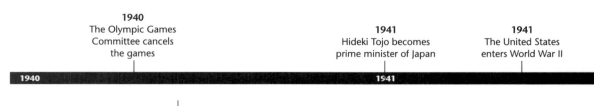

1940
The Olympic Games Committee cancels the games

1941
Hideki Tojo becomes prime minister of Japan

1941
The United States enters World War II

1940   1941

1942: The Battle of Midway is fought from June 4 to 7; the Americans inflict a severe defeat on the Japanese fleet in one of the most decisive naval battles in history.

1942: August 7, in the first American offensive operation of the war, American troops land on Guadalcanal in the Solomon Islands in the mid-Pacific.

1942: September 13, Germany begins its attack on the Soviet city of Stalingrad.

1942: November 8, the Allies launch Operation Torch, an invasion of German-occupied North Africa that ends with the Germans being chased from the region.

1943: January 31, the Germans surrender to the Russian troops at Stalingrad, marking a major turning point in the war.

1943: The Warsaw Ghetto uprising begins on April 19.

1943: American, British, and Canadian troops land on Sicily, a large island south of the Italian mainland, on July 10.

1943: Italian dictator Benito Mussolini is removed from office by the Fascist Grand Council on July 25; with German leader Adolf Hitler's help, Mussolini tries to establish a separate government in northern Italy.

1943: The Allies invade the southern Italian mainland on September 3; the Italian government surrenders to the Allies on September 8. German troops in Italy continue fighting.

1944: January 22, the Allies land at Anzio, Italy.

1944: June 4, the U.S. Army enters Rome, the capital of Italy.

1944: June 6, Allied forces land in Normandy in northern France in the largest sea invasion in history, called Operation Overlord. After heavy fighting, the Allies break out of Normandy and sweep eastward across France.

1944: On the third anniversary of the German invasion of the Soviet Union, June 22, the Soviets launch a mas-

Army nurses in a field hospital in France. *(Reproduced by permission of the National Archives and Records Administration)*

American troops on an amphibious landing craft heading for the Normandy coast. *(Reproduced by permission of the Corbis Corporation [Bellevue])*

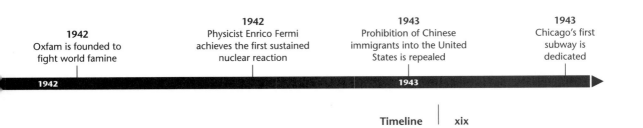

1942
Oxfam is founded to fight world famine

1942
Physicist Enrico Fermi achieves the first sustained nuclear reaction

1943
Prohibition of Chinese immigrants into the United States is repealed

1943
Chicago's first subway is dedicated

1942

1943

U.S. Marines raise the American flag on Mt. Suribachi in Iwo Jima.
(Reproduced by permission of the National Archives and Records Administration)

sive offensive called Operation Bagration along an 800-mile front in White Russia (Belarus). The Soviets inflict immense losses on the German army and drive them back almost 400 miles in one month.

1944: August 25, Paris is liberated by Free French and American forces.

1944: September 15, U.S. Marines land on Peleliu island, one of the Palau Islands in the western Pacific Ocean.

1944: The Battle of Leyte Gulf is fought in the Philippines from October 23 to 26. It is the largest naval battle in history and ends in the almost total destruction of the Japanese fleet.

1944: Franklin D. Roosevelt is elected to a fourth term as president of the United States.

1944: December 16, the Germans launch a major counteroffensive against the Americans in the Ardennes Forest region of Belgium and France, known as the Battle of the Bulge. After some initial success, the Germans are defeated.

1945: January 12, the Soviets begin an offensive along the entire Polish front. They enter Warsaw on January 17, and Lodz two days later.

1945: Soviet troops reach the Auschwitz concentration camp on January 27.

1945: British prime minister Winston Churchill, U.S. president Franklin D. Roosevelt, and Soviet leader Joseph Stalin meet at the Yalta Conference. The leaders establish postwar goals regarding future forms of government in Germany and the other parts of Europe and schedule the first United Nations conference.

1945: February 19, American marines land on Iwo Jima in the Pacific.

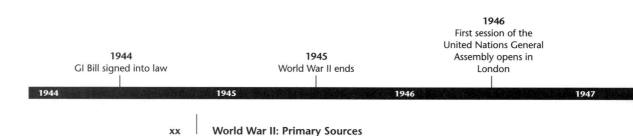

1944
GI Bill signed into law

1945
World War II ends

1946
First session of the United Nations General Assembly opens in London

1944   1945   1946   1947

1945: American troops land on Okinawa on April 1, beginning the largest land battle of the Pacific war. The Japanese forces are defeated by June.

1945: April 12, U.S. president Franklin D. Roosevelt dies; Harry S. Truman becomes president of the United States.

1945: April 20, Soviet troops reach Berlin, the capital of Germany.

1945: April 28, former Italian dictator Benito Mussolini is captured by resistance fighters and executed.

1945: April 30, Adolf Hitler commits suicide in his fortified bunker beneath Berlin. The new German government surrenders unconditionally to the Allies on May 8.

1945: The Potsdam Conference begins on July 16. U.S. president Harry S. Truman, British prime minister Winston Churchill, and Soviet leader Joseph Stalin confirm a four power occupation of Germany (by France, Great Britain, the Soviet Union, and the United States) and issue an ultimatum to Japan to surrender unconditionally.

1945: July 16, the first atomic bomb is tested in the desert near Alamogordo, New Mexico.

1945: August 6, the United States drops an atomic bomb on Hiroshima, Japan. A second bomb is dropped on Nagasaki, Japan, on August 9.

1945: August 8, the Soviet Union declares war on Japan; a large Soviet force invades Manchuria the following day.

1945: August 15, Allies accept the unconditional surrender of Japan. Formal surrender papers are signed aboard the USS *Missouri* in Tokyo Bay on September 2.

1945: War crimes trials begin in Nuremberg, Germany, in November.

1949: The Soviets establish East Germany as a Communist state called the German Democratic Republic; France,

Colonel Paul Tibbets, commander of the *Enola Gay*, on its atomic bomb mission over Hiroshima. *(Reproduced by permission of the Corbis Corporation [Bellevue])*

1948
Israel is declared an independent state

1949
The North Atlantic Treaty Organization (NATO) is created

1950
The Korean War begins; it ends in 1953

1948   1949   1950   1951

Dwight D. Eisenhower.
(Reproduced by permission of the National Archives and Records Administration)

England, and the United States join their power zones into a democratic state called the Federal Republic of Germany (West Germany).

1952: General Dwight D. Eisenhower becomes president of the United States.

1961: Communists build the Berlin Wall around East Berlin in order to stop East Germans seeking a higher standard of living from fleeing to West Germany through West Berlin.

1988: The U.S. Congress formally apologizes to Japanese Americans for interning them in concentration camps during World War II. Living persons who spent time in the camps are offered a one-time payment of $20,000.

1989: The Berlin Wall is destroyed.

1990: East Germany and West Germany are reunited.

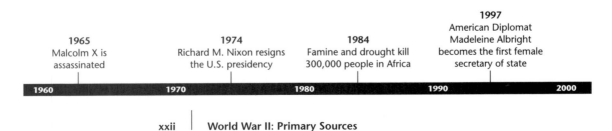

1997
American Diplomat Madeleine Albright becomes the first female secretary of state

1965
Malcolm X is assassinated

1974
Richard M. Nixon resigns the U.S. presidency

1984
Famine and drought kill 300,000 people in Africa

1960   1970   1980   1990   2000

Words to Know

A

Allies: The countries who fought against Germany, Italy, and Japan during World War II. The makeup of the Allied powers changed over the course of the war. The first major Allied countries were Great Britain and France. Germany defeated France in 1940 but some Free French forces continued to fight with the Allies until the end of the war. The Soviet Union and the United States joined the Allies in 1941.

Ammo: Ammunition—rifle and machine-gun bullets, high explosive shells, grenades, bombs, etc.

Anti-Semitism: The hatred of Jews, who are sometimes called Semites.

Appeasement: Making compromises in order to stay on neutral terms with another party or country.

Ardennes: A large forested area in southeastern Belgium. It was the site of the 1944-45 campaign known as the Battle of the Bulge.

Artillery: Missiles.

Atlantic Charter: An agreement signed in 1941 by President Franklin D. Roosevelt and British prime minister Winston Churchill in which the United States and Great Britain stated their commitment to worldwide peace and democracy.

Atom bomb: A weapon of mass destruction in which a radioactive element such as uranium is bombarded with neutrons to create a chain reaction called nuclear fission, releasing a huge amount of energy.

Axis: During World War II, Germany, Italy, and Japan formed a coalition called the Axis powers. Eventually, they were joined by Hungary, Romania, Slovakia, Finland, and Bulgaria.

B

Battalion: A large body of troops.

Blackout: Darkness (mandatory "lights out") enforced during wartime to discourage enemy air raids.

Blitzkrieg: Meaning "lightning war" in German, this is the name given the German's military strategy of sending troops in land vehicles to make quick, surprise attacks while airplanes provide support from above. This strategy was especially effective against Poland and France.

Bombardier: Member of a bomber crew who releases the bombs.

Bombardment: Assault or attack with bombs.

C

Cavalry: Originally referred to horse-mounted troops. In modern times cavalry refers to troops using armored vehicles such as tanks.

Chancellor: In some European countries, including Germany, the chief minister of the government.

Communism: An economic system that promotes the ownership of most property and means of production by the community as a whole. By 1939, the Soviet Union was a harsh dictatorship run by the Communist Party and its all-powerful leader, Joseph Stalin.

Company: A unit of soldiers.

Concentration camps: Places where the Germans confined people they considered enemies of the state. These included Jews, Roma (commonly called Gypsies), homosexuals, and political opponents.

Convoys: Large groups traveling together, sometimes with military protection, for safety.

D

D-Day: Usually refers to June 6, 1944, the day the Normandy Invasion began with a massive landing of Allied troops on the beaches of northern France, which was occupied by Germany; also called Operation Overlord. D-Day is also a military term designating the date and time of an attack.

Death camps: Concentration camps built by the Nazis for the single purpose of killing Jews.

Deportation: Banishment; being sent out of a country.

Depression: An economic downturn with falling industrial production, lower prices, and increasing unemployment. The United States experienced the worst depression in its history from 1929 to 1939, which is referred to as the Great Depression.

Depth charges: Drum-encased explosives aimed at submerged submarines.

Destroyers: A small, fast, heavily armed warship.

Dictator: A ruler who holds absolute power.

Division: A large unit of an army, usually about fifteen thousand men.

E

Escort: An armed protector ship that accompanies another sailing vessel.

Executive Order 9066: President Franklin D. Roosevelt's order directing all Japanese Americans living on the West Coast of the United States to be sent to internment camps.

Extermination camps: Concentration camps built by the Nazis with the single purpose of killing Jews.

F

Final Solution: The code name given to the Nazi plan to eliminate all the Jews of Europe.

Foxholes: Pits that provide cover from enemy fire.

Front: Battle zone.

Führer: The German word meaning "leader"; the title Adolf Hitler took as dictator of Germany.

Furlough: A soldier's leave of absence from duty.

G

GI: Standing for government issue, GI has become a nickname for enlisted soldiers or former members of the U.S. armed forces.

Genocide: The deliberate, systematic destruction of a racial, national, or cultural group.

Gestapo: An abbreviation for Germany's *Geheime Staats Politzei* or Secret State Police.

H

Half-track: A military vehicle with wheels in the front and tanklike tracks in the back.

Holocaust: The period between 1933 and 1945 when Nazi Germany systematically persecuted and murdered millions of Jews, Roma (commonly called Gypsies), homosexuals, and other innocent people.

I

Infantrymen: Soldiers fighting on foot.

Internment camp: A guarded facility usually used to hold citizens of an enemy country during wartime. The United States had ten camps located throughout the western part of the country to which about 120,000 Americans of Japanese ancestry were forced to move due to the ungrounded suspicion that they were not loyal to the United States.

Isolationism: A country's policy of keeping out of other countries' affairs. Isolationism was a strong force in American politics after World War I (1914-18) and continued to be an important factor until Japan attacked the United States in December 1941.

L

LCVP: Landing craft, vehicle and personnel; also called amphibian (land and water) tractors and assault amphibians.

Lebensraum: German term meaning "room to live." The Nazis told the German people that they needed expanded living space to survive and used this idea as justification for invading and occupying other countries.

Lend-Lease Program: A program that allowed the United States to send countries fighting the Germans (such as Great Britain and the Soviet Union) supplies needed for the war effort in exchange for payment to be made after the war.

LST: Landing ship, tank; amphibious (land and water) ships that can drive onto a beach to unload their cargo.

Luftwaffe: The German air force.

M

Magazine: A holder for cartridges that are fed into the chamber of a firearm.

Maginot Line: Defensive fortifications built to protect France's eastern border.

Manhattan Project: The project funded by the U.S. government that gathered scientists together at facilities in

Chicago, Illinois, Los Alamos, New Mexico, and other places to work on the development of an atom bomb.

Merchant ships: Commercial or trading ships.

Militarists: Extremists in the military and their supporters who believe the government should be controlled by the army and society should be organized on military principles.

N

Nationalism: Strong loyalty to one's nation, combined with a belief that one's country will benefit from acting independently and in its own best interest rather than in cooperation with other countries. Nationalism often leads to dislike of other countries.

Nazi: The abbreviated name for the National Socialist German Workers' Party, the political party led by Adolf Hitler, who became dictator of Germany. Hitler's Nazi Party controlled Germany from 1933 to 1945. The Nazis promoted racist and anti-Semitic ideas and enforced complete obedience to Hitler and the party.

O

Occupation: Control of a country by a foreign military power.

Operation Overlord: The code name for the Normandy Invasion, a massive Allied attack on German-occupied France; also called D-Day.

P

Pearl Harbor: Inlet on the southern coast of the island of Oahu, Hawaii, and the site of a Japanese attack on a U.S. naval base on December 7, 1941. The attack prompted the United States to enter World War II.

Perimeter: Boundary or outer limit.

Pillboxes: A roofed concrete compartment for machine guns and antitank weapons.

Prime minister: Chief executive of the government or of parliament.

R

Ration: To make something available in fixed amounts; limiting access to scarce goods; the allotted amount of something.

Reich: The German word meaning "empire"; Adolf Hitler's term as Germany's leader was called the Third Reich.

Reparations: Compensation required from a defeated nation for damage or injury during war.

S

Segregation: The forced separation of black and white people, not only in public places and schools but also in the U.S. military. The opposite of segregation is integration.

Shrapnel: Fragments of an exploded bomb or shell.

Soviet Union: Short for the Union of Soviet Socialist Republics or USSR, the country that the Communists had set up after overthrowing the Russian Empire.

SS: An abbreviation for *Schutzstaffel,* or security squad, the unit that provided German leader Adolf Hitler's personal bodyguards as well as guards for the various concentration camps.

Stormtroopers: Another name for members of the *Sturmabteilungen,* a special armed and uniformed branch of the Nazi Party.

Strafing: Firing at (with machine guns) in a long line and at close range.

T

Tommies: German nickname for British soldiers.

Tripartite Pact: An agreement signed in September 1940 that established an alliance among Germany, Italy, and Japan. The countries promised to aid each other should any one of them face an attack.

U

U-boat: Nickname given to German submarines because the German word for submarine is *unterseeboots.*

United Nations: Also referred to as the UN; an international peacekeeping organization formed in the spring of 1945 by representatives of fifty countries.

V

V-E Day: Victory in Europe Day, celebrated on May 8.

V-J Day: Victory over Japan Day, celebrated on September 2.

Versailles Treaty: The agreement signed by the countries who had fought in World War I that required Germany to claim responsibility for the war and pay money to other countries for damage from the war.

Veteran: A person who has served in the armed forces.

Vichy Government: The government set up in France after the Germans invaded the country; headed by Henri Petain, it was really under German control.

W

War crimes: Violations of the laws or customs of war.

World War II
Primary Sources

Intensification

Winston Churchill
...5

**Winston Churchill and
Franklin D. Roosevelt**
...21

Adolf Hitler
...31

Herbert A. Werner
...43

Franklin D. Roosevelt
...59

World War II (1939-45) grew out of a quest for power and territory in both Europe and Asia. On the European front, the war was sparked by the land-grabbing maneuvers of German dictator Adolf Hitler and his National Socialist German Workers' Party (or Nazi Party for short). (A dictator is a leader of a government in which absolute—and often unfair and oppressive—power is held by one ruler alone. In Germany's case, that leader was Hitler.)

Germany had been in a state of political and economic turmoil since its devastating loss to opposing forces in World War I (1914-18). In an attempt to restore the nation's former glory and expand German influence across Europe, Hitler launched an invasion of neighboring Poland on September 1, 1939. Great Britain and France responded with a show of solidarity (fellowship or unity), declaring war on Germany two days later. The Germans followed up with an attack on Belgium, the Netherlands, Luxembourg, and France in the spring of 1940.

The inspiring words of British prime minister **Winston Churchill** held Great Britain together as the prospect of a full-scale war in Europe became a reality. In his **"Blood, Toil, Tears** and Sweat" speech, his **"Be Ye Men of Valour"** speech, and his **"Finest Hour"** speech—all delivered in the spring of 1940—Churchill calls for total commitment to the war effort and an ultimate victory over Hitler's forces, "however long and hard the road may be."

Germany, Italy, and Japan had joined forces as the Axis Powers in September of 1940. The forces that fought against Germany—including France, Britain, and later the Soviet Union and the United States—were known as the Allied Powers. In the summer of 1941, as the threat to democracy (government by the people) escalated worldwide, U.S. president **Franklin D. Roosevelt** met with Churchill to discuss future war plans. From this meeting came the **Atlantic Charter**, a joint declaration by Roosevelt and Churchill that stressed the importance of human rights and charted a course for peace.

Around the same time, Germany and the Soviet Union became embroiled in armed conflict. Germany's relationship with the Soviet Union had deteriorated rapidly during 1940. Soviet leader Joseph Stalin's desires to further Soviet expansion in central Europe alarmed Hitler. He came to view Stalin—his former ally—as an obstacle to Germany's territorial growth. On June 22, 1941, more than three million German troops invaded the Soviet Union. **Adolf Hitler's Order of the Day to the German Troops on the Eastern Front**, issued October 2, 1941, vividly illustrates Hitler's menacing and manipulative nature.

World War II was fought on land, in the air, and on the high seas. German attempts to cut off British supply lines in the Atlantic Ocean fueled the brutal six-year-long Battle of the Atlantic. The key to Germany's early dominance in this battle was the German navy's use of U-boats, or submarines. U-boat commander **Herbert A. Werner**, a veteran of the war in the Atlantic, offers compelling insights from the German perspective in his memoir *Iron Coffins: A Personal Account of the German U-Boat Battles of World War II.*

U.S. attempts to remain neutral in the growing global conflict came to an end on December 7, 1941, when Japanese forces launched a surprise and unprovoked attack on American naval bases at Pearl Harbor, Hawaii. Japanese attacks on the Philippines, Guam, and Wake Island followed shortly after the raid on Pearl Harbor. President Roosevelt delivered his war message, better known as his **"Day of Infamy"** speech, to the

U.S. Congress the next morning. In his speech he requested that an official congressional declaration of war be made against the Japanese Empire. "We are now in this war," Roosevelt stated in a later radio address to the nation. "We are all in it—all the way."

Winston Churchill

"Blood, Toil, Tears, and Sweat"

"Be Ye Men of Valour"

"Their Finest Hour"

**Excerpts from selected speeches delivered
in the spring of 1940
Printed in *Blood, Toil, Tears and Sweat:
The Speeches of Winston Churchill*
Published in 1990**

After Adolf Hitler was named chancellor (chief officer) of Germany in 1933, the German government stepped up efforts to expand its territory in Europe. An extremely dangerous leader who seemed to have a spellbinding grasp on his followers, Hitler had spent the previous decade building up the National Socialist German Workers' Party (or Nazi Party for short). The Nazis encouraged the growing nationalist movement in Germany—a movement that glorified all things German and demanded blind devotion to the party's beliefs.

British prime minister Neville Chamberlain (the chief officer of the British government) sought to avoid war between Germany and Britain. To appease Hitler, he gave in to his demands to add the German-speaking sections of Czechoslovakia to his territory. As it turned out, this alone did not satisfy the cunning German leader's appetite for power and land. By March 1939 Germany claimed the rest of Czechoslovakia. It became clear that Hitler could not be trusted. Chamberlain resigned his post and Winston Churchill, unyielding and bold, was appointed prime minister of Britain on May 10, 1940.

"Let us therefore brace ourselves to our duties and so bear ourselves that, if the British Empire and its Commonwealth last for a thousand years, men will still say, 'This was their finest hour.'"

Churchill's first job was to form a new British government, called a coalition government. Members of all political parties—the tradition-minded Conservatives, the reform-seeking Liberals, and the workers' Labour Party—would play a role in the new government under Churchill.

World War II had already begun. In September 1939 Germany had invaded Poland. Great Britain and France responded to this aggression by declaring war on Germany. Eventually, the leading powers of the world would align (take sides) with Germany or with England. Germany, Italy, and Japan became known as the Axis Powers, and the forces that fought against Germany—France, Britain, and later the Soviet Union and the United States—were called the Allied Powers.

The Nazis' rise to power was tied directly to the staggering defeat suffered by Germany in World War I (1914-18). The First World War, sometimes referred to as the Great War, was a fight for power and influence. Germany tried to stake its claim as a leading European power through warfare. The long and bloody conflict concluded in 1918 with a full German retreat. World War I came to an official end with the signing of the Treaty of Versailles (named for the French palace where peace negotiations were conducted; pronounced "ver-SIGH") in 1919. The agreement stripped Germany of much of its territory, severely limited the size of its army and navy, demanded that Germany admit responsibility for starting the war, and required the defeated nation to make payments, or "reparations," to the opposing forces—especially to France—for the damage it had caused.

These penalties caused a serious economic decline, unemployment, and political turmoil in Germany. The Great Depression—a period of extreme economic slowdown that began in the United States in 1929 and spread to Europe in the early 1930s—only compounded problems.

Hitler took advantage of this chaos and suffering. He promised the German people that their nation would rise up from disgrace and become all-powerful. World War II can be viewed as another struggle for power, an attempt by the Germans to shake off past defeats and achieve European—and eventually world—domination.

In August 1939 Germany and the Soviet Union signed the Nazi-Soviet Nonaggression Pact, an agreement that the two

countries would not fight each other. On September 1, 1939, only a week after the pact went into effect, Hitler launched a German attack on Poland. (Under the terms of the nonaggression pact, the Soviet Union would not interfere with Germany's actions in Poland.) Obligated by earlier guarantees to assist various Eastern and Central European nations in case of a German invasion, Britain and France declared war on Germany two days later. It was already too late to save Poland—Germany conquered it by September 24. The stunning victory was called *blitzkrieg* (pronounced "BLITS-kreeg," meaning "lightning war" in German).

On May 10, 1940, Germany attacked Belgium, the Netherlands, and Luxembourg (a very small territory surrounded by France to the south, Belgium to the west, and Germany to the north and east). According to a special British press cable published in the *New York Times,* it was "generally believed" that the German "objective [was] to take the Netherlands and Belgium, solidify their positions there and then concentrate their entire attack against Britain."

Part of the Nazi invasion force, complete with cars, horse cavalry, and men on foot, advance farther into Poland, September 1939. *(Reproduced by permission of Corbis/Hulton-Deutsch Collection)*

European borders before World War II.

Germany also invaded France on May 10, and conquered it in another *blitzkrieg.* The first bombing in France occurred in May at Bron Airdrom, an airport near the city of Lyon. German troops entered the capital city of Paris on June 14, 1940. Shortly thereafter, all of northern and western France was occupied by Germany (taken over by German troops and controlled by the German government). As reported in the *New York Times,* French government officials felt there was "no longer . . . any possibility for a nation within striking range of Germany to remain neutral." In the coming months more nations would be forced to join the war against Hitler.

Three speeches written by British prime minister Winston Churchill in the spring of 1940 embody the nation's fierce determination to fight Hitler to the very end. These speeches—titled "Blood, Toil, Tears and Sweat," "Be Ye Men of Valour," and "Their Finest Hour"—were delivered in a five-week period between May 13 and June 18, 1940. Together, they chronicle England's early role in the war, document the escalation of the conflict, and reflect the spirit of pride, purpose, and confidence that Churchill inspired in the British people.

Winston Churchill.
(Reproduced by permission of the Bettmann Archive)

Things to remember while reading the excerpts of Churchill's speeches:

- Note that each speech was named for a key line that best captured Churchill's point.

- Churchill was appointed prime minister of Britain on May 10, 1940, just three days before delivering the first of these speeches to the House of Commons. (The elected House of Commons and the nonelected House of Lords make up the British Parliament—the supreme legislative, or law-making, body in Britain. The more powerful House of Commons is considered the ruling chamber of the kingdom's legislature.)

- Churchill became prime minister of Britain when he was sixty-five years old—an age when most of his colleagues were retiring.

- The "Blood, Toil, Tears and Sweat" speech is considered a classic—a model of Churchill's gift for public speaking and a testament to his tireless pursuit of victory.

- A few days before Churchill gave this speech, Germany invaded the Netherlands, Belgium, France, and Luxembourg. Churchill was working to shape a unified Parliament that would best lead the nation through this perilous time. He wanted to prepare British citizens for the long ordeal ahead and used "Blood, Toil, Tears and Sweat" to convey a message of urgency and commitment to the war effort.

- In his "Be Ye Men of Valour" speech—his first speech to be broadcast to the whole nation since his appointment as prime minister—Churchill calls on the British people to rally around the cause of freedom. He assures them that Germany will be conquered.

- Prime Minister Churchill's "Their Finest Hour" speech is set against the realization that France had indeed been devastated by the Germans' violent and forceful attacks. After France fell (surrendered) to the Germans in late June of 1940, England was Hitler's next target in a larger scheme to dominate all of Europe. Recognizing England's need for support in the war, Churchill would forge close ties with U.S. president Franklin D. Roosevelt and with Soviet leader Joseph Stalin. Most observers rank "Their Finest Hour" among Churchill's best-remembered wartime speeches.

- Churchill was known for his fiery temper, caustic wit, and astounding sense of self-confidence. He used all of these qualities to his advantage as England's prime minister, denouncing Hitler as a "crocodile" and motivating crowds with his rousing speeches and two-fingered "V-for-victory" sign.

"Blood, Toil, Tears and Sweat"

Delivered to the House of Commons, May 13, 1940

*. . . It must be remembered that we are in the **preliminary** stage of one of the greatest battles in history, that we are in action at many points in Norway and in Holland, that we have to be prepared in the*

Preliminary: Introductory; early.

***Mediterranean**, that the air battle is continuous and that many preparations have to be made here at home. . . . I would say to the House, as I said to those [ministers] who have joined the Government: 'I have nothing to offer but blood, toil, tears and sweat.'*

*We have before us an ordeal of the most **grievous** kind. We have before us many, many long months of struggle and of suffering. You ask, what is our policy? I will say: It is to wage war, by sea, land and air, with all our might and with all the strength that God can give us: to wage war against a monstrous **tyranny**, never surpassed in the dark, **lamentable** catalogue of human crime. That is our policy. You ask, what is our aim? I can answer in one word: Victory—victory at all costs, victory in spite of all terror, victory, however long and hard the road may be. . . . '*

"Be Ye Men of Valour"

Broadcast by the British Broadcasting Corporation (BBC), May 19, 1940

*I speak to you for the first time as Prime Minister in a solemn hour for the life of our country, of our Empire, of our Allies, and, above all, of the cause of Freedom. A tremendous battle is raging in France and **Flanders.** The Germans, by a remarkable combination of air bombing and heavily armoured tanks, have broken through the French defences north of the **Maginot Line**, and strong columns of their armoured vehicles are **ravaging** the open country, which for the first day or two was without defenders. . . . The regroupment of the French armies to make head against, and also to strike at, this intruding wedge has been proceeding for several days, largely assisted by the magnificent efforts of the Royal Air Force.*

We must not allow ourselves to be intimidated by the presence of these armoured vehicles in unexpected places behind our lines. . . .

*It would be foolish, however, to disguise the **gravity** of the hour. It would be still more foolish to lose heart or courage or to suppose that well-trained, well-equipped armies numbering three or four millions of men can be overcome in the space of a few weeks, or even months. . . .*

Mediterranean: A sea that borders Europe, Asia, and Africa and surrounds the southern European nation of Italy. Also sometimes used to describe the countries surrounding the Mediterranean sea.

Grievous: Serious.

Tyranny: Unjust and severe use of power by a government.

Lamentable: Sorrowful; mournful; regrettable.

Flanders: Region extending along the coast of the Netherlands, Belgium, and Luxembourg.

Maginot Line: (Pronounced "mah-zhuh-NO") Defensive fortifications built to protect France's eastern border.

Ravaging: Damaging; devastating.

Gravity: Seriousness; significance.

Hitherto: Up to this point.

Western Front: Western Europe, namely France.

Hideous apparatus of aggression: Churchill is referring to the might of the German military forces.

Retaliate: To repay; to get revenge.

Abates: Reduces; subsides.

Indomitable: Unconquerable.

M. Reynaud: French politician Paul Reynaud (1878-1966), who would later be imprisoned by the Germans.

Nay: No.

His Majesty: King George VI.

Commission: Instructions; task.

Servitude: Lacking the freedom to pursue a chosen way of life.

Sublime: Of outstanding moral significance; worthy of dignity and honor.

Bludgeoned: Beaten.

Barbarism: Backwardness; an uncivilized world.

*In the air—often at serious odds—often at odds **hitherto** thought overwhelming—we have been clawing down three or four to one of our enemies; and the relative balance of the British and German Air Forces is now considerably more favourable to us than at the beginning of the battle. In cutting down the German bombers, we are fighting our own battle as well as that of France. . . .*

*We must expect that as soon as stability is reached on the **Western Front**, the bulk of that **hideous apparatus of aggression** which gashed Holland into ruin and slavery in a few days, will be turned upon us. I am sure I speak for all when I say we are ready to face it; to endure it; and to **retaliate** against it—to any extent that the unwritten laws of war permit. . . . If the battle is to be won, we must provide our men with ever-increasing quantities of the weapons and ammunition they need. . . .*

*Our task is not only to win the battle—but to win the War. After this battle in France **abates** its force, there will come the battle for our island—for all that Britain is, and all that Britain means. That will be the struggle. . . . The interests of property, the hours of labour, are nothing compared with the struggle for life and honour, for right and freedom, to which we have vowed ourselves.*

*I have received from the Chiefs of the French Republic, and in particular from its **indomitable** Prime Minister, **M. Reynaud,** the most sacred pledges that whatever happens they will fight to the end, be it bitter or be it glorious. **Nay,** if we fight to the end, it can only be glorious.*

*Having received **his Majesty's commission**, I have found an administration of men and women of every party and of almost every point of view. We have differed and quarrelled in the past; but now one bond unites us all—to wage war until victory is won, and never to surrender ourselves to **servitude** and shame, whatever the cost and the agony may be. This is one of the most awe—striking periods in the long history of France and Britain. It is also beyond doubt the most **sublime.** Side by side, . . . the British and French peoples have advanced to rescue not only Europe but mankind from the foulest and most soul-destroying tyranny which has ever darkened and stained the pages of history. Behind them—behind us—behind the armies and fleets of Britain and France—gather a group of shattered States and **bludgeoned** races: the Czechs, the Poles, the Norwegians, the Danes, the Dutch, the Belgians—upon all of whom the long night of **barbarism** will descend, unbroken even by a star of hope, unless we conquer, as conquer we must; as conquer we shall.*

*Today is **Trinity Sunday.** Centuries ago words were written to be a call and a spur to the faithful servants of Truth and Justice: 'Arm yourselves, and be ye men of **valour,** and be in readiness for the conflict; for it is better for us to perish in battle than to look upon the outrage of our nation and our altar. As the Will of God is in Heaven, even so let it be.'*

"Their Finest Hour"

Delivered to the House of Commons, June 18, 1940

*. . . . I made it perfectly clear [a **fortnight** ago] that whatever happened in France would make no difference to the **resolve** of Britain and the British Empire to fight on, 'if necessary for years, if necessary alone.' . . .*

*During the great battle in France, we gave very powerful and continuous aid to the French army, both by fighters and bombers; but in spite of every kind of pressure we never would allow the entire metropolitan fighter strength of the Air Force to be consumed. This decision was painful, but it was also right, because the **fortunes of the battle in France could not have been decisively affected even if we had thrown in our entire fighter force.** That battle was lost by the unfortunate **strategical opening**, by the extraordinary and unforeseen power of the armoured columns and by the great **preponderance** of the German army in numbers. Our fighter Air Force might easily have been exhausted as a mere accident in that great struggle, and then we should have found ourselves at the present time in a very serious plight. But as it is . . . our fighter strength is stronger at the present time relatively to the Germans, who have suffered terrible losses, than it has ever been; and consequently we believe ourselves possessed of the capacity to continue the war in the air under better conditions than we have ever experienced before. . . .*

*There remains, of course, the danger of bombing attacks, which will certainly be made very soon upon us by the bomber forces of the enemy. It is true that the German bomber force is superior in numbers to ours; but we have a very large bomber force also, which we shall use to strike at military targets in Germany **without intermission.** I do not at all*

Trinity Sunday: The eighth Sunday after Easter.

Valour: (Americanized as "valor") Bravery; strength in the face of danger.

Fortnight: Two weeks.

Resolve: Firm decision.

Fortunes . . . force: Churchill is saying that even if the full power of the Royal Air Force had been used against Germany, France still would have been lost to the enemy.

Strategical opening: Unprotected gap.

Preponderance: Superiority; dominance.

Without intermission: Continually.

Winston Churchill

Winston Spencer Churchill (1874-1965) was born in 1874 in Blenheim Palace near London, England. His parents, Lord Randolph Churchill and American Jennie Jerome, later known as Lady Randolph, lived the extravagant existence of the upper-class and had little time for their son. Young Churchill felt alienated from his mother and father but developed a special bond with the doting nanny who loved and raised him as her own.

Young Churchill had a gift for writing, but his general lack of ambition and inability to pass Latin and mathematics courses almost ruined his chances for admission to the Royal Military College at Sandhurst. With the help of a tutor he finally passed the entrance exams—on his third try. After graduating from Sandhurst in 1894, he became a second lieutenant in the Fourth Hussars (elaborately clad soldiers on horseback). Churchill distinguished himself as a courageous soldier and a keen-eyed war correspondent, serving in Britain's army in India and Egypt and covering the Boer War (1899-1902; a war fought between the British and the Dutch for control of South Africa) for England's *Morning Post.* (While in South Africa, Churchill was taken prisoner by the Boers, then escaped and made his way back to England.)

After an unsuccessful bid for a seat in Parliament in 1899, Churchill won election the following year as the Conservative Party's candidate from Oldham. He held a number of important government positions over the next decade, married Clementine Hozier in 1908, and became First Lord of the Admiralty (commander of the British navy) in 1911.

World War I (1914-18; a war in which Germany, Austria-Hungary, and Turkey fought against twenty-eight other countries including Britain, France, Russia, and the United States) erupted in Europe in 1914. England joined the war effort in August, following Germany's assault on Belgium. When a risky British naval attack against Turkish forces ended in defeat, Churchill—as head of the navy—was held largely responsible. He resigned his post as First Lord of the Admiralty in 1915. Around the same time he took up a new hobby: painting. Originally serving as a diversion

underrate the severity of the ordeal which lies before us; but I believe our countrymen will show themselves capable of standing up to it. . . .

In what way has our position worsened since the beginning of the war? It has worsened by the fact that the Germans have conquered

Underrate the severity: Underestimate the seriousness.

from his career troubles, it became a lifelong love.

The war ended in 1918, and over the next two decades Churchill held various political offices, heading the war department, then the treasury, and switching political parties several times as Britain tried to recover politically and economically from four years of fighting. Except for one lost election in the early 1920s, Churchill maintained a seat in Parliament throughout the late 1930s.

Churchill's fiery personality led to frequent opposition in Parliament. He was spirited, brash, quarrelsome, and, as a result, rather unpopular with his colleagues. Early on, Churchill recognized Hitler as a threat to European peace and cautioned against the German program of arms buildup throughout the 1930s. (The Germans had been stripped of most of their weapons after World War I.) His demands for British rearmament (the buildup of forces in anticipation of war) were largely ignored until Germany invaded Poland in 1939.

At the dawn of World War II, Churchill was again named First Lord of the Admiralty, serving this time under Prime Minister Neville Chamberlain. The failure of Chamberlain's appeasement strategy—yielding to many of Hitler's demands—prompted Chamberlain to resign his post in 1940. Churchill took over just as the fighting intensified, and he inspired the British nation with his strength and fearlessness throughout the war. Nicknamed the "defiant lion" for pledging "never to surrender," he was often quoted as saying, "In war you don't have to be nice, you only have to be right."

Churchill's Conservative Party was soundly defeated in Britain's general elections of 1945. The Conservative Party was the party in power during the war; by the mid-1940s the British nation was war-weary, sick of foreign policy, and more interested in domestic issues (focusing on matters within the country such as rebuilding the British economy). Shortly before the close of World War II, Churchill announced his resignation, but he served another term from 1951 to 1955. He died on January 24, 1965—seventy years to the day after his father's death.

---

a large part of the coastline of Western Europe, and many small countries have been overrun by them. This **aggravates** the possibilities of air attack and **adds to our naval preoccupations**. It in no way diminishes, but on the contrary definitely increases, the power of our long-distance blockade. . . . If [Germany's] invasion [of Great Britain] has

Aggravates: Makes worse.

Adds...preoccupations: increases Britain's concerns about the war with Germany being fought at sea.

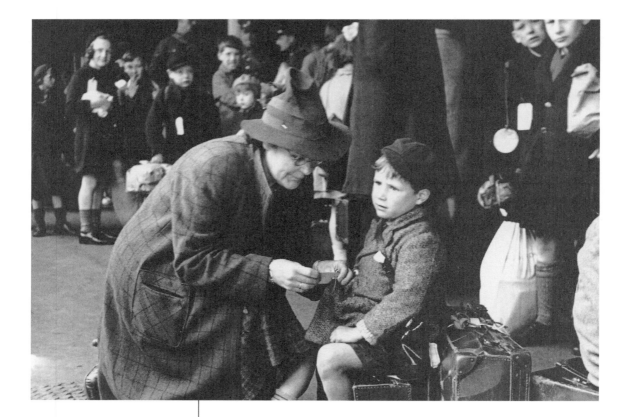

A British woman prepares a young boy for evacuation from London. *(Reproduced by permission of the Corbis/Hulton-Deutsch Collection)*

Imminent: Ready to take place.

Despotic: Ruling with unlimited power.

Dominions: Self-governing nations of the Commonwealth, namely Canada, Australia, New Zealand, and South Africa.

become more **imminent,** *as no doubt it has, we, being relieved from the task of maintaining a large enemy in France, have far larger and more efficient forces to meet it.*

If Hitler can bring under his **despotic** *control the industries of the countries he has conquered, this will add greatly to his already vast armament output. On the other hand, this will not happen immediately, and we are now assured of immense, continuous and increasing support in supplies and munitions of all kinds from the United States; and especially of airplanes and pilots from the* **Dominions** *and across the oceans, coming from regions which are beyond the reach of enemy bombers. . . .*

What **General Weygand** *called the Battle of France is over. I expect that the Battle of Britain is about to begin. Upon this battle depends the survival of Christian civilization. Upon it depends our own British life, and the long* **continuity** *of our institutions and our Empire. The whole fury and might of the enemy must very soon be turned on us. Hitler knows that he will have to break us in this island* *or lose the war. If we can stand up to him, all Europe may be free. . . . But if we fail, then the whole world, including the United States, including all that we have known and cared for, will sink into the **abyss** of a new Dark Age. . . . Let us therefore brace ourselves to our duties and so **bear** ourselves that, if the British Empire and its Commonwealth last for a thousand years, men will still say, 'This was their finest hour.' (Churchill, pp. 149, 151-54, 168, 172-78)*

General Weygand: French soldier Maxime Weygand (1867-1965), who commanded French forces during the 1940 invasion by Germany. He was later imprisoned by the Germans.

Continuity: Uninterrupted duration or existence.

Abyss: Hole; bottomless pit.

Bear: Withstand difficulty.

What happened next . . .

The German air force (called the Luftwaffe) and England's Royal Air Force (RAF) engaged in a string of air battles during the summer and fall of 1940, a period of the war now known as the Battle of Britain. The Germans tried to conquer England with waves of heavy bombing over the English Channel, but British forces held firm. Germany's efforts to gain control of the air were foiled.

On September 27, 1940, the governments of Germany, Italy, and Japan signed the Tripartite Pact, also known as the Axis or Three-Power Pact. Each nation pledged full cooperation and support—politically, economically, and militarily—to the others in case of attack by another power (namely, the United States) that might enter the war. The terms of the pact were to remain in effect for ten years.

Meanwhile, tensions were mounting between Germany and the Soviet Union. Hitler could not possibly achieve his goal of creating a vast European empire unless Stalin and the Soviet Union were defeated. It was inevitable that the nonaggression pact between the two countries would be broken. (See Adolf Hitler entry in chapter one for more information about the relationship between Hitler and Stalin.) The Soviets joined the Allied forces in 1941, after Germany invaded Russia. The United States entered the war that same year, following Japan's surprise attack on American forces at Pearl Harbor.

Winston Churchill giving
the two-fingered V-for-
victory sign. (Reproduced
by permission of AP/Wide
World Photos, Inc.)

Did you know . . .

- Churchill had a weakness for champagne, brandy, whiskey, and Cuban cigars. He acquired the cigar habit during his stint as a correspondent in Cuba back in 1895. (At the time the Cubans were seeking freedom from Spain; England, an ally of Spain, supported the Spanish effort to crush the Cuban rebellion.)

- During particularly stressful periods in his life, Churchill suffered severe and recurring bouts of melancholy (gloom and sorrow) and depression, a condition he referred to as his "Black Dog."

- Churchill was a night owl. He started his serious wartime planning each night at about 11:00 PM and continued working until dawn. A fanatic for cleanliness and comfort, he bathed twice daily and is said to have held many important meetings while wearing his bathrobe.

For More Information

Books

Churchill, Winston. *The Second World War.* 6 volumes. New York: Houghton, 1948-54. Reprinted, 1986.

Drieman, J.E., ed. *Winston Churchill: An Unbreakable Spirit.* Minneapolis, MN: Dillon Press, 1990.

Harris, Nathaniel. *Hitler.* North Pomfret, VT: Trafalgar, 1989.

Kimball, Warren F. *Forged in War: Roosevelt, Churchill, and the Second World War.* New York: Morrow, 1998.

Rose, Norman. *Churchill: The Unruly Giant.* New York: The Free Press, 1994.

Sainsbury, Keith. *Churchill and Roosevelt at War: The War They Fought and the Peace They Hoped to Make.* New York: New York University Press, 1994.

Shirer, William L. *Berlin Diary.* New York: Knopf, 1941.

Videos

Churchill and the Generals. BBC/LeVien International, 1981.

The Nazi Strike. Fusion Video, 1984.

Web Sites

The Churchill Center. *The Winston Churchill Home Page.* [Online] http://www.winstonchurchill.org (accessed on September 5, 1999).

Sources

Allen, Peter. *The Origins of World War II.* New York: Bookwright Press, 1992.

"Chamberlain Resigns, Churchill Premier." *New York Times,* May 11, 1940, pp. 1, 9.

Churchill, Winston. *Blood, Toil, Tears and Sweat: The Speeches of Winston Churchill.* Edited with an introduction by David Cannadine. Boston: Houghton Mifflin, 1990.

"German Army Attacks Poland." *New York Times,* September 1, 1939, p. 1.

Hills, Ken. *Wars That Changed the World: World War II.* New York: Marshall Cavendish, 1988.

Keller, Mollie. *Winston Churchill.* New York: F. Watts, 1984.

"Nazis Invade Holland, Belgium, Luxembourg by Land and Air." *New York Times,* May 10, 1940, p. 1.

Ross, Stewart. *World Leaders.* New York: Thomson Learning, 1993.

Severance, John B. *Winston Churchill: Soldier, Statesman, Artist.* New York: Clarion Books, 1996.

Winston Churchill and Franklin D. Roosevelt

The Atlantic Charter

Issued August 14, 1941. Printed by United Press in the *New York Times*, August 15, 1941, p.1.

After taking part in World War I (1914-18) the United States adopted a policy of isolationism, vowing to remain neutral (not take sides) in conflicts between foreign countries. But in the mid-1930s, soon after German dictator Adolf Hitler's rise to power in Germany (see Winston Churchill entry in chapter one), it became clear that every nation in the world was a potential target for power-hungry dictators. (A dictator is a leader of a government in which absolute—and often unfair and oppressive—power is held by one ruler alone.) In 1935 Italian dictator Benito Mussolini took steps to broaden his political power by attacking Abyssinia (the eastern African kingdom of Ethiopia). Two years later Japan invaded central China. With the outbreak of war in Europe in 1939, the defense of democracy (government by the people) became a very real concern worldwide.

In the fall of 1940 the U.S. Congress authorized the start of a peacetime draft to enlarge the American armed forces. The draft required men between the ages of twenty and thirty-five to enroll for military training. Meanwhile, American industries geared up for increased production of war supplies. On

"[Britain and the United States] respect the right of all peoples to choose the form of government under which they will live; and they wish to see sovereign rights and self-government restored to those who have been forcibly deprived of them."

May 27, 1941, U.S. president Franklin D. Roosevelt proclaimed that an "unlimited national emergency" existed, requiring military "readiness to repel any and all acts or threats of aggression directed toward any part of the Western Hemisphere."

By mid-1941 Germany controlled virtually all of Europe west of the Soviet Union. In August 1939, Germany and the Soviet Union had signed the Nazi-Soviet Nonaggression Pact, an agreement that the two countries would not fight each other. Despite this agreement, on June 22, 1941, the Germans launched a surprise attack, code-named Operation Barbarossa, on the Soviet Union. The Soviets were completely unprepared for the invasion and for the first few months the Germans won battle after battle and pushed deep into Soviet territory. With this action it was clear to world leaders that Hitler intended to conquer all of Europe.

Meanwhile, tensions were mounting between the United States and Japan throughout 1941. The Japanese were attempting to expand their empire in Asia and the Pacific. Japan's leaders planned to take over Asian and Pacific territories that had been controlled by Britain, France, and the Netherlands. These countries couldn't defend their outlying areas because they were defending their own countries from German attacks. The only other major power in the Pacific was the United States. When Japanese troops moved into French-controlled territory in southern Indochina (the modern country of Vietnam) in July, the United States and Britain took it as a sign that Japan was planning to move against the rest of the Allies' territories in the Pacific, which would lead to war with Japan.

In August 1941, Roosevelt and British prime minister Winston Churchill met secretly aboard ships anchored in the coastal waters of Newfoundland (an island in the Atlantic Ocean off the eastern coast of Canada) to discuss defensive measures and war goals. During their meetings they composed a joint declaration known as the Atlantic Charter, which stressed the supreme importance of human rights and outlined the key ingredients necessary for achieving peace. First made public on August 14, 1941, this "recipe for peace" set forth principles that would guide the actions of the Allies (the forces that fought against Germany in World War II, namely, France, Britain, and later the Soviet Union and the United States) in the

escalating global conflict. The charter also served as a foundation for the creation of the United Nations, an international peace organization formally established on October 24, 1945.

President Franklin D. Roosevelt led efforts by the United States to help Britain fight Germany. *(Reproduced by permission of the Library of Congress)*

Things to remember while reading the Atlantic Charter:

- After Germany conquered France in June 1940, Britain was the only European country left fighting the Germans. Four distant countries that had once been British colonies— Canada, Australia, New Zealand, and South Africa— offered their support. They declared war on Germany and sent supplies and troops to help Britain fight the war.

- In his January 6, 1941 message to Congress President Roosevelt pledged American support to the nations already fighting the Germans. In order to furnish this support, certain terms of earlier Neutrality Acts had to be changed. In addition, Congress passed the Lend-Lease Act (March

Franklin D. Roosevelt

Franklin D. Roosevelt (1882-1945) was born January 30, 1882, on his family's estate near Hyde Park, New York. He came from a wealthy and privileged family–U.S. president Theodore Roosevelt (1858-1919) was his cousin.

Roosevelt received his early education from his mother and father and from private tutors, then entered the prestigious Groton School in Massachusetts, where he excelled academically. He went on to attend Harvard University and Columbia Law School and married social crusader Eleanor Roosevelt, a distant cousin, in 1905.

Franklin Roosevelt first entered the political spotlight in 1910, winning election to the New York state senate as a democrat. A close political adviser to President Woodrow Wilson (1856-1924), he also served as assistant secretary of the navy from 1913 to 1920. Then, following an unsuccessful bid for the office of vice president of the United States, Roosevelt decided to put his political career on hold for a while. He never expected the dramatic turn that his life would take the next year.

In 1921 Roosevelt contracted a virus called poliomyelitis (pronounced "POH-lee-oh MIH-uh-LIH-tuss"; also known as polio or infantile paralysis) and lost the use of both his legs. He was only thirty-nine years old. From that point on, Roosevelt needed a wheelchair or steel leg braces and crutches to get around.

According to family members, friends, and other observers, Roosevelt's illness changed his entire outlook on life. He gained a greater understanding of people's problems and a newfound sense of compassion for others. Roosevelt did not want to be seen as disabled. He worked hard to develop the muscles in his upper body and even had special hand controls installed in his Ford convertible so he could drive on his own.

Roosevelt reemerged on the political scene in the late 1920s. He narrowly won election in 1928 to the first of two terms as governor of New York. His commitment to helping impoverished Americans brought him national prominence and, in time, fueled his political rise. Roosevelt defeated Herbert Hoover in the presidential election of 1932. At the

1941), making it easier for the United States to provide military aid to Great Britain and other nations at war against Hitler. By "loaning" war materials to these countries, Roosevelt hoped "to keep war away" from American shores.

time, America was in the midst of the Great Depression, a period of severe economic slowdown that began in the United States in 1929. By 1932 about twelve million Americans were unemployed. More and more people found themselves homeless and hungry.

Roosevelt took the oath of the office of president on March 4, 1933, and gave a memorable, moving speech that captured the hearts of the American people. "This great nation will endure as it has endured," he stated, "[and it] will revive and will prosper.... The only thing we have to fear is fear itself."

Roosevelt set out to use the powers of the government to spark social and economic reform (change for the better). Relief began with the creation of a number of agencies to assist and employ millions of Americans in a revolutionary program known as the "New Deal." Roosevelt's critics charged that government involvement in everyday American life had transformed the nation into a huge welfare state and created an enormous national debt. But the president's supporters maintained that his actions helped restore the nation's faith in its government.

With his easy charm and winning ways, Roosevelt revolutionized the way the president communicated with the American people. His "fireside chats"— informal updates on government business—were broadcast by radio to millions of homes. But by the late 1930s world events forced Roosevelt to focus mainly on foreign affairs. World War II had erupted in Europe, and German leader Adolf Hitler's alarming display of military force led the neutral United States closer and closer to direct involvement in the conflict.

Roosevelt was elected to his fourth and final term as president in November 1944. Some historians maintain that the stress of the war contributed greatly to his death just five months after the election. On April 12, 1945, while vacationing in Warm Springs, Georgia, Roosevelt suffered a cerebral hemorrhage (also known as a stroke). He was posing for a painting by artist Elizabeth Shoumatoff at the time of the stroke, and he never regained consciousness.

- Roosevelt stressed the need for "freedom of religion" and "freedom of information" throughout the world. He declared that the principles of the Atlantic Charter could not be achieved without these freedoms.

Franklin D. Roosevelt (seated, left) and Winston Churchill (seated, right) at the Atlantic Charter meeting. *(Reproduced by permission of AP/Wide World Photos, Inc.)*

• After World War I, the United States was strongly isolationist (not interested in getting involved in the problems of other countries). The Atlantic Charter moved the United States one step closer toward involvement in World War II and suggested that the United States would be taking a greater role in world politics in the years to come.

• The United States did not officially enter World War II until after the Japanese attack on Pearl Harbor in December 1941.

His Majesty: King George VI.

Aggrandizement: Appearance of greatness; expansion of power; enhancement of reputation.

The Atlantic Charter

*The President of the United States of America and the Prime Minister, Mr. Churchill, representing **His Majesty**'s Government in the United Kingdom, being met together, deem it right to make known cer-*

tain common principles in the national policies of their respective countries on which they base their hopes for a better future for the world.

FIRST, their countries seek no **aggrandizement**, territorial or other;

SECOND, they desire to see no territorial changes that do not **accord** with the freely expressed wishes of the peoples concerned;

THIRD, they respect the right of all peoples to choose the form of government under which they will live; and they wish to see **sovereign rights** and self-government restored to those who have been **forcibly deprived** of them;

FOURTH, they will **endeavor**, with **due respect** for their existing obligations, to further the enjoyment by all States, great or small, victor or **vanquished**, of access, on equal terms, to the trade and to the raw materials of the world which are needed for their economic prosperity;

FIFTH, they desire to bring about the fullest **collaboration** between all nations in the economic field with the object of securing, for all, improved labor standards, economic advancement, and social security;

SIXTH, after the final destruction of the **Nazi tyranny**, they hope to see established a peace which will **afford** to all nations the **means** of dwelling in safety within their own boundaries, and which will afford assurance that all the **men** in all the lands may live out their lives in freedom from fear and want;

SEVENTH, such a peace should enable all men to **traverse** the high seas and oceans without **hindrance**;

EIGHTH, they believe that all of the nations of the world, for realistic as well as spiritual reasons, must come to the abandonment of the use of force. Since no future peace can be maintained if land, sea or air **armaments** continue to be **employed** by nations which threaten, or may threaten, aggression outside of their frontiers, they believe...that the **disarmament** of such nations is essential. They will likewise aid and encourage all other **practicable measures** which will lighten for peace-loving peoples the crushing burden of armaments.

Franklin D. Roosevelt

Winston S. Churchill

Accord: Agree.

Sovereign rights: Rights of freedom and independence.

Forcibly deprived: Removed or taken away under threat of harm or violence.

Endeavor: Try; attempt.

Due respect: Rightful or appropriate consideration.

Vanquished: Conquered; defeated in battle.

Collaboration: Cooperation.

Nazi tyranny: The term "Nazi" is taken from the full name of the National Socialist German Workers' Party—the political party in power in Germany from 1933 to 1945. "Nazi tyranny" refers to Hitler's abusive use of power as head of Nazi Germany.

Afford: Give.

Means: A method or course of action used to achieve something.

Men: People.

Traverse: Travel across or over.

Hindrance: Restrictions; interference.

Armaments: Arms or weapons.

Employed: Used.

Disarmament: Removal of arms, armed forces, and means of attack.

Practicable measures: Possible steps.

The actions of dictators Adolf Hitler (right) and Benito Mussolini (Mussolini) caused democratic nations to fear for their safety.
(Reproduced by permission of Snark/Art Resource, NY)

What happened next...

On September 27, 1940, the governments of Germany, Italy, and Japan signed the Tripartite Pact, also known as the Axis or Three-Power Pact. Each nation pledged full cooperation and support—politically, economically, and militarily—to the others in case of attack by another power (namely, the United States) that might enter the war. The terms of the pact were to remain in effect for ten years.

The United States officially joined the war four months after Roosevelt and Churchill signed the Atlantic Charter. On December 7, 1941 the Japanese bombed an American naval base at Pearl Harbor, Hawaii. The United States and Britain declared war on Japan. A few days later Japan's allies, Germany and Italy, declared war on the United States. The United States was now fully in the war, which had truly become a world war. By the end of December, Japan controlled most of the Pacific region, including the Philippines, Guam, the Gilbert Islands, Malaya, and Singapore.

Did you know...

- Franklin D. Roosevelt was the first U.S. president to appoint a woman—Frances Perkins—to his cabinet. (A cabinet is a group of close advisers to the president. Perkins held the post of secretary of labor from 1933 to 1945.)

- The meeting in Newfoundland was the first face-to-face meeting between Churchill and Roosevelt.

- In addition to numerous meetings between the two leaders throughout the war, they constantly exchanged opinions, information, and arguments by coded radio messages. They exchanged more than eight hundred such messages over the course of the war.

- While meeting in Newfoundland, Roosevelt and Churchill had secretly discussed what the war strategy would be in the United States entered the war.

- A failed attempt to assassinate President Roosevelt occurred on February 15, 1933, in Miami, Florida.

- Roosevelt was the only president in U.S. history to serve more than two terms in office.

- Roosevelt did not live to see the Allied victory in Europe. He died on April 12, 1945, about three and a half weeks before the Germans surrendered.

For More Information

Books

Burns, James M. *Roosevelt: The Soldier of Freedom*. New York: Harvest/Harcourt, 1973.

Graham, Otis L., Jr., and Meghan Robinson Wander, eds. *Franklin D. Roosevelt, His Life and Times: An Encyclopedic View*. Boston: G.K. Hall & Co., 1985.

Hacker, Jeffrey H. *Franklin D. Roosevelt*. New York: F. Watts, 1983.

Larsen, Rebecca. *Franklin Delano Roosevelt: Man of Destiny*. New York: F. Watts, 1991.

Miller, Nathan. *FDR: An Intimate History*. Originally published in 1983. Reprinted. Lanham, MD: Madison Books/University Press of America, 1991.

Morgan, Ted. *FDR: A Biography*. New York: Simon & Schuster, 1985.

Perkins, Frances. *The Roosevelt I Knew*. New York: 1946.

Potts, Steve. *Franklin D. Roosevelt: A Photo-Illustrated Biography*. "Read and Discover Series." Mankato, MN: Bridgestone Books, 1996.

Ward, Geoffrey C. *Before the Trumpet: Young Franklin Roosevelt, 1882-1905*. Originally published in 1985. Reprinted. New York: Smithmark, 1994.

Videos

FDR. "The American Experience." WGBH Educational Foundation and David Grubin Productions, Inc., 1994.

Web Sites

Franklin D. Roosevelt Library and Digital Archives. [Online] http://www.academic.marist.edu/fdr/ (accessed on September 6, 1999).

The American Experience: The Presidents. [Online] http://www.pbs.org/wgbh/pages/amex/presidents/ (accessed on September 6, 1999).

Sources

Allen, Peter. *The Origins of World War II*. New York: Bookwright Press, 1992.

Freedmen, Russell. *Franklin Delano Roosevelt*. New York: Clarion Books, 1990.

Hills, Ken. *Wars That Changed the World: World War II*. New York: Marshall Cavendish, 1988.

Leckie, Robert. *The Story of World War II*. New York: Random House, 1964.

New York Times, May 7, 1941, p. 1; June 23, 1941, p. 1; July 3, 1941, p. 1; August 14, 1941, p. 1; October 4, 1941; October 10, 1941, p. 2.

Ross, Stewart. *World Leaders*. New York: Thomson Learning, 1993.

Adolf Hitler

Excerpt from "Hitler's Order of the Day to the German Troops on the Eastern Front"

Issued October 2, 1941
Excerpt taken from Associated Press release reprinted in the *New York Times*, October 10, 1941, p. 2

After Adolf Hitler was named chancellor (chief officer) of Germany in 1933, the German government stepped up efforts to expand its territory in Europe. In March 1938 the German army moved into Austria and united it with Germany. Soon, Hitler began demanding the return of land that Germany had lost after World War I (1914-18). His first target was a German-speaking section of Czechoslovakia, called the Sudetenland. Czechoslovakia didn't have a strong enough military to stand alone against Germany and prevent it from taking the territory. Czechoslovakia's allies, Britain and France, did not want to go to war over the territory, so they agreed to let Germany take over the Sudetenland. Hitler claimed that this would be his last territorial demand in Europe. In reality, he already had plans for conquering all of Europe.

By March 1939 Hitler's army had taken over all of Czechoslovakia. Soon after, Hitler made demands on Poland, specifically the port city of Danzig. Before World War I, Danzig was a German city. After World War I it became a "free city," which meant it didn't belong to Germany or to Poland, even though it now fell within Poland's borders. Poland had a right

"Your names, soldiers of the German armed forces, and the names of our brave allies, the names of your divisions and regiments, and your tank forces and air squadrons, will be associated for all time with the most tremendous victories in history."

German leader Adolf Hitler reviewing German cavalry troops as they march down a street in Warsaw, the capital of Poland.
(Reproduced by permission of the Corbis Corporation [Bellevue])

to use the port for its exports and imports. But the people of the city were almost all German. Hitler wanted Danzig returned to Germany and he also wanted to build a road through Polish territory that would connect Danzig and Germany. European leaders were no longer willing to give in to Hitler's demands. Poland refused to give up its right to use Danzig and England and France swore to defend Poland if Germany attacked it.

In August 1939 Germany and the Soviet Union signed the Nazi-Soviet Nonaggression Pact, an agreement that the two countries would not fight each other. On September 1, 1939, only a week after the pact went into effect, Hitler launched a German attack on Poland. (Under the terms of the nonaggression pact, the Soviet Union would not interfere with Germany's actions in Poland.) Britain and France declared war on Germany two days later. It was too late to save Poland—by September 24 Germany had conquered it. The stunning victory was called *blitzkrieg* (pronounced "BLITS-kreeg," meaning "lightning war" in German).

By mid-1941 Germany controlled virtually all of Europe west of the Soviet Union. In May and June it had conquered Norway, Denmark, the Netherlands, Belgium, Luxembourg, and France. Germany's quest for territory seemed unquenchable. Tensions were mounting between Hitler and Soviet leader Joseph Stalin. The *führer* (pronounced "FYOOR-uhr"; German term for "leader," the title Hitler gave himself) was infuriated by Stalin's moves to expand Soviet territory farther into central Europe. On June 22, 1941, more than three million German troops invaded the Soviet Union, thus launching the famous assault that Hitler named Operation Barbarossa. In a July 3 radio address Stalin warned his nation of the seriousness of Germany's aggressions. "A grave danger hangs over our country," he stated. "The enemy must be crushed. We must win." Italy sided with Germany, declaring war on the Soviet Union and setting the stage for a long conflict with the Soviets, the British, and the Americans.

Things to remember while reading the excerpt from Hitler's Order of the Day:

- In his July 3, 1941, radio broadcast Stalin predicted: "Our war for the freedom of our country will merge with the struggle of the peoples of Europe and America . . . . It will be a united front of peoples standing for freedom and against enslavement and threats of enslavement by Hitler's . . . armies."

- On July 12, 1941, the British and Soviet governments signed an agreement pledging mutual assistance in the war against Germany.

- Hitler's order to the German troops on the eastern front was issued on October 2, 1941, about three and a half months after Germany invaded the Soviet Union. At this time, Hitler felt confident that Germany had won the war against the Soviet Union.

- Notice how Hitler plays upon his soldiers' deepest emotions and rawest instincts—instincts of loyalty, courage, and survival—by telling them that Stalin had long planned a devastating invasion of Germany. He also calls on a higher power—God—to lead the German forces to victory in their war against the Soviet "beasts."

Hitler's Order of the Day to the German Troops on the Eastern Front

Issued October 2, 1941.

*Filled with the greatest concern for the existence and future of our people, I decided on June 22 to appeal to you to anticipate in the **nick of time** threatening aggression by one opponent [the Soviet Union].*

*It was the intention of the **Kremlin** powers—as we know today— to destroy not only Germany but all Europe....*

*God's mercy on our people and the entire European world if this **barbaric** enemy had been able to move his tens of thousands of tanks before we moved ours!*

All Europe would have been lost, for this enemy does not consist of soldiers, but a majority of beasts....

*Soldiers, when I called on you on June 22 to ward off the terrible danger **menacing** our homeland you faced the biggest military power of all times....*

*Within a few weeks his three most important industrial regions will be completely in our hands. Your names, soldiers of the German armed forces, and the names of our brave **allies**, the names of your divisions and **regiments** and your tank forces and air squadrons, will be associated for all time with the most tremendous victories in history.*

*You have taken more than 2,400,000 prisoners, destroyed or captured more than 17,500 tanks and more than 21,600 pieces of **artillery**. Fourteen thousand two hundred planes were brought down or destroyed on the ground.*

*The world **hitherto** never has experienced similar events.... Since June 22 the strongest fortifications have been penetrated, tremendous streams have been crossed, innumerable localities have been stormed and **fortresses** and **casemate** systems have been crushed or smoked out.*

*From far in the north, where our superbly brave Finnish allies gave evidence of their courage a second time, down to Crimea you stand today together with Slovak, Hungarian, Italian and Rumanian divisions roughly **1,000 kilometers** deep in the enemy's country.*

Nick of time: At the final moment; just in time.

Kremlin: The Soviet government.

Barbaric: Primitive; backward.

Menacing: Threatening.

Allies: In this case, Hitler is referring to the countries fighting on Germany's side.

Regiments: Military units.

Artillery: Weapons for discharging missiles.

Hitherto: Up to this point in time.

Fortresses: Strong, secure, fortified places or towns.

Casemate: An enclosed portion of a warship from which guns are fired.

1,000 kilometers: Approximately 620 miles.

Adolf Hitler

Austrian-born German leader Adolf Hitler (1889-1945) rose from obscurity to become one of the most threatening figures in world history. Disinterested in the technical training courses his father had forced him to take, he left school at the age of sixteen and eventually ended up in Austria. Although Hitler fancied himself a budding young artist, he was denied admission to the Vienna Academy of Fine Arts. While living in poverty in Vienna, the frustrated artist began lecturing to crowds on the virtues of German nationalism and anti-Semitism (the hatred of Jews).

Hitler fought in the German army during the First World War. In 1920 he joined the German Workers' Party, which would soon become the National Socialist German Workers' Party, called Nazis. Hitler became very powerful in the party. In the midst of the political and economic chaos that enveloped Germany after the war, he played on the emotions of the German people and portrayed himself as their sole savior. Hitler focused all of his attention on politics, establishing a strong foundation for the rise of the Nazi Party in Germany.

The self-proclaimed *führer* (pronounced "FYOOR-uhr"; German term for "leader") envisioned a world ruled by a a pure, white German race. To achieve his goal of racial dominance, he ordered the murder of six million Jews, as well as all political opponents and other so-called enemies of the state. These hideous mass murders—most of them carried out in the gas chambers of concentration camps—are now collectively referred to as the Holocaust.

Hitler's invasion of Poland in 1939 ignited World War II. Germany continued to fight under the *führer*'s leadership until the spring of 1945. Rather than surrender and face judgment, he reportedly committed suicide in his underground bunker (a fortified chamber) in Berlin on April 30, 1945.

Spanish, Croat and Belgian units now join you and others will follow. This fight—perhaps for the first time—is recognized by all European nations as a common action to safeguard the future of this most **cultural** continent....

This outstanding achievement of one struggle was obtained with sacrifices that, however painful in individual cases, in the total amount to not yet five percent of those of **the World War**. . . .

Cultural: Highly developed intellectually and morally.

The World War: World War I.

A German tank rolls through Soviet territory during Operation Barbarossa. *(Reproduced by permission of the Corbis Corporation [Bellevue])*

Decisive battle: The battle that will end the war.

Instigator: An often underhanded force that urges another to take action.

Reich: (Pronounced "RIKE") German word for "empire" or "kingdom."

Huns: A brutal tribe from western Asia who took over central and eastern European lands around the year 400 B.C.

Mongol: Asian peoples.

Ensuing: Following.

With bated breath: An expression used to convey a feeling of anxiety or uneasiness; holding one's breath while waiting for a decision or outcome.

During these three and a half months, my soldiers, the precondition, at least, has been created for a last mighty blow that shall crush this opponent before Winter sets in.

All preparations . . . have been made. . . . We can now strike a deadly blow.

*Today begins the last great **decisive battle** of this year. It will hit this enemy destructively and with it the **instigator** of the entire war, England herself. For if we crush this opponent, we also remove the last English ally on the [European] Continent.*

*Thus we will free the German **Reich** and entire Europe from a menace greater than any since the time of the **Huns** and later of the **Mongol** tribes.*

*The German people, therefore, will be with you more than ever before during the few **ensuing** weeks. What you and allied soldiers have achieved already merits our deepest thanks.*

***With bated breath**, the blessing of the entire German homeland accompanies you during the hard days ahead. With the Lord's* *aid you not only will bring victory but also the most essential condition for peace.*

The Fuehrer's Headquarters: Oct. 2, 1941.

Adolf Hitler, Fueher and Supreme Commander of the Armed Forces.

What happened next...

Even though German forces captured the Soviet city of Kiev in September of 1941, their December advance on Moscow failed. Stalin used the unbearably cold Russian winters to his advantage, launching his counterattack just as temperatures plunged to a bitter -40°F. The Germans retreated, but the conflict was far from over. Fierce fighting in the cities of Leningrad and Stalingrad broke out in 1942. Food was scarce. Once-thriving towns were reduced to rubble. Thousands of Soviet citizens died of starvation; others fell into the hands of the Nazis and became prisoners of war. By December, however, Soviet forces surrounded the German troops occupying Stalingrad, isolating them in the heart of the city. The German campaign in the Soviet Union ended on January 31, 1943, with the surrender of German forces. The Soviets' triumphant defense of Stalingrad was a staggering blow to Hitler and his supposedly unbeatable army.

In December 1941, the United States officially joined the war after Japanese forces attacked an American Naval base in Pearl Harbor, Hawaii. The United States declared war on Japan, and then Japan's allies, Germany and Italy, declared war on the United States. Britain, the Soviet Union, and the United States established a unified strategy for defeating Germany. Almost immediately the United States and Britain launched an offensive against the Germans in North Africa. Britain and the United States also planned to launch an assault in western Europe (the western front) as soon as possible, while the Soviets kept fighting in the east (the eastern front). By forcing Hitler to fight on many fronts, the Allies hoped that the Ger-

Joseph Stalin

Soviet political leader Joseph Stalin (1879-1953) was born December 21, 1879, in Gori, Georgia, a southwest Asian territory that was then part of the Russian empire. He survived a difficult childhood—including an infection with smallpox, a life-threatening virus, and cruel beatings by his father—to become absolute ruler of the Soviet Union.

An enthusiastic student of Georgian history, Stalin displayed a revolutionary spirit early. His philosophies clashed with those of the theological seminary (a training ground for future priests) he attended in the Georgian capital of Tbilisi (pronounced "tuh-bih-LEE-see") in the mid-1890s.

Stalin joined a Marxist political group in 1898. (Marxism is a political philosophy professed by nineteenth-century German philosopher Karl Marx, who believed that a revolution by the working class would lead to the formation of a classless society.) Stalin was eventually expelled from the seminary and then pursued a path of political rebellion against Russia's czarist (pronounced "ZARR-ist") system of government. (At the time, a single ruler called a *czar* exercised unlimited power over the Russian people. Stalin's hometown, Georgia, had been independent before being taken over by czarist Russia.)

By the turn of the century Stalin had joined Russia's Social Democratic Party (the political party opposed to the czar). When a militant, or more extreme, wing of the party developed, Stalin became an active member. Members of this more aggressive, radical wing were known as the Bolsheviks. They led the Russian Revolution of 1917, which resulted in the overthrow of the czar and the formation of the communist Soviet Union. (Communism is a system of government in which the state controls almost all the means of production and the distribution of goods. Communism clashes with the American ideal of capitalism, which is based on private ownership and a free market system.)

Following the death of Bolshevik leader Vladimir Lenin, Stalin eliminated all of his political opponents and managed to establish himself as the premier (chief official; first in rank) of the Soviet Union. He held this position until his own death in 1953.

man army would be spread too thin and could be more easily defeated. The plan was to advance from the east, west, and south and squeeze the Germans between the Allied armies advancing from three directions.

Joseph Stalin. *(Reproduced by permission of the Corbis Corporation/Bettmann)*

Stalin's brand of Marxism was particularly harsh, leaving no room for economic freedom or for political dissent (disagreement; opposition). He transformed the Soviet Union's economy by implementing a program of rapid industrialization and collectivizing agriculture (outlawing private ownership of farms and making them communal or state-controlled). As restrictions on freedom were tightened, feelings of discontent and conflict spread among the Soviet people. Resistors (those who opposed Stalin's ideas and policies) were shot or imprisoned in labor camps.

When World War II broke out in Europe in 1939, Stalin aligned himself with German leader Adolf Hitler, hoping to gain more European territory for the Soviet Union. In time, however, Hitler came to view Stalin as an obstacle to the German goal of world dominance. The German leader ordered an invasion of the Soviet Union in June of 1941. After many long and bloody battles, Soviet forces finally defeated the Germans in 1943 in the Battle of Stalingrad (1942-1943).

In the years following World War II, Stalin's efforts to expand Soviet influence throughout Eastern Europe weakened his relationship with England and the United States. The Soviet Union's apparent quest for European—even world—domination led to intense anti-Soviet and anticommunist sentiment in the United States from the 1950s through the 1980s, a time known as the Cold War.

Did you know...

- As a young man Hitler spent a few years in Vienna making money by painting portraits, postcard scenes, and store posters.

- While serving in the German army in World War I Hitler suffered a poison gas attack, during which he claimed to have a vision of himself as an Aryan (white) hero called upon by the gods to lead his country in a glorious 1000-year reich (reich means empire).

- In 1944, some high-ranking officers in the German military tried, unsuccessfully, to assassinate Hitler. Hitler responded to the attack by having approximately five thousand people he suspected of being involved in the plot killed.

- Hitler spent his last days in an underground bunker in Berlin. As the Russian army was overtaking Berlin, the final blow in Germany's defeat, Hitler was in a state of extreme nervous exhaustion. It is reported that he shuffled around the bunker, stooped over, with trembling limbs, talking incoherently, and planning new war strategies for divisions of the German army that had long been defeated.

For More Information
Books

Fuchs, Thomas. *The Hitler Fact Book*. Los Angeles: Fountain Books, 1990.

Marrin, Albert. *Hitler*. New York: Viking Kestrel, 1987.

Skipper, G. C. *The Battle of Stalingrad*. Chicago: Children's Press, 1981.

Stein, R. Conrad. *Invasion of Russia*. Chicago: Children's Press, 1985.

Stein, R. Conrad. *Siege of Leningrad*. Chicago: Children's Press, 1983.

Warth, Robert D. *Joseph Stalin*. New York: Twayne, 1969.

Whitelaw, Nancy. *Josef Stalin: From Peasant to Premier*. New York: Macmillan, 1992.

Videos

Stalin. HBO, 1992.

Sources

Allen, Peter. *The Origins of World War II*. New York: Bookwright Press, 1992.

Hills, Ken. *Wars That Changed the World: World War II*. New York: Marshall Cavendish, 1988.

Leckie, Robert. *The Story of World War II*. New York: Random House, 1964.

Hoobler, Dorothy, and Thomas Hoobler. *World Leaders Past and Present: Joseph Stalin*. New York: Chelsea House, 1985.

New York Times, May 7, 1941, p. 1; June 23, 1941, p. 1; July 3, 1941, p. 1; August 14, 1941, p. 1; October 4, 1941; October 10, 1941, p. 2.

Ross, Stewart. *World Leaders*. New York: Thomson Learning, 1993.

Herbert A. Werner

Excerpt from Iron Coffins: A Personal Account of the German
U-Boat Battles of World War II
First published in 1969; reprinted in 1998

Germany's invasion of Poland on September 1, 1939, marked the beginning of World War II (1939-45). Great Britain and France had promised to protect Poland if it were attacked and declared war on Germany two days later. On that same day the British passenger ship *Athenia,* traveling westward across the Atlantic Ocean toward Canada, was sunk by a German submarine. The attack had come without warning. Over one hundred of the ocean liner's thirteen hundred passengers perished. The Battle of the Atlantic—a deadly, six-year-long campaign—had begun.

Great Britain (England, Scotland, and Wales) is surrounded by water: the Atlantic Ocean to the west and north, the North Sea to the east, and the English Channel to the south. Throughout World War II, Great Britain relied on the Atlantic waterways as paths for receiving much-needed food, fuel, manpower, military supplies, and equipment to fight the Germans. German forces sought to cut off these supply lines.

U-boats (German submarines) were the key to Germany's early dominance in the Battle of the Atlantic: they could launch both surface and underwater attacks. (The U-

"The idea of a convoy with its own air defense smashed our basic concept of U-boat warfare. No longer could we mount a surprise attack or escape without meeting savage counterattacks."

A rescuer assists survivors of the German attack on the passenger ship *Athenia.*
(Reproduced by permission of Corbis/Hulton-Deutsch Collection)

boat takes its name from the word *unterseeboot,* which is German for "submarine.") British prime minister Winston Churchill asserted that during the war "everything happening elsewhere, on land, at sea, or in the air, depended ultimately on [the] outcome" of the Battle of the Atlantic.

The convoy system—in which nonmilitary merchant boats sailed together in groups, protected by an armed navy escort—was used to keep war supplies flowing into the British Isles from the United States. It was the job of the submarines and battleships of the *Kriegsmarine* (the German navy) to destroy the convoys before they reached Great Britain.

The Battle of the Atlantic was in full swing very early in the war. While patrolling the Atlantic for submarines in September of 1939, the British aircraft carrier *Courageous* was torpedoed by a German U-boat. The *Courageous* exploded and sank, killing hundreds of British sailors. The next month the German U-boat *U-47,* commanded by U-boat ace Günther Prien, slipped into a Scottish harbor under the cover of darkness and sank

HMS *Royal Oak,* a huge British battleship. More than eight hundred British sailors died. (HMS stands for "His Majesty's Ship," or "Her Majesty's Ship,"referring to the British king or queen.)

In addition to its submarines and standard battleships, the *Kriegsmarine* had two lightweight, high-speed "pocket battleships" in its arsenal. One of these, the *Graf Spee,* was sent into the South Atlantic to destroy British ships. It sank nine merchant ships in the fall of 1939. But a punishing encounter with three British cruisers—the *Exeter,* the *Ajax,* and the *Achilles*—proved to be the *Graf Spee*'s undoing. (Cruisers are smaller than battleships and very fast.) After taking shelter in a harbor in Uruguay (a country in south east South America) and assessing his chances for a successful escape, *Graf Spee* captain Hans Langsdorff destroyed his own ship with massive explosives to avoid capture by the British. The next night he committed suicide.

Around this time, Admiral Karl Dönitz, commander of the German U-boat force, formulated a plan to assure German victory in the Atlantic. He felt that the fighting power of the submarines would be unbeatable if the boats traveled in clusters. These so-called "wolf packs"—usually five or six U-boats working together to destroy the same convoy—began traveling together in the summer of 1940 and proved highly effective. U-boats also worked in cooperation with German bomber aircraft, which scouted for enemy ships from the air.

The Allied powers (the countries fighting against Germany and its allies, called the Axis powers) used air power for protection. A U-boat that was above water typically dived for cover whenever an aircraft approached. Once submerged, a U-boat was far less capable of detecting and tracking enemy ships.

German battleships continued to play a key role in the Battle of the Atlantic throughout 1940. The British merchant cruiser *Jervis Bay* was escorting more than three dozen ships through the North Atlantic in November of 1940 when it encountered the German pocket battleship the *Admiral Scheer.* The *Jervis Bay* took on the much larger and more heavily armed *Scheer,* giving the ships in the British convoy a chance to scatter and reach safety. The *Jervis Bay* was sunk, but the heroic action of her captain and crew saved thirty-two of the thirty-seven ships in the convoy from a similar fate. By the end of 1940, the Germans had destroyed approximately one thousand British ships.

The HMS *Hood* was sunk by the German battleship *Bismark* in May 1941. Only three members of the fourteen-hundred-member crew survived. *(Reproduced by permission of AP/Wide World Photos, Inc.)*

The German navy dominated the Battle of the Atlantic in 1941. The sinking of HMS *Hood* (see box) in May of 1941 was a stunning blow for the British. By midsummer 1941 American ships had joined in efforts to convoy merchant ships bound for Britain. Up until this point the United States had allowed its navy to serve only as a patroller of neutral waters. But in September U.S. president Franklin D. Roosevelt declared that American naval convoys could and would attack German war vessels. On October 30, 1941, a German submarine sank the American destroyer *Reuben James*. This event marked America's first real loss in the Battle of the Atlantic.

Things to remember while reading the *Iron Coffins* excerpt:

- After conquering Norway and France in the spring of 1940, the Germans were able to use the Atlantic coastal waters of these nations for U-boat bases. The bases gave the German navy a distinct advantage over the Allies on the high seas throughout 1941 and 1942. In 1942 alone, U-boats sank more than twelve hundred Allied ships.

- In the early phases of the battle it was next to impossible to detect German submarines lurking in the Atlantic Ocean. The Allied forces realized that the war against the U-boats could be won only with advanced tracking methods. Technological breakthroughs such as radar and sonar gave the Allies the upper hand in the later stages of the battle. (Radar is short for "RAdio Detection And Ranging," and sonar is short for "SOund NAvigation Ranging." Radar and sonar made use of reflected radio and sound waves, respectively, to pinpoint the location of enemy subs.)

- Between 1941 and 1945 the author, Herbert A. Werner, served on five different German submarines. He used his wartime notes and letters to compose *Iron Coffins*.

- In his introduction to *Iron Coffins,* Werner wrote: "Because I was one of the few U-boat commanders who fought through most of the war and who managed to survive, I felt it was my duty to my fallen comrades to set the record straight. . . . This book belongs to my dead comrades, stricken down wholesale in the prime of youth. I hope it pays them the honor they deserve. If I have succeeded in handing down to the reader the ancient lesson that each generation seems to forget—that war is evil . . . then I consider this my most constructive deed."

Hood and Bismarck Sinkings

The *Bismarck* was a huge German battleship, the most powerful ship in the German naval fleet. In May 1941 it paired up with the German cruiser *Prinz Eugen* to search the North Atlantic for British convoys. The ships found their target—two patrolling British cruisers—on May 23. The cruisers called for assistance, and the British battleships HMS *Hood* and HMS *Prince of Wales* responded. A short but fierce battle followed between the *Bismarck* and the *Hood.* The *Hood* exploded after being hit by enemy fire in the early morning hours of May 24, 1941. The ship broke into pieces and sank. Only three members of the fourteen-hundred-person crew survived. The incident was a huge defeat for Britain's Royal Navy.

In response, the British sent out battleships, cruisers, destroyers, torpedo planes, aircraft carriers, and flying boats to find the *Bismarck.* After searching for two days through foggy, dark, wet skies, the Royal Navy finally located the German battleship. On May 27, 1941, after repeated attacks, the *Bismarck* sank. More than two thousand German sailors on board died.

- Werner took part in his first U-boat battle in May 1941, when he was just twenty-one years old. The following excerpt describes a grueling two-day clash that occurred in May of 1943, after the Allies had gained superiority in the Battle of the Atlantic. Werner was then the executive officer of *U-230,* second in command to the captain.

- The four-digit numbers in the paragraphs below are times—the first two digits represent hours and the last two represent minutes. Military time is measured on a twenty-four-hour scale. The first twelve hours in a day are recorded as "0100" (for the first hour after midnight) through "1200" hours. The afternoon and evening hours are recorded as "1300" (for 1:00 P.M.) through "2400" hours (for midnight).

Excerpt from Iron Coffins

May 12. 0716: . . . Before we could risk resurfacing to race into a new attack position, we had to put distance between us and the **convoy***. . . . For almost two hours we traveled diagonally away from the giants of steel.*

0915: U-230 surfaced. Mounting the bridge while the deck was still **awash,** *I took a hurried look in a circle. Far to the northeast,* **mastheads and funnels** *moved along the sharp line which divided the ocean from the sky. U-230 forged through the sea, parallel to the convoy's track, in an attempt to reach a forward position before dusk. . . .*

0955: . . . I saw a twin-engined plane dropping out of the sun. The moment of surprise was total.

"Alarrrmmm!" We plunged head over heels into the **conning tower***. The boat reacted at once and shot below the surface. . . .*

Four short, ferocious explosions shattered the water above and around us. The boat trembled and fell at a 60-degree angle. Water splashed, steel shrieked, ribs moaned, valves blew, deck-plates jumped, and the boat was thrown into darkness. As the lights flickered on, I saw astonishment in the . . . eyes of the men. They had every right to be astounded: the attack out of the sun was a complete

Convoy: A group of Allied merchant ships (nonmilitary boats carrying cargo and sometimes passengers) sailing together, protected by a navy escort.

Awash: Flooded.

Mastheads and funnels: The tops of the Allied ships.

Alarrrmmm!: The alarm indicates that the submarine is going to dive below the surface of the water.

Conning tower: Raised structure situated on a submarine deck.

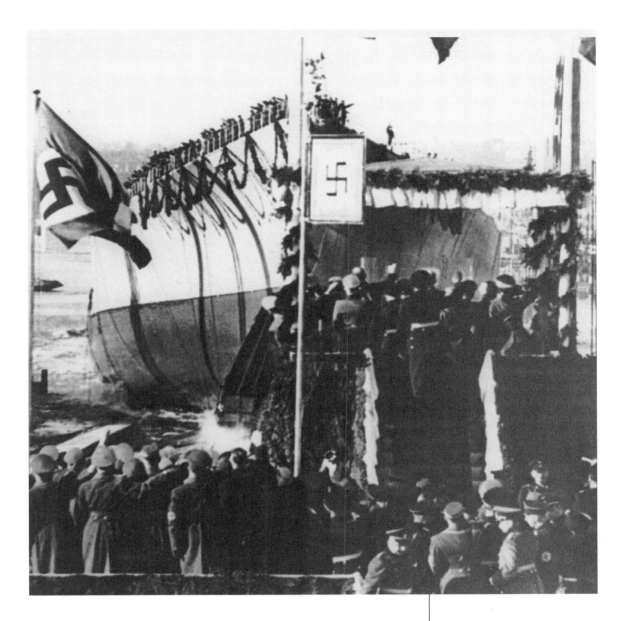

mystery. Where had the small plane come from? It did not have the range to fly a round-trip between the nearest point of land and the middle of the Atlantic. The conclusion was inescapable that the convoy launched its own airplanes. . . . The idea of a convoy with its own air defense smashed our basic concept of U-boat warfare. No longer could we mount a surprise attack or escape without meeting savage counterattacks. . . .

Launching of the Bismarck, Germany's largest battleship. *(Reproduced by permission of AP/Wide World Photos, Inc.)*

1035: U-230 *came up to periscope depth. A careful check with our "sky scope," an instrument similar to the periscope, revealed no aircraft. We surfaced at high speed.*

The hunt went on. We pressed forward obstinately. . . . I glanced only occasionally at the …horizon and concentrated on the sky. . . .

1110: I detected a glint of metal between the clouds. It was a small aircraft, and it was diving into the attack.

"Alarrrmmm!"

Fifty seconds later, four explosions nearby taught us that the pilot was a well-trained **bombardier***. . . .*

1125: U-230 *surfaced. We drove forward and clung to the fringes of the convoy with grim determination . . .*

1217: "Aircraft dead **astern***, alarrrmmm!"*

U-230 *dived once more and descended rapidly. I bit my lip and waited for the final blast. At forty-five seconds, four booms whipped the boat with violent force. Every second we were able to snatch from the pursuing aircraft brought us closer to the convoy and success. But if we dived a second too late, bombs would end our hunt with sudden death. . . .*

1323: Our radio mate delivered an urgent message to the Captain: ATTACKED BY AIRCRAFT. UNABLE TO DIVE. SINKING. . . . HELP. U-456.

"Have **Prager** *check position,"* **Siegmann** *shouted back. "Maybe we can save the crew."*

The captain's impulse to rescue our comrades might well result in suicide. We were closer to death than to life ourselves. But help was **imperative***—we would have expected the same. Moments later, Prager reported that U-456 was only twelve miles ahead. . . . Immediately, the Captain changed course.*

1350: We spotted a plane circling four miles ahead. Then my **glasses** *picked up the* **bow** *of U-456 poking out of the rough sea. The men clung to the slippery deck and to the steel cable strung from bow to bridge. Most of them stood in the water up to their chests. The aircraft kept circling above the sinking boat, making it* **foolhardy** *for us to approach. Another danger prevented rescue: astern, a* **corvette** *crept over the horizon, evidently summoned by the plane. Now our own lives were in jeopardy. We turned away from the aircraft, the* **escort***, and U-456, and fled in the direction of the convoy.*

Bombardier: Member of a bomber crew who releases the bombs.

Astern: Behind a ship.

Prager: U-230's navigator.

Siegmann: U-230's captain.

Glasses: Binoculars.

Bow: Forward part of a ship.

Foolhardy: Reckless; unwise.

Corvette: A small, fast escort ship that is well armed with machine guns and explosive depth charges.

Escort: An armed protector ship that accompanies another sailing vessel.

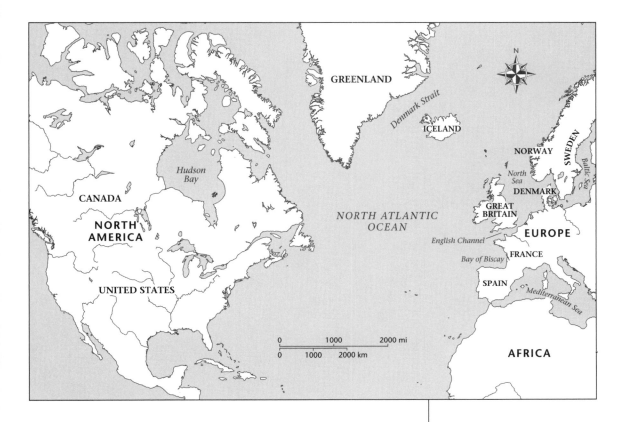

1422: "Aircraft astern!"

*. . . It was too late to dive. The single-engined plane came in low in a straight line [over us]. I fingered the trigger of my gun. . . . [It] was jammed. I kicked its **magazine**, clearing the jam. Then I **emptied the gun at the menace**. The mate's automatic bellowed. Our boat veered to **starboard**, spoiling the plane's bomb run. The pilot revved up his engine, circled, then roared toward us from dead ahead. As the plane dived very low, its engine sputtered, then stopped. Wing first, the plane crashed into the surging ocean, smashing its other wing on our superstructure as we raced by. The pilot, thrown out of his cockpit, lifted his arm and waved for help, but then I saw him disintegrate in the explosion of the four bombs which were meant to destroy us. Four violent shocks kicked into our starboard side astern, but we left the horrible scene unharmed. . . .*

*1545: A report from the radio room put our small victory into proper perspective: **DEPTH CHARGES** BY THREE **DESTROYERS**. SINKING. U-186. This new loss was the 11th we had heard of since our patrol began. . . .*

During the Battle of the Atlantic, German U-boats tried to stop supplies from North America from reaching Great Britain.

Magazine: A holder for cartridges that are fed into the chamber of a firearm.

Emptied the gun at the menace: Used up all his bullets firing at the Allied bomber.

Starboard: The right side of a ship or aircraft.

Depth charges: Drum-encased explosives aimed at submerged submarines.

Intensification: Herbert A. Werner   51

A German submarine sinking after a combined attack by several aircraft.
(Reproduced by permission of the Corbis Corporation [Bellevue])

1600: U-230 cut into the **projected** path of the convoy. I saw four columns of ships creep over the sharp horizon in the southwest, headed in our direction. We had to halt them. . . .

1638: . . . Siegmann . . . cried, "Down with the boat, Chief, take her down for God's sake, destroyer in **ramming position.** . . . "

. . . As the boat swiftly descended, the harrowing sound of the destroyer's engines and propellers hit the steel of our **hull.** *It grew so*

fast, and echoed so deafeningly, that we were all unable to move. Only our boat was moving, and she went downward much too slowly to escape the blow.

An earshattering boom ruptured the sea. A **spread** of six depth charges lifted the boat, tossed her out of the water, and left her on the surface at the mercy of four British destroyers. The screws of U-230 rotated in highest revolutions, driving us ahead. For seconds there was silence. For seconds the British were baffled and stunned. After a whole eternity, our bow dipped and the boat sank—and sank.

A new series of exploding charges lifted our stern with a mighty force. Our boat, entirely out of control, was catapulted toward the bottom five miles below. . . . U-230 tumbled to 250 meters before [we were] able to reverse her fall. . . .

1716: A new spread deafened us and took our breath away. . . . The steel knocked and shrieked and valves were thrown into open position. . . . Water everywhere. Its weight forced the boat deeper into the depths. In the meantime, the convoy crawled in a thunderous procession over our boat.

1740: The uproar was at its peak. A sudden splash told us that we had 10 or 15 seconds to brace against another barrage. The charges went off just beyond lethal range. . . . Perhaps we should risk going deeper. I did not know where our limit was, where the hull would finally crack. No one knew. Those who had found out **took their knowledge into the depths.** For hours we suffered the punishment and sank gradually deeper. In a constant pattern, spreads of twenty-four charges battered our boat every twenty minutes. . . .

2000: [A] new group [of escorts] launched its first attack, then another, and another. We sat helpless 265 meters below. . . . Our bodies were stiff from cold, stress, and fear. . . . The **bilges** were flooded with water, oil, and urine. Our washrooms were under lock and key; to use them then would have meant instant death, for the tremendous outside pressure would have acted in reverse. . . . Added to the stench of waste, sweat, and oil was the stink of the battery gases. The increasing humidity condensed on the cold steel, dropped into the bilges, dripped from pipes, and soaked our clothes. By midnight, the Captain realized that the British would not let up in their bombardment, and he ordered the distribution of **potash cartridges** to supplement breathing. Soon every man was equipped with a large metal box attached to his chest, a rubber hose leading to his mouth, and a clamp on his nose. . . .

Destroyers: A small, fast, heavily armed warship.

Projected: Planned or estimated.

Ramming position: Ready to drive or force with impact; set to crash violently and deliberately into another structure (in this case, into Werner's U-boat).

Hull: Main body of a ship.

Spread: A scattering of explosives.

Took their knowledge into the depths: Died finding out.

Bilges: Lowest points of the body of a ship.

Potash cartridges: Devices that deliver potassium compounds to assist in breathing.

Smoke and flames billow from a tanker torpedoed by Axis forces.
(Reproduced by permission of Corbis/Bettmann)

May 13. . . . [As of] 0400 . . . we had been under assault for 12 hours and there was no sign of relief. This day was my birthday and I wondered whether it would be my last. . . .

May 14. By midnight, we had approached the limit for boat and crew. We had reached a depth of 280 meters and the boat was still sinking. I dragged myself through the aisle, pushing and tossing men around, forcing them to stay awake. Whoever fell asleep might never be awakened.

*0310: A thunderous spread rattled down, but without effect. We were closer to being crushed by the mounting pressure than by the exploding canisters. As the echo of the last blast slowly subsided, something else attracted our attention. It was the thrashing of retreating propellers. For a long time we listened to the fading sound, unable to believe that the **Tommies** had given up the hunt.*

0430: . . . U-230 broke through to air and life. We pushed ourselves up to the bridge. Around us spread the infinite beauty of night, sky, and ocean. . . . We could not believe that death had kept his finger on us for thirty-five gruesome hours.

Tommies: British soldiers.

Refuse: (Pronounced "REH-fyoos") Garbage.

Abruptly I felt the impact of the oxy-gen-rich air upon my system. Almost losing consciousness, I sagged to my knees and slumped over the rim of the bridge. . . .

The diesels coughed to life. Since the convoy had disappeared long ago, we trav-eled south, toward our last position. The engines muttered reassuringly. . . . The bilges were emptied, the foul air expelled, and the accumulated **refuse** *thrown over-board. When the darkness dissolved and a new day dawned, U-230 was again ready for combat. (Werner, pp. 119-26)*

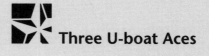

Three U-boat Aces

Among the leading names in U-boat warfare are Otto Kretschmer, Günther Prien, and Erich Topp. Together, these German commanders sank 106 ships during the Battle of the Atlantic. Admiral Topp's *Odyssey of a U-Boat Commander* is considered a classic wartime memoir.

What happened next . . .

Werner was promoted to commander in December of 1943 and began his training in January 1944. By that time the Germans were losing the Battle of the Atlantic. British, Ameri-can, and Canadian bombers were working together to provide air cover over the Atlantic from North America to Europe.

In April of 1944 Werner took command of his own U-boat, *U-415.* He and his crew successfully evaded heavy bomb-ing raids that spring, only to sink in July while docked at Brest Harbor, a seaport off France's northwestern coast. (The subma-rine activated a mine that had been laid in the port by the British.) In August Werner assumed command of *U-953,* a dilapidated boat with an inexperienced crew. They managed to survive until war's end.

Did you know . . .

- British prime minister Winston Churchill was quoted as saying, "The only thing that really frightened me during [World War II] was the U-boat peril."

Winston Churchill (center) with officers of the Royal Canadian Air Force. The American and Royal Canadian air forces helped Britain defend its ships in the Battle of the Atlantic.
(Reproduced by permission of AP/Wide World Photos, Inc.)

- In the first half of 1942 German U-boats sank more than two hundred merchant ships in the western part of the Atlantic, bringing the war closer to American shores than ever before.

- By the time World War II was over some twenty-eight thousand of the thirty-nine thousand men in Germany's U-boat force had died in battle. In addition, about eight hundred U-boats were lost by the end of the war. "One by one, our crews sailed out obediently, even optimistically, on ludicrous missions that ended in death," wrote Werner in his introduction to *Iron Coffins.* "When hostilities finally ceased in May 1945, the ocean floor was littered with the wreckage of the U-boat war." Of all the subs that had seen battle duty, only three remained afloat when Germany surrendered in 1945. One of these three, *U-953,* was under Werner's command. Werner attributes his survival, in large part, to luck.

- Werner immigrated to the United States in 1957 and later became an American citizen.

For More Information

Books

Buchheim, Lothart-Günther. *Das Boot.* Originally published in 1975. Published in English translation as *The Boat.* New York: Dell, 1988.

Burn, A. *Fighting Captain: The Story of Frederic John Walker and the Battle of the Atlantic.* Philadelphia: Trans-Atlantic Publications, 1993. Reprinted, 1998.

Hirschfeld, Wolfgang. *Hirschfeld: The Story of a U-Boat NCO, 1940-1946.* U.S. Naval Institute, 1996.

Lane, T. *The Merchant Seaman's War.* UK/New York: Manchester University Press, 1990.

Thomas, D.A. *The Atlantic Star: 1939-45.* UK: W.H. Allen, 1990.

Topp, Erich. *The Odyssey of a U-Boat Commander: Recollections of Erich Topp.* Translated by Eric C. Rust. Westport, CT: Praeger, 1992.

Vause, Jordan, and Jurgen Oesten. *Wolf: U-Boat Commanders in World War II.* Osceola, WI: Airlife, 1997.

Videos

The Boat. From the book *Das Boot* by Lothart-Günther Buchheim. Radiant Film, 1982.

Web Sites

Uboat.net: the U-boat War 1939-1945. [Online] http://uboat.net (accessed on September 6, 1999).

The Career of Battle Cruiser Hood [Online] http://www.geocities.com/SoHo/Workshop/2966/History/Timeline.html (accessed on September 6, 1999).

Heydt, Bruce. "The Hunt for *Bismarck.*" *British Heritage.* June/July 1998. [Online] http://www.thehistorynet.com/BritishHeritage/articles/1998/0798_cover.htm (accessed on September 6, 1999).

Sources

Allen, Kenneth. *Battle of the Atlantic.* London: Wayland, 1973.

Ballard, Robert D. *Exploring the Bismarck.* Toronto: Madison Press, 1991.

Black, Wallace B., and Jean F. Blashfield. *Battle of the Atlantic.* "World War II 50th Anniversary Series." New York: Crestwood House, 1991.

Heydt, Bruce. "The Hunt for *Bismarck.*" *British Heritage* (June-July 1998) [Online] http://www.thehistorynet.com/BritishHeritage/articles/1998/0798_cover.htm (accessed on September 6, 1999).

Pitt, Barrie, and the editors of Time-Life Books. *The Battle of the Atlantic.* Alexandria, VA: Time-Life Books, 1977.

Shirer, William L. *The Sinking of the Bismarck*. New York: Random House, 1962.

Skipper, G.C. *Battle of the Atlantic*. Chicago: Children's Press, 1981.

Werner, Herbert A. *Iron Coffins: A Personal Account of the German U-Boat Battles of World War II*. New York: H. Holt, 1969. Reprinted. New York: Da Capo Press, 1998.

Woodrooffe, T. *The Battle of the Atlantic*. New York: Faber, 1965.

Franklin D. Roosevelt

"A Date Which Will Live in Infamy"
**War message delivered to U.S. Congress
December 8, 1941**

Intensification: Franklin D. Roosevelt

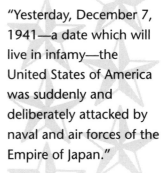

In the years leading up to World War II (1939-45), the government of Japan was run by its military leaders. These men sought to expand Japan's power on the eastern Asian mainland, forming an enormous empire in Asia.

Japanese forces had been fighting in China since July 1937 and by 1940 had taken over much of Southeast Asia. Japan's next targets were the island groups in the southwest Pacific ocean. Alarmed by the Japanese government's quest to dominate Asia, the United States took steps to restrict—but not totally ban—trade with Japan and demanded the nation withdraw its troops from China and French Indochina (now Vietnam). Although the U.S.-imposed trade restrictions interfered with their manufacture of war materials, the Japanese did not buckle under the economic pressure. Japan's military steadfastly refused to remove troops from occupied areas. As a result, U.S. president Franklin D. Roosevelt took more definitive action in the summer of 1941, cutting off *all* U.S. trade with Japan—including oil, which was vital to fuel the Japanese war effort. Shortly thereafter, the governments of Great Britain and the Netherlands did the same.

"Yesterday, December 7, 1941—a date which will live in infamy—the United States of America was suddenly and deliberately attacked by naval and air forces of the Empire of Japan."

59

The USS *Arizona* after Japan's attack on Pearl Harbor. *(Reproduced by permission of UPI/ Corbis-Bettmann)*

The United States had been on the brink of war with the Axis Powers (Germany, Italy, and Japan) for months, but the events that occurred on the morning of Sunday, December 7, 1941, propelled the nation into the very heart of the growing global conflict. During the early morning hours of that Sunday, the Japanese Fleet launched a surprise attack on the U.S. naval base at Pearl Harbor, Hawaii. (Pearl Harbor is located on the southern coast of the Hawaiian island of Oahu [pronounced oh-AH-hoo]. The torpedo planes and bombers that attacked the harbor were launched from Japanese aircraft carriers stationed about 200 miles north of Oahu.)

The raid on Pearl Harbor lasted less than two hours. In that time eighteen American warships were hit. The USS *Arizona* was destroyed in a fiery explosion. The *Nevada* and *West Virginia* were sunk. Approximately 200 planes—most of them on the ground—were destroyed and another 150 were damaged. The Pearl Harbor attack left nearly 2,500 Americans dead and 1,200 wounded. In a radio address to the nation on December 9, 1941, President Roosevelt declared: "We are now in this war. We are all in it—all the way."

Things to remember while reading "A Day Which Will Live in Infamy":

- Japan had signed the Tripartite Pact on September 27, 1940, thus pledging support to the governments of Germany and Italy. Together, the three nations became known as the Axis Powers.

- Throughout the autumn of 1941 the United States expected Japan to attack somewhere in the Pacific. Many U.S. officials suspected the Philippine Islands—not Pearl Harbor—to be the prime target for an enemy assault.

- In 1941, although the United States had not declared war against Germany, a significant portion of the American naval fleet was already engaged in battles with German U-boats in the Atlantic while protecting U.S. and British merchant ships. (See Herbert Werner entry in chapter one for more information about the Battle of the Atlantic.)

- The attack on Pearl Harbor was the idea of Japanese Admiral Isoroku Yamamoto, commander in chief of Japan's navy.

- By sidelining the U.S. Pacific Fleet at Pearl Harbor (putting it out of action by launching a surprise attack), Admiral Yamamoto thought he would clear the way for a Japanese conquest of islands in the western and southern Pacific.

- Japanese attacks on the Philippines, Guam, and Wake Island followed shortly after the raid on Pearl Harbor.

"A Day Which Will Live in Infamy"

War message delivered to the U.S. Congress, December 8, 1941

*Yesterday, December 7, 1941—a date which will live in **infamy**— the United States of America was suddenly and deliberately attacked by naval and air forces of the Empire of Japan.*

*The United States was at peace with that nation and, at the **solicitation** of Japan, was still in conversation with its government and its Emperor looking toward the maintenance of peace in the Pacific. Indeed, one hour after Japanese air squadrons had **commenced** bombing in **Oahu**, the Japanese ambassador to the United States and his colleague delivered to the Secretary of State [Cordell Hull] a formal reply to a recent American message. While this reply stated that it seemed useless to continue the existing **diplomatic negotiations**, it contained no threat or hint of war or armed attack.*

*It will be recorded that the distance of Hawaii from Japan makes it obvious that the attack was deliberately planned many days or even weeks ago. During the **intervening** time the Japanese Government has deliberately sought to deceive the United States by false statements and expressions of hope for continued peace.*

The attack yesterday on the Hawaiian Islands has caused severe damage to American naval and military forces. Very many American lives have been lost. In addition American ships have been reported torpedoed on the high seas between San Francisco and Honolulu.

Yesterday the Japanese government also launched an attack against Malaya.

Last night Japanese forces attacked Hong Kong.

Last night Japanese forces attacked Guam.

Last night Japanese forces attacked the Philippine Islands.

Last night the Japanese attacked Wake Island.

This morning the Japanese attacked Midway Island.

*Japan has, therefore, undertaken a surprise **offensive** extending throughout the Pacific area. The facts of yesterday speak for themselves. The people of the United States have already formed their opinions and well understand the **implications** to the very life and safety of our nation.*

Infamy: Disgrace; being known forever as an evil act.

Solicitation: Request.

Commenced: Began.

Oahu: Hawaiian island.

Diplomatic negotiations: Talks of a possible compromise between the United States and Japan.

Intervening: Occurring between two points in time; in the meantime.

Offensive: Attack.

Implications: Consequences; significance; meaning.

The character of the onslaught: Roosevelt is referring to the underhanded nature of the attack by the Japanese.

Premeditated: Thought about beforehand; planned ahead.

Righteous might: Strength or power that goes with being right, just, and good.

As Commander-in-Chief of the Army and Navy, I have directed that all measures be taken for our defense.

Always will we remember **the character of the onslaught** against us.

No matter how long it may take us to overcome this **premeditated** invasion, the American people in their **righteous might** will win through to absolute victory.

USS *West Virginia* in flames during the attack on Pearl Harbor. *(Reproduced by permission of the National Archives and Records Administration)*

The Attack on Pearl Harbor: A Sequence of Events

1. The Japanese Fleet set out from a harbor in the North Pacific at 6:00 A.M. on November 26, 1941 (in Japan).

2. Twelve days later (having crossed the international date line in the Pacific, adding one day) the aircraft carriers reached their launching point, a little more than 200 miles north of Oahu.

3. Government officials in Washington, D.C., sent a war-alert message to Hawaii on December 6. The United States was bracing for war with Japan, but an attack on the American naval base at Pearl Harbor was hardly considered.

4. Two representatives of the Japanese government were in Washington, D.C., carrying on talks with U.S. Secretary of State Cordell Hull (1871-1955) on Sunday, December 7, 1941. Peace talks were still going on after the attack on Pearl Harbor had begun.

5. Japanese bombers began their infamous December 7 run on Pearl Harbor at 7:50 A.M. Hawaii time. Prior to the raid, Japan had not declared war on the United States.

6. The attack, which lasted 110 minutes, paralyzed the U.S. Pacific Fleet.

7. President Roosevelt delivered a message to Congress on the morning of December 8.

8. Two and a half hours after completing his message, Roosevelt signed a formal declaration of war against Japan.

*I believe I interpret the will of the Congress and of the people when I assert that we will not only defend ourselves to the uttermost but will make very certain that this form of **treachery** shall never endanger us again.*

Hostilities exist. There is no blinking at the fact that our people, our territory and our interests are in grave danger.

*With confidence in our armed forces—with the **unbounding** determination of our people—we will gain the **inevitable** triumph—so help us God.*

*I ask that the Congress declare that since the **unprovoked** and **dastardly** attack by Japan on Sunday, December 7th, a state of war has existed between the United States and the Japanese Empire. (Roosevelt, pp. 302-3)*

Treachery: Betrayal of faith or trust; deception.

Unbounding: Limitless.

Inevitable: Unavoidable.

Unprovoked: Not aroused to action; not brought on or stirred up on purpose.

Dastardly: Cowardly; acting secretly and deceptively.

What happened next...

On December 11, 1941, Germany and Italy declared war on the United States. While America was scrambling to recover from the raid on Pearl Harbor, the Japanese staged a series of invasions in the Pacific. U.S. military bases on Guam (a U.S. territory in the western Pacific) and Wake Island (located northeast of Guam) were attacked the same day as Pearl Harbor. Japanese forces captured Guam on December 10 and Wake Island on December 23, 1941. On December 25, following a week of steady bombing, Hong Kong fell to Japan. Manila, the capital city of the Philippine Islands, surrendered to the Japanese eight days later, and the southeast Asian island of Singapore, located at the southern tip of the Malay Peninsula, followed suit in February of 1942.

President Franklin D. Roosevelt signing the declaration of war against Japan, Dec. 8, 1941. *(Reproduced by permission of the National Archives and Records Administration)*

The American fight against Japanese forces in the Philippines reached a fever pitch in March of 1942. U.S. troops surrendered to Japan at Bataan (a key island in the northern part of the Philippines) on April 9, 1942, and a nightmarish "Death March" of American and Filipino prisoners of war (POWs) ensued. The captured soldiers were forced to hike 65 miles across the rocky, dusty terrain to their prison camp. By the time it was over, seven thousand of the seventy thousand POWs on the march had died.

But the naval battle at Midway, which took place during the first week in June 1942, marked a turning point in the war in the Pacific. Midway Island is located in the northern Pacific Ocean between Hawaii and Japan. On June 3, 1942, one hundred Japanese warships staged what was supposed to be a surprise attack. Two factors gave American forces the upper hand in the Battle of Midway: (1) Japanese military codes had been deciphered, or broken, by the United States,

Hideki Tojo

General Hideki Tojo (1884-1948) was the dominant figure in the Japanese government during World War II. Always aggressive and militant, he earned the nickname "Kamisori," meaning "The Razor," for his keen mind. As chief of staff of the Japanese army (1937), minister of war (beginning 1940), and prime minister of Japan (from October 1941 through July 1944), Tojo pushed hard for the expansion of Japanese influence throughout Asia. He authorized the Japanese attack on the American naval base at Pearl Harbor in 1941. Four years later, following Japan's surrender to Allied forces (the United States, Great Britain, and the Soviet Union) at war's end, Tojo attempted to commit suicide. He was arrested later in 1945, tried by the Allies as a war criminal, and hanged in Tokyo on December 23, 1948.

revealing Japan's battle plan, and (2) American aircraft carriers had not been at Pearl Harbor at the time of the attack. Five were at sea and one was in a California harbor.

Consequently, U.S. aircraft carriers (called "flattops") and bombers were well prepared for the Japanese assault on Midway. After losing four of their own carriers in the battle against American forces, the Japanese retreated. The American victory at Midway was considered revenge for the attack on Pearl Harbor. From that point on, a Japanese invasion of the continental United States was no longer a threat.

In the first half of 1942 the Japanese also captured the Solomon Islands, located north of Australia, and used them as bases to launch further attacks in the Pacific. U.S. Marines landed on Guadalcanal, one of the Solomon Islands, on August 7, 1942. For six months Americans fought on the ground, in the air, and in the shark-infested waters to win control of the Japanese-held island. By January 1943 the Japanese had lost Guadalcanal.

Did you know...

- When Japan invaded China in 1937—before World War II had even started—a Japanese plane attacked and sank the USS *Panay* in the Yangtze River. The United States did not launch a counterattack. Later, the Japanese government apologized and promised to end its bombing raids over China. When the air bombings continued, the U.S. government cut exports to Japan.

- Radio communications between Washington D.C. and Pearl Harbor were hampered by the bad weather on the morning of December 7, 1941.

Hideki Tojo, prime minister of Japan from October 1941 through July 1944.

(Reproduced by permission of AP/Wide World Photos, Inc.)

- A "Declaration by the United Nations," issued on January 1, 1942, pledged the full cooperation and assistance of twenty-six member nations in the fight against the Axis Powers.

- When the USS *Arizona* exploded at Pearl Harbor, 1,177 Americans were killed. In 1962 a memorial bridge and shrine were constructed over the remains of sunken battleship.

- Admiral Yamamoto, the man behind the attack on Pearl Harbor, was killed on April 18, 1943, when U.S. fighter pilots shot down his plane over the South Pacific.

For More Information
Books

Prange, Gordon W. *At Dawn We Slept: The Untold Story of Pearl Harbor.* New York: Viking Penguin, 1982.

Shapiro, William E. *Pearl Harbor.* New York: F. Watts, 1984.

Videos

Pearl Harbor: 50 Years Later. Turner Entertainment, 1991.

Pearl Harbor: Two Hours That Changed the World. MPI Home Video, 1991.

Web Sites

Pearl Harbor Remembered. [Online] http://www.execpc.com/~dschaaf/mainmenu.html (accessed on September 6, 1999).

The History Place. *December 7, 1941 - Japanese Bomb Pearl Harbor* [Online] http://www.historyplace.com/worldwar2/timeline/pearl.htm (accessed on September 6, 1999).

Sources

Allen, Peter. *The Origins of World War II.* New York: Bookwright Press, 1992.

Dunnahoo, Terry. *Pearl Harbor: America Enters the War.* New York: F. Watts, 1991.

Harris, Mark Jonathan, Franklin Mitchell, and Steven Schechter, eds. *The Homefront: America during World War II.* Introduction by Studs Terkel. New York: G. P. Putnam's Sons, 1984.

Newsweek, March 8, 1999, pp. 42-4, 49.

New York Times, December 8, 1941, pp. 1, 8.

Roosevelt, Franklin Delano. *Nothing to Fear: The Selected Addresses of Franklin Delano Roosevelt, 1932-1945.* Edited by B. D. Zevin. New York: Houghton, 1946.

Ross, Stewart. *World Leaders.* New York: Thomson Learning, 1993.

Zich, Arthur, and the editors of Time-Life Books. *The Rising Sun.* "Time-Life Books World War II Series." Alexandria, VA: Time-Life Books, 1977.

The American Home Front

2

Catherine "Renee"
Young Pike
...71

Jerry Stanley
...85

A merica's accomplishments during World War II were fueled largely by the collective efforts of ordinary citizens on the home front. After declaring war on Japan, and then on Germany, in December of 1941, the United States assembled and trained the largest military force in its history. As most of the nation's men joined the ranks of the armed forces, American women stepped into the jobs "the boys" had left vacant on the home front.

Wartime production pulled the American economy out of a twelve-year slump known as the Great Depression (1929-1939). The Great Depression was a period of severe economic decline. Many factories and banks closed; many people lost their jobs. Large numbers of people were homeless and had no way to get food. As World War II heated up in Europe, the economic situation in the United States began to improve. But after the United States actually entered the war in December 1941, unemployment plummeted as more and more manufacturing jobs were created. Factories churned out planes, tanks, ships, jeeps, weapons, and other war materials in record numbers. Money to cover the incredibly high cost of the war was raised through the sale of war bonds, through added taxes, and through mandatory conservation measures, most notably rationing scarce food items, rubber, gasoline, and heating oil.

The hopes and fears of one woman on the home front, Catherine "Renee" Young Pike are captured in a series of letters she wrote over a two-year period to her husband, George Pike, an American soldier. These letters are excerpted from the collection *Since You Went Away: World War II Letters from American Women on the Home Front.*

In the wake of the Japanese attack on American naval bases at Pearl Harbor, Japanese Americans on the home front became victims of intensified discrimination and abuse. Law-abiding Japanese American citizens were treated as potential threats to national security—solely because of their race. In February 1942 President Roosevelt signed Executive Order 9066. This move led to the confinement of Japanese Americans in shoddily constructed internment camps that had been set up in Arizona, Arkansas, California, Colorado, Idaho, Oregon, Utah, Washington, and Wyoming. Relocated Japanese Americans lost their homes, their jobs, and virtually everything they owned. *I Am an American: A True Story of Japanese Internment,* written by Jerry Stanley, tells the story of Shiro Nomuri, an American citizen of Japanese ancestry who was sent to the Manzanar Relocation Center in eastern California.

Catherine "Renee" Young Pike

Excerpt from **Since You Went Away: World War II Letters from American Women on the Home Front**

Edited by Judy Barrett Litoff and David C. Smith
Published in 1991

T hose Americans who were not fighting on the front lines during World War II worked on a different front—the home front, which fueled the entire war effort. The decade before the war had been a particularly bleak one for most Americans. The Great Depression, a period of severe economic slowdown, began in the United States in 1929. By 1932 approximately twelve million Americans were unemployed. But the nation's entry into World War II in December of 1941 brought a swift end to nearly twelve years of hardship and deprivation. High unemployment in the United States disappeared as government office positions and manufacturing jobs opened up in record numbers.

U.S. president Franklin D. Roosevelt has been credited with inspiring the nation to reach phenomenal wartime production goals. "To change a whole nation from a basis of peace time production of implements of peace to a basis of war time production of implements of war is no easy task," noted Roosevelt in his January 6, 1941 message to Congress. According to Russell Freedman in *Franklin Delano Roosevelt*, "As late as 1940, the United States was so poorly prepared for

"The cab driver must have sensed my feelings as he drove me to the train station. He said to me, 'Is your husband going overseas?' I looked out into that deep, dense fog where you had gone, and I said, 'Tonight may be the last time I will see him for a long, long time.'"

We Can Do It!

WAR PRODUCTION CO-ORDINATING COMMITTEE

Rosie the Riveter became an inspirational figure for women who were taking on new roles and contributing to the war effort. *(Courtesy of the National Archives and Records Administration)*

war that soldiers trained with broomsticks for rifles and pieces of cardboard marked 'Tank.' And yet the nation's factories and shipyards were swiftly converted to produce planes, tanks, ships, and weapons."

War production boosted the American economy more than any government relief program ever could. Factories began churning out ammunition, bombers, jeeps, and other war supplies. As American men were drafted into or voluntarily signed up for service in the armed forces, the nation's women stepped into the workforce in unprecedented (never before seen) numbers. American production allowed Great Britain and the Soviet Union to battle against Germany's forces. And between 1942 and 1944, after the United States entered the war (see Franklin D. Roosevelt entry in chapter one for more information on America's entry into the war), American industry doubled its aircraft production from 4,800 military aircraft per year to more than 9,600 per year. The fabled image of tireless airplane assembler "Rosie the Riveter" became the archetype for female defense plant workers.

Fighting World War II cost the United States a whopping $200 billion. Funds were raised for the war effort through the sale of U.S. savings bonds, known as "war bonds," beginning in 1941, and through the addition of a 5 percent "victory tax" on all income taxes. Money and materials were saved through rationing—making goods available in fixed amounts, limiting access to scarce goods.

The U.S. government's Office of Price Administration (OPA) directed the rationing of scarce items. American shoppers were issued ration books that allowed each family member a limited share of certain products each month. Goods in especially short supply were rationed more strictly. Rationing

of sugar, coffee, automobile tires, gasoline, and heating oil began in 1942. Americans had to keep their thermostats at a chilly 65° through the harsh winter of 1942-43. By 1943 shoes, cheese, fats, canned goods, and meat were being rationed. A pound of scarce items like sirloin steak, pork tenderloin, cheddar cheese, or even butter could cost an individual his or her entire weekly meat allotment.

Men lining up for the gas ration coupons in 1942.
(Reproduced by permission of Corbis/Bettmann)

Things to remember while reading the excerpt from *Since You Went Away: World War II Letters from American Women on the Home Front*:

- Letters from home were a soldier's only link to loved ones and the "normalcy" of life in the States. Regular mail delivery was so important to American troops overseas that mail even got through to the beachheads of islands in the Pacific.

- The following excerpt features letters from Catherine "Renee" Young Pike to her husband, George Pike. The letters span a two-year period between February 1943 and January 1945, when Renee was living with her parents and younger brother and sister in Esmond, Rhode Island. Renee and George were married shortly before the Japanese attacked U.S. naval bases at Pearl Harbor in December of 1941. George was drafted into the army in August of 1942. Renee was pregnant with their first child at the time. Little "Georgie" was born in March of 1943.

- Note Renee's comments on the butter shortage in February of 1943—there wasn't enough available to meet the ration allotments.

Excerpt from Since You Went Away: World War II Letters from American Women on the Home Front

Esmond, Feb. 3, 1943

My darling Husband,

Last night I had a whole mix-up of dreams. But one thing I dreamed was that I was eating banana splits one right after the other and were they good! When I awakened I thought to myself "Boy, what I wouldn't give for a nice banana." But that is just wishful thinking. I don't think anyone in America has seen a banana for over six months.

*Well, George, the **civilian population** is certainly feeling the shortage of food-stuffs now. Last week we didn't have a scratch of*

Civilian population: People who were not in the military; Americans on the home front.

butter in the house from Monday until Friday—and how I hate dry bread! It's a lot worse on we people in the country than it is on the city folks. They can go out and get some kind of meat every day while we have plenty of meatless days up here. They can also stand in line for 2 or 3 hours for a pound of butter, but up here there are no lines as there is no butter and when there is a little butter everyone gets a 1/4 of a pound. So you can imagine how far a 1/4 of a pound goes in this family of five adults. And that's suppose to last us for a week.

Yesterday I didn't take any meat not because we didn't have any but because I'm sick of the same thing. You see, the thing that they have the most of is sausages, but people can't keep eating the same thing every day. . . .

I received a swell letter from you yesterday. Gee, it seems that all the letters I 've got from you recently have been the nicest letters. . . . I love you, George, more than anything in the whole, wide world.

Yours forever, Renee

Esmond, March 4, 1943

My Darling.

I've just been thinking that you'll miss getting my letters when I go the hospital, won't you? . . .

I'm beginning to get weary now and nervous. I want to go and get it over with. You see, Darling, I've gained 25 pounds since I first started [the pregnancy] and at the end like this you get sort of miserable. Last night after I got to bed I had what is known as "false labor." I had quite bad pains in my stomach but I didn't tell anyone and I dropped off to sleep after awhile. But it makes you think that your time has come, believe me. . . .

Honey, whether I've had the baby or whether I haven't why don't you ask for a **furlough** *when you're through with your schooling. Of course you know better than me if you should but let me know what you think about it. O.K.?*

I want to see you so much, Honey, and I miss you something awful, especially lately. I love you with all my heart and soul and body.

Yours forever, Renee

Furlough: A soldier's leave of absence from duty.

Women helped with the war effort in a number of ways. These women are sorting scrap metal that will be melted down and used for war supplies. *(Reproduced by permission of AP/Wide World Photos, Inc.)*

The Invasion: A reference to the Allied Invasion of France at Normandy on D-Day—June 6, 1944.

Up their sleeve: Secretly planned.

Esmond, June 6, 1944

My Darling,

*. . . 6:45 a.m. The phone just rang about ten minutes ago. It was your mother. She told me that **the Invasion** had started. I just put on the radio and this time it's real. I don't quite know what to say, Sweetheart. It goes without saying that I feel very nervous and very afraid. I do feel though, that you weren't in this first wave. I hope and pray, Darling, that if I am right you will never have to go in. I suppose I want too much. . . .*

*As I listen to the radio here I can't understand why the Germans haven't given more opposition. Either they're pretty weak or they have something **up their sleeve.***

Well, Darling, for all I know you may be in combat when you receive this. I pray not. But if you are, please be careful and try and take care of yourself as well as is possible in battle.

Georgie just woke up so I'll have to go get him.

I love you, Sweetheart, and I'll always love you. I miss you terribly and I'll pray for you night and day. Georgie is saying, "Da-da" as loud as he can. Come back to us, Darling.

Yours now and forever, Renee

Esmond, June 9, 1944

My Dearest,

It is a beautiful day here today. It's not too warm and not too cool. I just got through hanging out the baby's washing and as I stand in the yard looking up at the sky in the distant horizon I wondered where my Darling was and if he was all right. Three big four-motored bombers roared over about then. But you'd never know to look at this quiet calm little village that there was a terrible bloody conflict going on over there. You'd never know to look at this little village that there was a sad, heavy-hearted girl living in it, namely me.

I received two letters from you last night, Honey. They were written on Friday and Saturday, the 19th and 20th of May. I'd be very happy about it if the invasion hadn't started. I'm happy about it anyway, of course, but I wish the letter written on or before June 6th would hurry and come through. . . .

Yours now and always, Renee

P.S. Kisses and hugs from Georgie and me.

Esmond, Aug. 24, 1944

My Dearest,

. . . I guess when I received the letter from you last night I nearly went hysterical for a minute. I felt so terrible to think that you had been hurt and even as I read your letter I was thanking God that that was all that was the matter, bad as it is.

*After I had read your letter over about three times, I called your folks and told them to come up. George, I hate to cry in front of anyone so through will-power I kept myself **composed** while they were here. But I didn't go to bed until 2:30 and I didn't sleep until about*

Composed: Calm.

Eleanor Roosevelt: In Her Own Words

Anna Eleanor Roosevelt (1884-1962), the first lady of the United States from 1933 to 1945, is probably best remembered for her commitment to the improvement of human rights worldwide. Eleanor Roosevelt's memoirs include thought-provoking commentary on the World War II era.

- On British prime minister Winston Churchill . . . "I shall never cease to be grateful to Mr. Churchill for his leadership during the war [World War II]; his speeches were a tonic to us here in the United States as well as to his own people."

- On the Japanese attack on Pearl Harbor . . . "I think it was steadying to know finally that the die was cast. One could no longer do anything but face the fact that this country [the United States] was in a war."

- On the presidency of her husband, Franklin D. Roosevelt . . . "[The] President of the United States must think first of what he considers the greatest good of the people and the country. . . . Franklin . . . always gave thought to what people said, but I have never known anyone less really influenced by others."

- On her own role during Roosevelt's presidency . . . "I think I sometimes acted as a spur, even though the spurring was not always wanted or welcome."

- On Roosevelt's death . . . "Though this was a terrible blow, somehow you had no chance to think of it as a personal sorrow. It was the sorrow of all those to whom this man . . . had been a symbol of strength and fortitude."

4:30. I wanted to write to you but I didn't know what to say. My thoughts were all jumbled. . . .

Well Sweetheart, I'll write again this afternoon or tonight as the mail from Esmond goes out in half an hour and I want this to go as soon as possible.

I hope your leg takes long enough to heal so that Germany will be finished. Don't be like you always are and pretend you can walk on it . . . before you really can. Please don't Darling. . . .

So until this afternoon God bless you and keep you and speed your safe return to me.

Yours forever and always, Renee

My Darling,

It is very cold here today and a thin blanket of snow covers the ground. As I hung out Georgie's wash this A.M. my hands became so cold that I could hardly move them. It made me think about you. Gosh, Honey, how can you shoot when your hands are stiff? I wonder if you'd like me to send you a couple of pairs of gloves? You could wear them when you're not shooting maybe. I don't want to send anything that's foolish, you understand. . . .

Well, Darling, no mail, no lovin,' no kissin,' no nothin'—so I guess I'll close for today. . . .

Yours for always, Renee

Esmond, Jan. 10 [?], 1945

My Dearest,

My thoughts tonight are far-reaching. I know my thoughts of you are very tender ones. Perhaps it is the classical music on the radio, or perhaps it's just because it is Saturday night—our night that has prompted me to write tonight (my second letter to you today). Whatever the reason, I know I love you and miss you so terribly tonight. . . .

[My thoughts take] me back to a cold, windy night in Maryland. We were standing together in the darkness beside a building at Ft. Meade. It was almost time to say our last good-bye—almost time. You ran your fingers through my hair and said, "Whenever I feel cold, Honey, I'll think of you and I'll feel warm." I thought of how you hated to be cold, and I thought that soon you'd be leaving me, and I tried so hard not to cry and I said, "Oh no, don't ever be cold George; don't be cold, Honey." You ran your fingers through my hair again, "I'll be cold lots of times, Renee, but I'll just think of you."

I watched you until you were out of sight in the heavy fog that lay over Ft. Meade that night. There were terrible emotions fighting within me. I wanted to run after you; I wanted to call out your name, and I wanted to cry and cry and cry until I couldn't cry anymore.

Later, the cab driver must have sensed my feelings as he drove me to the train station. He said to me, "Is your husband going overseas?" I looked out into that deep, dense fog where you had gone, and I said, "Tonight may be the last time I will see him for a long, long time."

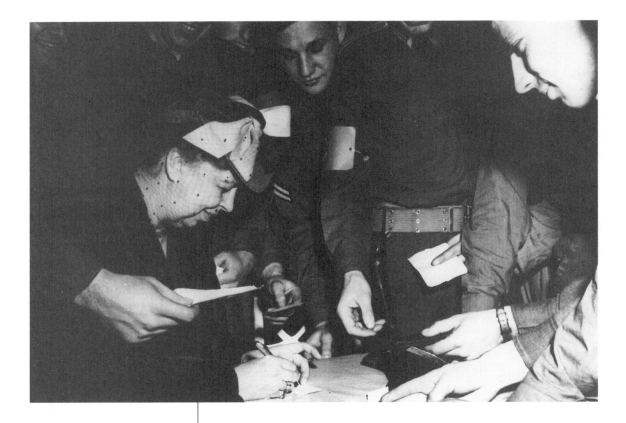

Eleanor Roosevelt signing autographs for U.S. soldiers. *(Reproduced by permission of AP/Wide World Photos, Inc.)*

I hope this letter doesn't make you feel "blue," but just once I had to put my true feelings on paper. There will be more "cheery" letters tomorrow.

All my love, all my life—until that day when God brings you home safely to me. Renee

Esmond, Jan. 31, 1945

My Darling,

I really feel terrible to think that I'm sitting here in a nice warm, cozy house and you're out in that terrible cold fighting. Yes, I know you're fighting, Darling. I figure that you must have gone into action on January 30th before dawn. Your division has been mentioned in the paper as one of them. Your division has also been mentioned on the radio as one of the **"crack"** *divisions. . . . They also told about your unit receiving the Presidential Citation. . . .*

"Crack": Possessing superior ability.

This lonesomeness for you just gnaws at my heart continually. Oceans of love, Darling, and a kiss on every wave.

God bless you and keep you and speed your safe return to me.

All my love, all my life, Cathie (Litoff and Smith, pp. 84-90)

What happened next . . .

The war in Europe ended in May 1945 with the surrender of Germany to the Allied forces (the countries fighting against Germany, Italy and Japan, primarily the Great Britain, the Soviet Union, and the United States). Fighting continued in the Pacific until shortly after the United States dropped atomic bombs on the Japanese cities of Hiroshima and Nagasaki. (See Harry S. Truman excerpt concerning the Manhattan Project and the Rodney Barker excerpt from *The Hiroshima Maidens* in chapter three for more information concerning the atomic bomb.) Devastated by the bombings, Japan signed formal surrender papers on September 2, 1945, bringing the long and bloody war to an official close.

After George's discharge from the army, the Pikes bought a house in Greenville, Rhode Island, opened up a bakery, and had two more children.

Did you know . . .

- More than twenty million wartime vegetable gardens—known as "victory gardens"—were planted by Americans in 1943. That year, the food grown in those gardens provided about a third of all the vegetables consumed in the United States.

- At the height of the war the U.S. armed forces had fifteen million people in its ranks.

- America's industrial workforce increased by more than 35 percent between 1940 and 1944.

During World War II, women found many new job opportunities. This woman is working on an assembly line building airplanes. *(Courtesy of the National Archives and Records Administration)*

- Executive Order 8802, issued by Franklin D. Roosevelt in 1941, banned discrimination in the government and defense industries. The order paved the way for the passage of the Fair Employment Practices Act by U.S. Congress.

- During World War II about 6.5 million women on the American home front held war-related jobs. The number of African American women in industry increased by a little more than 11 percent. But millions of women—black and white—found themselves unemployed in the fall of 1945, when the war ended and war industry production came to a grinding halt.

For More Information

Books

Gluck, Sherna. *Rosie the Riveter Revisited: Women, the War, and Social Change.* New York: Twayne, 1987.

Goodwin, Doris Kearns. *No Ordinary Time: Franklin and Eleanor Roosevelt-The Homefront in World War II.* New York: Simon & Schuster, 1994.

Green, Anne Bosanko. *One Woman's War.* St. Paul: Minnesota Historical Society, 1989.

Litoff, Judy Barrett, and David C. Smith, eds. *Miss You: The World War II Letters of Barbara Wooddall Taylor and Charles E. Taylor.* Athens: University of Georgia Press, 1990.

Litoff, Judy Barrett, and David C. Smith, eds. *Dear Boys: World War II Letters from a Woman Back Home.* Jackson: University Press of Mississippi, 1991.

Roosevelt, Anna Eleanor. *The Autobiography of Eleanor Roosevelt.* New York: Harper, 1961. Reprinted. New York: Da Capo, 1992.

Videos

Fly Girls. "The American Experience." PBS/WGBH, 1999.

Women at War: From the Home Front to the Front Lines. Atlas Video, 1989.

Web Sites

The Homefront Magazine. [Online] http://www.homefrontmag.org (accessed on September 6, 1999).

What Did You Do in the War, Grandma? [Online] http://www.stg.brown.edu/projects/WWII_Women/WWTWref.html (accessed on September 6, 1999).

Group E: Rosie the Riveter and other Women World War II Heroes. [Online] http://www.u.arizona.edu/~kari/rosie.htm (accessed on September 6, 1999).

Sources

Bailey, Ronald H., and the editors of Time-Life Books. *The Home Front: USA.* "Time-Life Books World War II Series." Alexandria, VA: Time-Life Books, 1978.

Barck, Oscar Theodore, Jr., and Nelson Manfred Blake. *Since 1900: A History of the United States in Our Times.* 3rd ed. New York: Macmillan, 1959.

Brokaw, Tom. *The Greatest Generation.* New York: Random House, 1998.

Freedmen, Russell. *Franklin Delano Roosevelt.* New York: Clarion Books, 1990.

Harris, Mark Jonathan, Franklin Mitchell, and Steven Schechter, eds. *The Homefront: America during World War II.* Introduction by Studs Terkel. New York: G. P. Putnam's Sons, 1984.

Hoopes, Roy, ed. *Americans Remember the Home Front: An Oral Narrative.* New York: Hawthorn Books, 1977. Reprinted, 1992.

Litoff, Judy Barrett, and David C. Smith, eds. *Since You Went Away: World War II Letters from American Women on the Home Front.* New York/UK: Oxford University Press, 1991.

Roosevelt, Eleanor. *This I Remember.* New York: Harper, 1949.

Roosevelt, Franklin Delano. *Nothing to Fear: The Selected Addresses of Franklin Delano Roosevelt, 1932-1945.* Edited by B. D. Zevin. New York: Houghton, 1946.

Jerry Stanley

Excerpt from I Am an American: A True Story of Japanese
Internment
Published in 1994

When the American naval base at Pearl Harbor was
bombed by Japanese fighter planes on December 7, 1941
(see Franklin D. Roosevelt entry for more information about
Pearl Harbor), approximately 125,000 Japanese Americans
resided in the United States. Japan's surprise attack on U.S.
forces plunged the United States into World War II (1939-45).
Within a few months, more than 115,000 Japanese Americans—two-thirds of them born in the United States—were
forced to leave their West Coast homes. (At the time, about
ninety-five percent of the Japanese in the States lived in the
coastal states of Washington, Oregon, and California.)

Americans of Japanese ancestry were easy targets of
discrimination because of their distinctive Asian features. "We
looked like the enemy," noted Japanese American author
Yoshiko Uchida in her book *The Invisible Thread.* In no time
Japanese Americans were being treated like the enemy—the
so-called "Japs" who had brought the war so close to America's
shores. (The disparaging term "Jap" was used widely during
World War II to refer to Japanese soldiers.)

Fear and racism sparked a wave of hysteria that over-
whelmed the nation in the wake of the Pearl Harbor attack.

"With 18,000 men,
women, and children,
Santa Anita was the
largest assembly center.
The horses had been
removed only four days
before the Japanese
started to arrive."

A Japanese American grocer who was forced to sell his grocery store reminds others in the community that he is an American citizen. *(Courtesy of the National Archives and Records Administration)*

Throughout 1942 "No Japs Wanted" signs became familiar across the United States. Newspapers regularly reported stories of Japanese restaurants being boycotted, businesses being vandalized, and other Japanese-American-owned property being destroyed.

In February 1942 President Franklin D. Roosevelt signed Executive Order 9066, which allowed the U.S. Army to confine Japanese Americans in special holding places called internment camps. In his book *The Greatest Generation,* broadcast journalist Tom Brokaw referred to the order as "one of the most shameful documents in American history"—a document clearly racist in nature. In 1942 America was also at war with Japan's allies, Italy and Germany, but Americans of European ancestry were not treated as shamefully as the Asian American population. Brokaw pointed out: "Italian and German immigrants were picked up and questioned closely" during the frenzy that accompanied America's entry into World War II. "They may have had some uncomfortable moments during the war," he continued, "but they retained all their rights. Not so for the Japanese Americans."

Any American with a Japanese ancestor, including any American of mixed racial heritage who had just one Japanese great-grandparent, was affected by Executive Order 9066. Stripped of their rights as citizens of the United States, the Japanese Americans were subject to curfews, travel restrictions, illegal searches, seizure of their property, complete violation of the right to privacy, and, ultimately, relocation to detention centers. Once there, these loyal Americans faced a frightening and uncertain future.

Evacuation orders (orders to the Japanese Americans to leave or vacate their homes) were issued by the U.S. Army in the late winter and early spring of 1942. The War Relocation Authority (WRA), established by executive order in March, directed the assembly and relocation process. The Japanese Americans had to give up their homes, their property, their businesses, and even their pets. Families were identified by number, not name, and packed onto buses headed for temporary holding areas called assembly centers. By the fall they were transferred to war relocation camps in Arizona, Arkansas, California, Colorado, Idaho, Oregon, Utah, Washington, and Wyoming.

Internees were expected to live in uninsulated shacks furnished only with cots and coal-burning stoves. (All other furniture was made by the residents from scrap wood and other materials.) Limited amounts of hot water were available in the common bathroom and laundry facilities. Worst of all, the camps were surrounded by barbed wire and armed guards.

Interned Japanese Americans struggled to establish some sense of community at the camps. They set up schools,

Japanese Americans arriving at the Santa Anita Assembly Center. *(Reproduced by permission of the National Archives and Records Administration)*

churches, farms, and newspapers. Children tried to escape the monotony of life at the camps by engaging in competitive sports, scouting, and arts and crafts. But the relocation process took its toll on the Japanese American population. Interned children were forced to spend their formative years in an atmosphere of tension, suspicion, and hopelessly mixed messages: instructors at the camp schools tried to teach the students to be loyal Americans, but their Japanese heritage automatically brought their loyalty into question. Internment, after all, was the U.S. government's way of dealing with a potential threat to national security. As Japanese forces stormed the Pacific in late 1941 and early 1942, the U.S. government feared that America's western states would be the next site for an enemy invasion. It was widely thought that Japanese Americans living on the coast would aid the Japanese if such an attack ever took place.

Things to remember while reading
the excerpt from *I Am an American:*

- Author Jerry Stanley interviewed Japanese Americans Shiro and Mary Nomuri in 1986 and 1993. He used their firsthand accounts of the internment experience to write *I Am an American.*

- Some Japanese Americans were born in Japan. These people, called Issei (pronounced "EE-say,") were Japanese citizens who had come to the United States in the early 1900s. They were denied U.S. citizenship because of their race. (Not until 1952, with the passage of the Immigration and Nationality Act, were the Issei allowed to become naturalized citizens.) American-born Nisei (pronounced "NEE-say") were the children of the Issei. The Nisei could not be denied citizenship because they were born in the United States.

- Shiro Nomuri was the son of Issei farmers who grew fruits and vegetables first in northern and later in southern California.

- Nomuri—nicknamed Shi (pronounced "Shy")—was a high school senior when he and his family were forcibly removed from their home in April 1942. A popular student and gifted athlete, he never really thought of himself as anything but an American citizen. Shi was sent to the Manzanar Relocation Center (pronounced "MANN-zuh-nahr") in eastern California.

- Shi was about to propose to his girlfriend, Amy Hattori, just before receiving his evacuation notice. The internment experience altered his plans.

- Japanese American internees could leave the camps by (1) joining the armed forces or (2) contributing to the war effort through work. Shi had been injured in an accident prior to internment, so he was unable to join the military.

Excerpt from I Am an American

Shi's family was evacuated to Manzanar on April 25, 1942. Earlier that month, Amy and her family had been sent to an assembly

A Japanese American girl awaiting internment.
(Courtesy of the National Archives and Records Administration)

Sentries: Soldiers standing guard.

center at the Santa Anita racetrack. Built to confine the Japanese until permanent camps were constructed, the assembly centers were created in just twenty-eight days. Fashioned from fairgrounds, racetracks, and other open areas, they were enclosed by barbed wire and guarded by armed **sentries** in towers. In April and May 110,723 Japanese were escorted into the assembly centers, while another 6,393 were sent straight to permanent relocation camps.

With 18,000 men, women, and children, Santa Anita was the largest assembly center. The horses had been removed only four days before the Japanese started to arrive. [Some] families were housed in horse stalls heavy with manure dust. . . .

After their baggage and clothes were searched, Amy's family moved into an open **barrack**, where they slept on mattresses stuffed with straw. The army had used raw lumber in hastily constructing the building. As the boards dried, gaping cracks appeared in the walls and floors. Within three weeks mushrooms were growing through the floor. Every day Amy went to the main gate where the buses unloaded, until she received word that Shi had been sent to Manzanar.

Manzanar was one of ten permanent relocation centers, or internment camps, built and supervised by the War Relocation Authority. It was located just south of the town of Independence, in Inyo County in eastern California. Two more camps were in Arizona, at Gila River and Poston. Temperatures reached 115 degrees at the **latter**, and the Japanese poured water on their canvas cots to keep cool in what they jokingly renamed Camp Roastin'. At Minidoka, in Idaho, the average summer temperature was 110 degrees. . . . At Amache, in Colorado, and Heart Mountain, in Wyoming, winter temperatures fell to minus thirty degrees. In November 1942 thirty-two Nisei children were arrested for sneaking out of the Heart Mountain camp and sledding on a nearby hill. **At Topaz, in Utah, an elderly Issei was shot** and killed in broad daylight for walking too close to the camp's fence. An eight-foot barbed wire fence, a thousand armed soldiers, and six tanks guarded the Japanese interned at the Tule Lake camp in California. The other two camps, Rohwer and Jerome, were in the damp, swampy, lowlands of Arkansas, where the most poisonous snakes in North America lived.

Manzanar was modeled after an army base designed to house single men. It was one mile square and divided into thirty-six blocks

A Tradition of Racism: African Americans in the U.S. Air Force

During World War II the U.S. armed forces were segregated by race. African American air force trainees received instruction at the 66th Air Force Flying School at Alabama's Tuskegee Institute and at Tuskegee's Army Air Field. The all-black 99th Squadron, later incorporated into the 332nd Fighter Group, became known as the Tuskegee Airmen. The exemplary performance of these black fighter pilots in missions over Europe and North Africa led to the slow but eventual desegregation of the U.S. military. For more information on the Tuskegee Airmen, see the following web sites: www.afroam.org/history/tusk/ tuskmain.html (AFRO-Americ@) and www. kent.wednet.edu/KSD/SJ/TuskegeeAirmen/ Tuskegee_HomePage.html

Barrack: A shed or barnlike structure used for temporary housing; soldiers' lodgings.

Latter: Last mentioned; in this case, Poston.

At Topaz, in Utah, an elderly Issei was shot . . . : The author is referring to the shooting death of James H. Wakasa. On April 11, 1943 Wakasa—a 63-year-old Issei who more than likely suffered some degree of hearing loss—was shot for walking too close to the barbed-wire fencing that surrounded the Topaz camp. Apparently, he failed to acknowledge the armed guard's calls to move away from the fence. According to Michael O. Tunnell and George W. Chilcoat in *The Children of Topaz,* the guard did not fire a warning shot before shooting Wakasa to death.

Motor pool: Government-controlled vehicles kept at the camp and used when necessary for camp business.

Perimeter: Boundary or outer limit.

Brush: Shrub-covered land.

Firebreak: Cleared land that acts to stop the progress of grass or forest fires.

with twenty-four barracks to a block. Each barrack was twenty feet wide and 120 feet long. Laundry and bathroom facilities were located in the center of each block, each of which had an open mess hall. There was a hospital in one corner of the camp, but the **motor pool,** *warehouses, and administrative offices were located beyond the barbed wire* **perimeter.** *At night, searchlights scanned the* **brush.** *One of the largest internment camps, Manzanar held over 10,000 men, women, and children guarded by eight towers with machine guns. No area within the camp was beyond the reach of a soldier's bullet.*

When Shi arrived at Manzanar, he was greeted by "a great ball of dirty fog." Because of the dust storm, created by the fierce Manzanar wind, Shi did not see the guard towers with their mounted machine guns or the barbed wire fence until the next day. Visibility was near zero, he recalled. "The strong wind picked up rice-sized sand from the construction areas and pelted the buses like buckshot."

The buses rolled to a stop in the middle of a **firebreak** *between Blocks 14 and 15. . . .*

Soldiers marched the new arrivals to a mess hall, where their numbers were recorded. Guards searched them, seizing anything they considered dangerous—kitchen knives, knitting needles, even hot plates for warming babies' milk. Each internee was issued a cot, an army blanket, and a sack to be filled with straw for a mattress; then families were assigned to a barrack according to size and number of children. Childless couples had to live in an open barrack, with only sheets hung up as partitions to separate them from strangers. . . . (Stanley, pp. 37-43)

What happened next . . .

Amy was transferred to Camp Amache in Colorado later in 1942. Thinking that he might have a chance to see her, Shi enrolled in a 60-day program that allowed selected Manzanar internees to leave camp and perform agricultural work in Colorado, Idaho, Utah, and Montana. Western American farmlands were nearly ruined in the early 1940s because so many farm workers had been drafted into the military. Interned Nissei were asked to help save certain farms in the West by harvesting

The barracks at Manzanar.
(Reproduced by permission of the Corbis/Hulton-Deutsch Collection)

remaining crops before they froze. Many agreed because they knew they would be freed from the barbed-wire camps, if only for two months. Shi was accepted into the program, but he was not sent to Colorado. Instead, he and the rest of his crew ended up in the icy sugar beet fields of Great Falls, Montana.

In the summer of 1943 Shi and Amy were finally able to see each other, but the time apart had changed them both. Realizing that they would not be able to renew their relationship, they broke up. In 1945 Shi married Mary Kageyama, a beautiful singer who had gained a reputation as the Songbird of Manzanar. He later ran his own fish market and grocery. Amy married Tatsumi Mizutani, a former Manzanar internee, in 1947.

Relocation ended officially in December of 1944. Evacuees were expected to vacate the camps just as quickly as they had been rounded up and herded into them. They then faced the difficult task of reestablishing themselves in society—rebuilding their lives, their homes, and their jobs.

Kaun Onodera, a Japanese American veteran who fought with the 442nd Infantry Regiment, holding the Bronze Star he earned in World War II.
(Reproduced by permission of the Corbis/Dean Wong)

In the postwar years anti-Japanese sentiment continued to exist in the United States. In 1990—forty-five years after the relocation program had ended—then-President George Bush issued letters of apology to camp survivors along with token redress payments (small offers of compensation or repayment) of $20,000 each.

Did you know . . .

- Many Japanese Americans contributed to the war effort even while interned, sending handmade blankets to the American Red Cross and purchasing war bonds with the little money they were allotted by the U.S. government.

- For a little over a year after Japan attacked Pearl Harbor, Nisei were not allowed to join the U.S. armed forces. Then, early in 1943, a segregated "all-Nisei" combat unit called the 442nd Regimental Combat Team was formed. Not until January 1944 were Japanese Americans included in the draft—and even then they were forced to make an official declaration of their loyalty to the United States and forsake any allegiance to Japan.

- U.S. senator Daniel Inouye, a decorated Nisei veteran of World War II who lost his right hand fighting the Germans in Italy, couldn't even get his hair cut when he returned from combat overseas. A racist barber in Oakland, California, told Inouye that he wouldn't "cut Jap hair."

- Not one Japanese American was ever accused of a war crime. The ten people who were accused, tried, and convicted of spying for the Japanese during World War II were white.

For More Information
Books

Daniels, Roger. *Concentration Camps USA: Japanese Americans and World War II.* New York: Holt, 1972.

Davis, Daniel S. *Behind Barbed Wire: The Imprisonment of Japanese Americans during World War II*. New York: Dutton, 1982.

Myer, Dillon. *Uprooted Americans: The Japanese Americans and the War Relocation Authority during World War II*. Tucson: University of Arizona Press, 1971.

Weglyn, Michi. *Years of Infamy: The Untold Story of America's Concentration Camps*. New York: Morrow, 1976.

Videos

Children of the Camps. First broadcast on PBS-TV, 1999. Video copies available through the National Asian American Telecommunications Association (NAATA; http://www.naatanet.org/distrib).

Web Sites

The Camps. [Online] http://www.geocities.com/Athens/8420/camps.html (accessed on September 6, 1999).

War Relocation Authority Camps in Arizona. [Online] http://www.library.arizona.edu/images/jpamer/wraintro.html (accessed on September 6, 1999).

Japanese-Americans Internment Camps During World War II. [Online] http://www.lib.utah.edu/spc/photo/9066/9066.htm (accessed on September 6, 1999).

National Japanese American Historical Society. [Online] http://www.nikkei-heritage.org/main.html (accessed on September 6, 1999).

Remebering Manzanar. [Online] http://www.qnet.com/~earthsun/remember.htm (accessed on September 6, 1999).

Japanese-American Internment Camps. [Online] http://www.umass.edu/history/internment.html (accessed on September 6, 1999).

Sources

Brokaw, Tom. *The Greatest Generation*. New York: Random House, 1998.

Fremon, David K. *Japanese-American Internment in American History*. Springfield, NJ: Enslow Publishers, 1996.

Stanley, Jerry. *I Am an American: A True Story of Japanese Internment*. New York: Crown, 1994.

Tunnell, Michael O., and George W. Chilcoat. *The Children of Topaz*. New York: Holiday House, 1996.

Uchida, Yoshiko. *Journey to Topaz*. New York: Scribner, 1971.

Uchida, Yoshiko. *Journey Home*. New York: Macmillan, 1978.

Uchida, Yoshiko. *The Invisible Thread*. New York: J. Messner, 1991.

The Human Cost

3

Ruth Minsky Sender
...101

Harry S. Truman
...117

Rodney Barker
...129

Ernie Pyle
...143

World War II Nurses
...159

G erman leader Adolf Hitler was a staunch anti-Semite—he harbored an intense hatred for Jewish people. He and his Nazi Party (pronounced "NOHT-see"; taken from the full German name of the National Socialist German Workers' Party) blamed Germany's post-World War I (after 1918) political and economic woes on the Jews. After becoming chancellor (supreme leader) of Germany in 1933, Hitler instituted a ruthless campaign of terror against the Jews of Europe. As Germany invaded neighboring countries and became enmeshed in World War II (1939-45), the Nazis made plans for the "Final Solution" to what they called the "Jewish problem." The Final Solution was to completely eliminate European Jews through mass extermination. This murderous crusade is now referred to as the Holocaust.

The Nazi-engineered Holocaust resulted in the deaths of six million Jewish men, women, and children. *The Cage*, a powerful autobiographical account by Holocaust survivor **Ruth Minsky Sender**, gives voice to the overwhelming fear that swept through the Jewish communities of Europe during World War II. In the book, the author recounts with stunning clarity her haunting memories of abuse and segregation in a Jewish ghetto in Poland, the hellish week she spent at the Auschwitz-Birkenau death camp, and the nightmare of life in Nazi-run work camps. Sender was liberated from Camp Grafenort, a forced labor camp in Germany, just as the Germans were preparing to surrender to the Allied Powers (the countries fighting against Germany, Italy, and Japan, primarily Great Britain, the United States, and the Soviet Union) in May of 1945.

After the death of Franklin D. Roosevelt in 1945, **Harry S. Truman** was sworn into the office of the president of the United States. Only then did Truman learn of the Manhattan Project, a top secret venture to build and test an atomic weapon for use in war. The excerpt from ***Memoirs by Harry S. Truman,*** **Volume 1:** *Year of Decisions* traces the final stages in the evolution of the atomic bomb and Truman's intention to use the newly developed weapon to hasten the end of World War II.

The decision to drop the atomic bomb on Japan came after the long and bloody battles for the Pacific islands of Iwo Jima and Okinawa. Plans were being made for the much-dreaded U.S. invasion of the Japanese home islands—an invasion that, according to military experts, would result in the injury or death of another five hundred thousand American soldiers and the prolongation of the war by at least another year. "I gave the final order," reflected Truman after the bombing of the Japanese cities of Hiroshima and Nagasaki. "I did what I thought was right."

An incredible amount of controversy accompanied the development and use of atomic weaponry during World War II. The effect of a nuclear power blast on human beings was uncertain before the Hiroshima and Nagasaki bombings but it became horribly apparent in the aftermath. *The Hiroshima Maidens: A Story of Courage, Compassion, and Survival,* written by **Rodney Barker**, chronicles the experiences of a group of Japanese women who were in Hiroshima on August 6, 1945, the fateful day of the bombing. They were among the thousands of Japanese whose lives were changed forever in a matter of seconds. The agonizing injuries sustained by the *hibakusha* (survivors of the atomic blast) has generated decades-long debate over the use of the bomb.

Excerpts from war correspondent **Ernie Pyle's *Ernie's War: The Best of Ernie Pyle's World War II Dispatches*** offer firsthand insights into the horrors of war on the front lines. Pyle covered the war as it was being fought in England, North Africa, Sicily, Italy, France, and the Pacific. His penetrating accounts of World War II combat brought the reality of the war home to the American people. Pyle was killed by a sniper's bullet on April 18, 1945, on the tiny Pacific island of Ie Shima. His last columns were published after his death.

Throughout the war the sixty thousand nurses of the Army Nurse Corps (ANC) provided wounded soldiers with the best care possible under the very worst conditions. From the rain-soaked fields of France to the mosquito-infested islands of the Pacific, they healed and comforted GIs by the thousands—and jeopardized their own lives in the process. Their remarkable stories are collected in ***No Time for Fear: Voices of American Military Nurses in World War II***, edited by **Diane Burke Fessler.**

Ruth Minsky Sender

Excerpt from **The Cage**
Published in 1986

G ermany was in a state of political and economic chaos at the end of World War I (1914-18). (See Winston Churchill entry in chapter one for more information on Germany before World War II.) Future German leader Adolf Hitler (1889-1945) spent much of the 1920s building up the Nazi Party (pronounced "NOHT-see"; taken from the full German name of the National Socialist German Workers' Party) to restore order and glory to the German nation. The Nazis organized a strong nationalistic movement in Germany—a movement that glorified all things German—and demanded blind devotion to their party's teachings.

After becoming the leader of Germany in 1933, Hitler launched a frightening campaign of suppression built on fear and hatred. Hitler was an ardent anti-Semite, meaning he held a deep-seated hatred for Jewish people. He blamed the Jews for the depressed economy in Germany and the nation's stunning defeat in World War I. The Holocaust was the Nazi campaign to persecute—and eventually eliminate—all Jews from Europe.

Although Hitler's wrath was directed primarily against the Jews of Europe, he also targeted his political adversaries (so-

"They are calling our group. Panic seizes me. This is it. We are going into the cattle cars for a journey to the unknown. The guards are getting very impatient. They are already bored with the game of loading Jews into the wagons."

called "enemies of the state"), Roma (often called Gypsies), homosexuals, Poles (including Polish Jews and Catholics), Jehovah's Witnesses (a Christian denomination), the physically and mentally disabled, and others he deemed "racially inferior." Hitler and his Third Reich sought to completely dominate Europe by silencing their perceived opponents and removing all obstacles that lay in their path to power. (The Third Reich was the name given to the Nazi-controlled government in Germany, which held power from 1933 to 1945. The word *reich*, pronounced "RIKE," means "empire" or "kingdom.")

With the growth of the Nazi Party came a renewed emphasis on German expansionism (adding to a nation's territory) and rearmament (building up arms for warfare). Hitler demanded more *Lebensraum* (space for living) for the German people, whom he deemed a superior "master race," and set out to claim chunks of European territory for Germany. His armies moved into Austria, which had voted to become part of Germany, in March of 1938. Then the Germans occupied the Sudetenland (the western section of Czechoslovakia, where most people spoke German). By March of 1939 the Nazis had taken over the rest of Czechoslovakia. About six months later, on September 1, 1939, German forces invaded Poland, triggering declarations of war from Great Britain and France against Germany.

Persecution of German Jews had begun in earnest even before the start of World War II (1939-45). Widespread anti-Jewish sentiment had fueled an extensive anti-Jewish movement in Germany. Jews were stripped of their citizenship and their political rights and even forced to give up their jobs. Approximately three hundred thousand Jews left Germany in the 1930s. But after 1939 it was virtually impossible for the Jews of German-occupied territories to escape from the Nazis. The Gestapo (the Nazi secret police) gathered up all the Jews in Germany and in the territories they had conquered and segregated them in ghettos. (The Jewish ghettos were isolated sections of various cities in Poland and other German-occupied territories in Eastern Europe. The most infamous of these ghettos were located in Warsaw and Lodz, both in central Poland.)

In 1942 the Nazis began implementing what they called the Final Solution to the so-called "Jewish problem." The Final Solution called for the extermination (mass murder)

A victim of a Nazi gas chamber still in the position he died in. *(Reproduced by permission of the National Archives and Records Administration)*

of Jews in all the German-occupied territories of Europe. Jews in the ghettos were rounded up and transported by rail to death camps in out-of-the-way sections of Poland. Equipped with murderous gas chambers and crematoriums (huge ovens for burning dead bodies), the death camps were designed specifically to murder all the European Jews. The Nazi-engineered genocide (a deliberate and systematic effort to destroy an entire body of people) had begun.

Things to remember while reading the excerpt from *The Cage:*

- More than one hundred concentration camps were established by the Nazis during World War II. Jewish prisoners of the concentration camps faced a harsh future. They were starved, overworked, beaten, humiliated, and exposed to all kinds of filth and disease. Prisoners who became ill or weak were killed. Aside from the concentration camps, the Nazis set up six special "death camps": the notorious Auschwitz-Birkenau and five others—Belzec, Chelmno, Majdanek, Sobibor, and Treblinka. An estimated three million adults and children were killed at these six extermination centers; about 1.25 million died at Auschwitz alone.

- Camp survivor Ruth Minsky Sender named her moving wartime memoir *The Cage* because of the Nazis' practice of housing Jews behind barbed-wire fencing. *The Cage* recounts the author's haunting memories of the Holocaust.

- Sender's book is filled with a host of characters. The following is a guide to the names that appear in the excerpted text: Riva Minska is the author; Motele and Moishele are her brothers; Mrs. Boruchowich is the mother of Sender's friends Laibish and Rifkele; Mrs. Mikita is the mother of Sender's friends Karola and Berl; Tola is another friend of Riva's.

- After Riva's mother is taken away by the Nazis in September of 1942, Riva and her brothers are left to mourn and to survive the best they can in the Lodz ghetto. In time the remaining family members are herded off to Auschwitz and separated.

- The words of Riva's mother—"If hope is lost, all is lost. As long as there is life, there is hope"—stand as a symbol of strength and comfort for Riva as she struggles to endure each day of her captivity.

Excerpt from *The Cage*

The railroad station is packed with people. Bundles, sacks, cartons, neatly tied packages all around us. A whole city is leaving on a mass **pilgrimage.** "Where to? Where are we all going? What is the name of the place? Does anyone know?"

"Please stay together," Motele urges us. "Let's not lose one another in this crowd."

"Children, my dear children, hold on to one another," pleads Mrs. Boruchowich. "We must stay together, children. We must."

On the tracks, freight trains are waiting. They are cattle cars.

"Why cattle cars?" someone asks, full of panic. "We will suffocate in there from the heat. It is mid-August. The heat will kill us."

"What did you expect?" I hear another voice. "You thought **they** would send us first class?"

"To them we are animals," one voice cuts in sarcastically. "Besides, they want to make sure that these animals cannot escape. They need our hands to make them uniforms. They need our skilled labor. . . . "

"Keep still! Keep quiet! Do not push! You will all get into the wagons! We have plenty of trains for you!" call the guards.

I look around me, search for familiar faces. We wave good-bye to people we know. They wave back. Eyes meet, **petrified, aghast.**

"What choice do we have? What can we do other than go into the cattle cars? We have no way out, no choice."

People all around me, desperately trying to find an answer. Clinging to tiny sparks of hope. Optimistically spreading rumors: "They stopped the **deportation.** The **Russian front** is too close. They are sending us back home. They need us. They will not hurt us as long as they need our labor."

But the trains keep filling up with people. Each wagon is locked. One train pulls away, and another pulls up, ready to be loaded. We wait our turn, holding on to one another.

"Next. Hurry up! Get your bundles! Move! Move! Get into the wagons! You there, hurry, you stupid Jews."

They are calling our group. Panic seizes me. This is it. We are going into the cattle cars for a journey to the unknown. The guards

Pilgrimage: Journey.

They: The Nazis.

Petrified: Made lifeless from fright.

Aghast: Shocked; struck with terror.

Deportation: Banishment; being sent out of a country.

Russian front: The Russian line of battle.

Jewish women and children, carrying clothes and belongings, wait outside a train for deportation.
(© Archive Photos, Inc. Reproduced by permission)

are getting very impatient. They are already bored with the game of loading Jews into the wagons. They are angrier and louder now: "Jew, make it faster!"

Laibish is helping his mother up into the wagon. She slips. He pulls her quickly into the wagon before the whip of the angry Nazi can touch her body. "You cursed old Jew," the Nazi guard shouts, swinging his whip in all directions.

We move fast, trying to duck the whip. So many families are being separated. We must try to stay together. We must try. We are at the end of the line. The train is almost full.

Whatever happens, please let us stay together, I pray silently. Just let us be together.

Someone reaches out to help me up into the cattle car. Motele and Moishele are behind me, lifting me up. They jump in after me.

"Are we all here?" I call out to Laibish.

"Yes. Yes. We all made it into the same wagon. There is Karola, Berl, Mrs. Mikita, my mother, and my sister." He points to the corner of the car. "Let's try to make our way toward them."

We squeeze through the crowded wagon. We sit down on the floor, worn out from the horrible ordeal but relieved to be all together again. We can hardly move our arms. We are just like one big mass of tired flesh, hot and steaming. The doors are about to close. I hear someone scream: "I am part of a family. Don't leave me behind!"

"Here, stay with your family!" I hear a sarcastic remark in German, and someone is pushed into the wagon. The doors close. We are all in total darkness. Some cry out hysterically; others pray aloud.

Slowly my eyes penetrate the darkness. From some cracks in the walls rays of light break through, throwing ghastly shadows on our terrified faces.

"Is this what a grave feels like?" someone wonders aloud.

"In a grave you have more room than this," a sobbing voice answers.

"We must have hope. We must not give up hope." . . .

I cannot see any faces. They are all covered in darkness. I see only shadows around me. But the voices are clear, painfully clear.

"So, where is God? Why does he not answer us? Have we not suffered enough? What is he waiting for?"

"You are sinning with that kind of talk. We must pray, pray."

"Maybe I have sinned, but what about my little children? What sins can little children commit? They were only babies. Why did they take them from us? Why did God allow this to happen?"

Bitter voices, angry, heartbroken, wailing.

We sit huddled together, listening to the voices around us. Mrs. Boruchowich puts her head on her daughter's lap, mumbling something to herself. Rifkele caresses her mother's head, whispering, "It's all right, Mama."

"Riva." Motele turns toward me, taking my hands in his. His voice sounds so strange. "Riva, they may separate us. They may separate the men from the women. Remember, if this happens, stay with Karola and Rifkele. You must look out for one another. You must be strong. We must live. We must survive. I'll take care of Moishele, I *promise. Laibish, Berl, and I are the older boys. We'll keep Moishele between us so he'll look older than thirteen. We'll take care of Moishele. I promise you."*

I pull them both close to me. We cry silently together.

Mrs. Boruchowich raises her head from her daughter's lap. "I will watch over my children. I will watch over my children," she says with sudden determination. "Don't worry, my children. Don't worry."

Moishele turns suddenly toward Rifkele. He puts his hand on Rifkele's shoulder. "Rifkele, please take care of my sister," he says. "You are the oldest of the girls here. You are their big sister. Riva is not very strong. She always had us to watch over her. We are leaving her in your hands. Please, look after her."

"I will, Moishele. I will," she whispers softly.

Days turn to nights and nights into days again. The cracks in the walls let in some rays of sunlight to tell us it is a new day. The rays of moonlight coming through the cracks let us know it is night again. We doze, resting our heads on one another's shoulders, awaken startled by nightmares to find that the nightmares are real.

The stench of human secretion mixed with the sweltering heat makes it hard to breathe. The buckets used as toilets are overflowing. People faint from the smell, from the heat, from exhaustion. The trains stop several times, but no doors are opened.

"How much longer? How much more can we endure?"

"Hold on. Do not give up. We will survive." Voices of strangers, trying to comfort one another. Searching for the courage to stay alive.

It has been three long, horrible days and three terrifying nights. "Where are we going? Where are we going?"

The train stops. The doors finally open. The sudden sunlight is blinding, but our ears are filled with music. Music all around us.

"Where are we? What is this place?"

"Welcome to Auschwitz, Jews." A German voice comes through the loudspeaker. "Welcome to Auschwitz, Jews."

The living crawl out. The dead are pulled out.

"Men to the right! Women to the left! Quickly! Quickly!" The guards push us with their rifles. "Faster! Move! Faster! Move! Left! Right! Left! Right!"

Everything is happening so fast, like in a horrible dream. The people behind me are pushing me forward toward the women's group, but where is Moishele? Where is Motele? They were near me only a moment ago.

"Moishele! Motele!" I cry out hysterically. "Where are you? Don't leave me. Let's stay together. Don't leave me alone. Motele! Moishele! Motele! Moishele!"

They are lost in the crowd of dazed people. I cannot see them anymore. I keep on calling, "Where are you, my brothers? Where are you, my children? Don't leave me alone. Motele! Moishele!"

I hear names being called out all around me. Children calling their mothers. Mothers calling their children. Husbands calling to wives their last good-byes. And above it all the German commands: "Left! Right! Left! Right!"

A man in a Nazi uniform is pointing with a white baton toward Mrs. Boruchowich. She is pulled out from our group and to the left of us, where a group of older women and mothers with small children are gathered. Her daughter follows her and is kicked back by a Nazi guard toward our group. I grab Rifkele before she can fall and get trampled by the moving crowd. I hear Mrs. Boruchowich's cries as she, too, disappears from my sight.

"Faster! Faster! Left! Right! Faster! Faster!" I am being carried forward.

"I think I saw my brother, Berl, with Motele and Moishele. They marched by with a group of men." I hear Karola's voice behind me. "They will try to stay together. We must also try to stay together."

Karola is holding her mother's arm. Then we hear "Left!"—and her mother is pulled away from her. "Hold on, my child. Don't lose your courage. Hold on, my child!" And she, too, is gone.

Ruth Minsky Sender

Holocaust survivor and author Ruth Minsky Sender (1926-) was born Riva Minska, May 3, 1926, in Lodz, Poland. She came from a tightly knit family headed by a strong, loving, and deeply devoted mother. While living out the nightmare of the Holocaust in the Lodz ghetto, at Auschwitz, and later at German work camps, Riva never forgot her mother's words of inspiration: "As long as there is life, there is hope." *The Cage* tells Riva's story.

Riva married Morris Sender (himself a survivor of the Nazis' brutal reign) in 1945, moved to the United States in 1950, and became a naturalized U.S. citizen. The couple had four children of their own—children, Sender writes, of "the Jewish generation that was not to be, proud human beings, the new link in an old chain." Among Sender's other works are *To Life* and *The Holocaust Lady*.

From all sides I hear people calling: "You must not lose hope! You must not lose hope!"

"You must live!" a woman calls to her daughter as she is pulled toward the group on the left.

My eyes are blurred from burning tears. My head is spinning. And through it all come the voices of strangers calling, commanding: "You must live! You must hope!"

I hope that it is all a horrible nightmare. I'll wake up soon. The nightmare will be gone. My brothers will stand beside me. We will be in a free world.

But the nightmare continues. We are pushed forward toward the unknown by whips whistling in the air, their sharp blows landing on the heads and shoulders of the women. Outcries of pain echo all around us.

Karola, Rifkele, and I try desperately to hold on to one another. We are pushed into a long barrack and ordered to undress: "Drop all your clothes and put them in neat piles! Leave all your belongings! Remove your eyeglasses and leave them here! Move forward! Move!"

I move like a zombie. I remove my eyeglasses, which I have worn for the last few years, and feel as if I am suddenly blind, left all alone in the darkness. I am pushed forward, forward.

My head is shaven by a woman in striped prison clothes. "This is to keep the lice out of your hair," she says sarcastically, while cutting into my long, brown hair with her shaver. I stare at her without really seeing her.

There are mountains of hair all around us: blond, brown, black. Piles of shoes, clothing, eyeglasses surround us, each pile growing bigger and bigger with each passing row of new arrivals.

"Quickly! Quickly! Forward to the showers! Move!" We are pushed into a large room filled with showers. Suddenly the water from the shower head comes at me in full force. The cold spray helps to bring me out of the stupor I have been in. I look at my friends, at their shaven heads, at their horror-filled eyes.

I grab Karol's hand. "Karola, is that you?" I whisper. We stare at each other for a long moment.

"Is that you, Riva? Is that you?" She gasps, transfixed by the sight of my shaven head.

"Out! Out! Quickly! Out!" We are herded outside. The sound of

*the whip makes us move as fast as we can. We are pushed into the bright sunlight of the warm August air stark naked. With my arms I try to cover my nakedness. My cheeks are hot from embarrassment. I feel so **degraded**.*

*Someone is handing out one piece of clothing to each girl to cover our naked bodies. I receive a **petticoat** big enough to wrap myself in. I look at Rifkele next to me. She is tall, and the blouse she received hardly reaches to the end of her buttocks. I pull off my petticoat and hand it to Rifkele. "I am small, Rifkele. Take this. Your blouse will be big enough to cover me to the knees."*

She takes off her blouse and puts it on me lovingly. With tears in her eyes she says, "We are not animals yet. We still have our pride."

"March into the barrack! Quickly!"

*We walk hurriedly into the huge barrack. It is filled with triple-decker bunks. On most decks lie five **shriveled** bodies with hungry, horror-stricken eyes. Some bunks are not filled yet.*

*"Where are you from?" parched lips whisper. "Are there still Jews alive outside this hell? Did you see the smoke? Did you see the chimneys? Do you feel the **Angel of Death** touching you? Can you smell the burning flesh?"*

Those eyes, those voices are so unreal, so ghastly. This has to be a nightmare.

"Leave them alone." The voices go on and on. "Leave them alone. They will know soon enough about the smoke, about the smell. . . . "

Why doesn't the nightmare end? It cannot be true. I will not listen to them. I will not look at them. I cover my ears, but the voices are within me now. I am part of them now.

Rifkele grabs hold of a small, skinny woman in her late twenties wearing a dress that is much too big. She looks familiar to her. They stare at each other in disbelief. "Tola? Tola?" Rifkele cries out. "Is that you? I am Rifkele, Rifkele Boruchowich. My God, what did they do to you?"

Tola's eyes fill with tears. "Rifkele? Rifkele? The beautiful, elegant Rifkele without hair, wrapped in rags. This cannot be you."

They fall into each other's arms, sobbing: "What did they make of us? What did they do to us? Dear God, help us remain human. Help us."

Degraded: Lowered or dragged down.

Petticoat: Underskirt.

Shriveled: Wrinkled; shrunken.

Angel of Death: A messenger said to appear before a death; a sign of impending doom.

"I lost my children, Rifkele," Tola says suddenly through her tears. "They took them from me. I lost them." She buries her head in Rifkele's chest, howling like a wounded animal.

Rikele hugs her close. "I'll stay with you, Tola. We'll stay with you, Riva, Karola, and I."

She is the only one in her bunk. We slide into her bunk and hold one another close. (Sender, pp. 139-55)

What happened next . . .

Sender spent seven days at Auschwitz in 1944 before being transferred to the first of two forced labor camps in Germany (first to Camp Mittelsteine and then, just before war's end, to Camp Grafenort). Soviet soldiers liberated Grafenort on May 7, 1945.

It was late 1944 when the tide turned decisively against Germany's military forces. As Soviet troops approached the German capital of Berlin from the east, the *Schutzstaffel* (or SS; the Nazi protection squad) began to evacuate the concentration camps and death camps of Poland, leaving the bodies of hastily executed victims in heaps. In January 1945 the prisoners of Auschwitz who were still able to walk were forced on a "death march" across Poland's frozen countryside. Nearly seventeen thousand of the sixty-six thousand marchers died before completing the westward trek to Germany.

By the spring of 1945 American and British armies were closing in on the Germans from the west. Realizing that Germany had lost the war, Hitler reportedly committed suicide in his underground bunker (a fortified chamber) on April 30, 1945.

An untold number of people died in the Nazi-run ghettos, concentration camps, labor camps, and death camps; approximately six million of the victims were Jews. British prime minister Winston Churchill concluded that the Nazi's Final Solution was the "most horrible crime ever committed in the whole history of the world."

Did you know . . .

- The word *holocaust* means "destruction by fire."

- The swastika (pronounced "SWAHS-tick-uh")—a cross with bent arms—is really an ancient religious symbol or ornament representing good luck and well-being. Hitler made it the emblem of the Nazi Party and the national symbol of the German nation; since then, the swastika has

Rows of dead inmates fill the yard of a concentration camp. The bodies of hastily executed victims were left in piles while German troops fled the approaching Allies. *(Photograph by Myers. Reproduced by permission of Corbis.)*

taken on a negative meaning and is frequently associated with intolerance, white supremacy, and hate crimes.

- Between 1934 and 1939, SS membership grew from 50,000 to 250,000.

- Dachau, the first Nazi concentration camp, was established in March 1933. Located near Munich, Germany, Dachau originally housed the Nazi Party's political opponents.

- The United States Holocaust Memorial Museum (USHMM) was established in Washington, D.C., as a testament to Holocaust history and as a memorial to the Nazis' millions of victims.

- The USHMM reports that the "stated intention [of the United States and Great Britain] to defeat Germany militarily took precedence over rescue efforts" even after reports of the Nazis' Final Solution had been confirmed in 1942. "No specific attempts to stop or slow the genocide were made until [1944, when] mounting pressure eventually forced the United States to undertake limited rescue efforts."

For More Information
Books

Arad, Yitzhak. *The Pictorial History of the Holocaust.* New York: Macmillan, 1990.

Boas, Jacob, ed. *We Are Witnesses: Five Diaries of Teenagers Who Died in the Holocaust.* Foreword by Patricia C. McKissack. New York: Holt, 1995.

Frank, Anne. *The Diary of a Young Girl.* New York: Doubleday, 1952.

Friedman, Ina. *The Other Victims: First Person Stories of Non-Jews Persecuted by the Nazis.* New York: Houghton, 1990.

Friedman, Ina. *Escape or Die: True Stories of Young People Who Survived the Holocaust.* Cambridge, MA: Yellow Moon, 1991.

Friedman, Ina. *Flying against the Wind.* Brookline, MA: Lodgepole Press, 1995.

Greenfield, Howard. *The Hidden Children.* New York: Ticknor & Fields, 1993.

Gutman, Israel, ed. *Encyclopedia of the Holocaust.* New York: Macmillan, 1990.

Lengyel, Olga. *Five Chimneys: A Woman's True Story of Auschwitz.* Chicago: Academy Chicago Pubs., 1995.

Niewyk, Donald L. *Fresh Wounds: Early Narratives of Holocaust Survival.* Chapel Hill: University of North Carolina Press, 1998.

Perl, Lila, and Marion Blumenthal Lazan. *Four Perfect Pebbles: A Holocaust Story.* New York: Greenwillow, 1996.

Rittner, Carol, and John K. Roth, eds. *Different Voices: Women and the Holocaust.* New York: Paragon House, 1993.

Rogasky, Barbara. *Smoke and Ashes: The Story of the Holocaust.* New York: Holiday House, 1988.

Sender, Ruth Minsky. *To Life.* New York: Macmillan, 1988.

Videos

Auschwitz: If You Cried, You Died. Indianapolis: Impact America Foundation, 1991.

Genocide, 1941-1945. "World at War Series." Produced and directed by Michael Darlow. South Burlington, VT: A&E Home Video, 1982.

Shoah. Directed by Claude Lanzmann. Los Angeles: Simon Wiesenthal Center, 1985.

Triumph of Memory. Produced by Robert Gardner, Sister Carol Rittner, R.S.M., and Sondra Myers. Directed by Robert Gardner. Alexandria, VA: PBS Video, 1972.

Witness to the Holocaust. Produced and directed by C.J. Pressma. New York: National Jewish Resource Center, 1984.

Web Sites

MiamiLINK. [Online] http://www.lib.muohio.edu/inet/subj/history/holoc.html (accessed on September 6, 1999).

A Cybrary of the Holocaust. [Online] http://www.remember.org/ (accessed on September 6, 1999).

United States Holocaust Memorial Museum. [Online] http://www.ushmm.org/ (accessed on September 6, 1999).

Sources

Adler, David A. *We Remember the Holocaust.* New York: Henry Holt, 1989.

Allen, Peter. *The Origins of World War II.* New York: Bookwright Press, 1992.

Ayer, Eleanor H. *The United States Holocaust Memorial Museum: America Keeps the Memory Alive.* New York: Dillon Press, 1994.

Dolan, Edward F. *America in World War II: 1945.* Brookfield, CT: Millbrook Press, 1994.

Sender, Ruth Minsky. *The Cage*. Originally published in 1986. Reprinted. New York: Aladdin Paperbacks, 1997.

Severance, John B. *Winston Churchill: Soldier, Statesman, Artist*. New York: Clarion Books, 1996.

Something about the Author. Volume 62. Detroit: Gale, 1990.

Additional information for this entry was obtained from the United States Holocaust Memorial Museum website (www.ushmm.org).

Harry S. Truman

Excerpt of Truman's comments on the Manhattan Project from
Memoirs by Harry S. Truman *Volume 1:* **Year of Decisions**

Published in 1955

In the late 1930s Austrian and German physicists (scientists who study matter and forces) made major breakthroughs in the field of nuclear energy, the energy released during nuclear reactions. The term "nuclear" refers to the nucleus, or core, of an atom. Atoms, the building blocks of all elements, are held together by incredibly powerful forces.

Nuclear energy research in the early World War II era centered on experiments with uranium atoms. Firing just one neutron (an uncharged particle found within the nucleus of most atoms) at the nucleus of a uranium atom caused the release of three new neutrons and a large amount of energy. Physicists believed that bombarding a larger sample of uranium with neutrons would trigger a powerful chain reaction: an enormous release of energy would accompany the splitting of the uranium atoms. It wasn't long before scientists in Germany and the United States were thinking about how they could harness this overwhelming burst of energy in a military weapon.

Serious research on atomic weapon development began in the United States in late 1941, around the time of Japan's

"The final decision of where and when to use the atomic bomb was up to me. Let there be no mistake about it. I regarded the bomb as a military weapon and never had any doubt that it should be used. . . . "

Harry S. Truman, who was famous for saying of his job as president "The buck stops here," had to make the final decision whether to drop atomic bombs on Japan. *(Reproduced by permission of AP/Wide World Photos, Inc.)*

surprise attack on American naval bases at Pearl Harbor. In 1942 Italian-born physicist Enrico Fermi, a professor at New York's Columbia University, created the first nuclear reactor in the United States. The device provided a controlled environment for the energy released from splitting atoms. Fermi settled in the United States during World War II (1939-45) because his wife was Jewish and Jews in Europe were facing severe persecution. (See Ruth Minsky Sender entry for background on Nazi treatment of Jews during the war). Fermi played a leading role in the burgeoning field of atomic weaponry.

Background work on the development of the atomic bomb took place in New York City. For this reason the venture became known as the Manhattan Project. U.S. Army general Leslie R. Groves supervised the project. He chose Dr. J. Robert Oppenheimer, a bright young nuclear physicist, to direct the team of scientists working first in New York, and later in a remote desert region of Los Alamos, New Mexico.

Uranium and another element called plutonium—the key ingredients in bomb research—were being processed in plants in Tennessee and Washington State, respectively. Only a special type of uranium known as uranium-235 would split easily enough to fuel a nuclear chain reaction. Scientists had found that for every one thousand atoms in a sample of uranium, only about seven of them turned out to be uranium-235. Special production plants were built to separate and gather uranium-235 atoms.

Final assembly of the first nuclear bombs occurred at the Los Alamos headquarters. The uranium bomb was known as "Little Boy." The plutonium-powered bomb, which weighed about 9,000 pounds, was nicknamed "Fat Man." The first atomic bomb ever tested—a "Fat Man"—was set off at Alamogordo, New Mexico, on July 16, 1945. The explosion rocked the test site with a force equal to the power of 20,000 tons (40 million pounds) of TNT, scorching the earth for miles around.

The war in Europe had ended a few months earlier with Germany's surrender on May 8, 1945, but fighting in the Pacific against the Japanese raged on. In July 1945 President Harry S. Truman set out for Potsdam, a Soviet-occupied city in Germany, where he and other Allied leaders (Prime Minister Winston Churchill of Great Britain and the Soviet leader, Joseph Stalin) would discuss the structure of Germany's new government. On the first day of the Potsdam Conference, Truman received word that the first atomic bomb had been tested at Alamogordo, New Mexico. The Manhattan Project had reached its goal. The test was a success.

All tolled, the project cost $2 billion, took nearly three years to complete, and required the combined efforts of a one-hundred-thousand-person workforce.

Things to remember while reading the excerpt from Truman's *Memoirs:*

- At the time of the Potsdam Conference, the U.S. military was focusing all its strength on defeating Japan. The battle for Iwo Jima in February 1945 had proved very costly to both the Japanese and Americans. (See Ernie Pyle entry in chapter three for more information about the war in the Pacific). By the time the U.S. Marine invasion of the island was over, more than twenty thousand Japanese soldiers had been killed; nearly seven thousand Americans died and another twenty thousand were wounded. Even more intensive fighting began on the island of Okinawa in April. (See Eugene B. Sledge entry in chapter four for more information about the battle at Okinawa). The three-month-long air and land battle was marked by streams of *kamikaze* (pronounced "kahm-ih-KAH-zee"; translated as "divine wind") attacks on American warships. (Kamikazes were suicide bombers—Japanese pilots who purposely crashed their planes into Allied ships, knowing that the planes would explode in the attack.) About 130,000 Japanese died defending Okinawa; 16,000 Americans were killed and 60,000 were injured.

- In the summer of 1945 preparations were under way for a land invasion of the Japanese home islands. After fighting the long and bloody battles for Iwo Jima and Okinawa, U.S. forces dreaded the prospect of the home island invasion, thinking it would mean another year of fighting and hundreds of thousands more American lives lost. (Military experts estimated that five hundred thousand American soldiers would be wounded or killed in the attack on Japan.)

- As long as they were alive, Japanese soldiers would keep on fighting. Their commitment to honor in battle drove many of them to choose death over surrender. Even after B-29 bombing raids had destroyed half of Tokyo, the Japanese military would not give in.

Excerpt from Memoirs by Harry S. Truman

*The historic message of the first explosion of an atomic bomb was flashed to me in a message from Secretary of War [Henry] Stimson on the morning of July 16 [1945]. The most secret and the most daring **enterprise** of the war had succeeded. We were now in possession of a weapon that would not only revolutionize war but could alter the course of history and civilization. This news reached me at Potsdam [Germany] the day after I had arrived for the conference of the **Big Three**.*

*Preparations were being rushed for the test atomic explosion at Alamogordo, New Mexico, at the time I had to leave for Europe, and on the voyage over I had been anxiously awaiting word on the results. I had been told of many predictions by the scientists, but no one was certain of the outcome of this full-scale atomic explosion. As I read the message from Stimson, I realized that the test not only met the most optimistic expectation of the scientists but that the United States had in its possession an explosive force of **unparalleled** power.*

Stimson flew . . . to Potsdam the next day to see me and brought with him the full details of the test. . . . We did not know as yet what effect the new weapon might have, physically or psychologically,

Enterprise: Risky, complicated project.

Big Three: Heads of the three leading Allied nations (the nations at war with Germany and Japan)—U.S. president Harry S. Truman, British prime minister Winston Churchill, and Soviet leader Joseph Stalin.

Unparalleled: Unequaled; unmatched.

The first atomic bombs were nick-named Fat Man (back) and Little Boy (front). *(Reproduced by permission of the Library of Congress)*

when used against the enemy. For that reason the military advised that we go ahead with the existing military plans for the invasion of the Japanese home islands....

If the test of the bomb was successful, I wanted to afford Japan a clear chance to end the fighting before we made use of this newly gained power. If the test should fail, then it would be even more important to us to bring about a surrender before we had to make a **physical conquest** *of Japan. [Chief of staff of the army] General [George C.] Marshall told me that it might cost half a million American lives to force the enemy's surrender on his home grounds.*

But the test was now successful. The entire development of the atomic bomb had been **dictated** *by military considerations. The idea of the atomic bomb had been suggested to President [Franklin D.] Roosevelt by the famous and brilliant Dr. Albert Einstein, and its development turned out to be a vast undertaking. It was the achievement of the combined efforts of science, industry, labor, and the military, and it had no parallel in history. . . .*

Physical conquest: Successful land invasion.

Dictated: Made necessary; required.

Harry S. Truman

Harry S. Truman (1884-1972), the eldest of three children, was born in Lamar, Missouri, on May 8, 1884. The "S" in "Harry S. Truman" doesn't stand for a particular middle name. Rather, it was added to Harry's name as a tribute to his grandfathers, Anderson Shippe Truman and Solomon Young.

When he was eight years old Truman contracted a serious case of diphtheria (pronounced "dip-THIR-ee-uh"; a once-common bacterial infection that restricts breathing, damages nerves, and often leads to heart damage) and nearly died. He also had very poor eyesight. Because of his expensive eyeglasses, Truman wasn't allowed to play sports and spent a lot of time reading.

After graduating from high school, Truman was unable to afford college tuition and went to work as an accountant and a bank clerk in Kansas City. Then in 1906 Truman took over the Young family farm. (Up to this point, it had been run by Truman's aging grandmother and his Uncle Harrison). Over the next ten years Harry successfully managed the large farm, doing much of the farm work himself.

Truman was a soldier in the U.S. Army during the last two years of World War I (1914-18). After returning home at war's end, he married Bess Wallace—his childhood playmate, school companion, and longtime sweetheart. In the early 1920s Truman embarked on a career in politics, beginning as a Missouri county judge in 1922 and becoming the Democratic senator from Missouri in 1934. Throughout his ten years in the Senate, he gained a sterling reputation as a plainspoken, honest, and efficient representative.

Despite every effort to avoid it, Truman reluctantly accepted U.S. president Franklin Roosevelt's invitation to be his running mate in the 1944 presidential election. (Truman liked his job in the Senate and wanted to stay there, but it was hard to say no to Roosevelt.) The duo won the election. President Roosevelt died less than three months later and Truman was sworn into the nation's highest office, the presidency, on April 13, 1945.

President Truman found himself in the most challenging role of his life. After Germany's surrender on May 8, 1945, he

Theoretically: Ideally; in this case, the splitting of an atom was believed to be possible, based on scientific evidence.

*Only a handful of the thousands of men who worked in these plants knew what they were producing. So strict was the secrecy imposed that even some of the highest-ranking officials in Washington had not the slightest idea of what was going on. I did not. Before 1939 it had been generally agreed among scientists that it was **theoretically***

was left with the monumental task of reorganizing postwar Europe. Truman met with British prime minister Winston Churchill and Soviet leader Joseph Stalin in Potsdam, Germany, to discuss bringing an end to the long years of fighting.

America's first successful atomic bomb test took place in July 1945, while Truman was in Potsdam. On Truman's order, U.S. forces dropped an atomic bomb on the Japanese city of Hiroshima on August 6; Nagasaki was bombed three days later. Japan surrendered to the Allies on September 2, 1945.

Foreign policy problems continued throughout the post-WWII years in America. Truman was committed to involving the United States in world affairs. He was especially concerned with controlling the spread of communism. Communism is a system of government in which the state controls most means of production and the distribution of goods. It contrasts with the American ideal of capitalism, which is based on private ownership and a free market system. The Soviet Union was a strong Communist country that sought to expand its influence throughout Eastern Europe and farther south into Greece and Turkey after World War II. Truman's opposition to communism was probably best reflected in the Truman Doctrine, a policy that provided military and financial aid to countries being threatened by the Communist Soviet Union in the late 1940s.

After winning a surprise victory over Republican candidate Thomas Dewey in the 1948 presidential election, Truman embarked on another term marked by international turmoil. In 1950 the Korean War (1950-1953) erupted. Forces from the Communist North invaded South Korea on June 24, 1950. Within hours Truman sent American troops to South Korea to put down the invasion. The United Nations backed his decision and sent forces to the war-ravaged nation, but the bloody conflict would not end until 1953, the year after Truman left office.

At the end of his second term Truman retired to his home in Independence with Bess and wrote his memoirs. He died December 26, 1972, in Kansas City.

possible to release energy from the atom. In 1940 we had begun to pool with Great Britain all scientific knowledge useful to war, although Britain was at war at that time and we were not. . . . We learned that the Germans were at work on a method to harness atomic energy for use as a weapon of war. This, we understood, was to be added to the

Albert Einstein warned Franklin Roosevelt that the Germans were working on an atomic bomb, encouraging the president to start research on atomic energy. *(Reproduced by permission of the Granger Collection)*

Providence: God or a higher power that guides human destiny.

V-1 and V-2 rockets with which they hoped to conquer the world. They failed, of course, and for this we can thank **Providence.** But now a race was on to make the atomic bomb—a race that became "the battle of the laboratories." . . .

We could hope for a miracle, but the daily tragedy of a bitter war crowded in on us. We labored to construct a weapon of such overpowering force that the enemy could be forced to yield swiftly once we could resort to it. This was the primary aim of our secret and vast effort. . . .

The task of creating the atomic bomb had been entrusted to a special unit of the Army Corps of Engineers, the so-called Manhattan District, headed by Major General Leslie R. Groves. The primary effort, however, had come from British and American scientists working in laboratories and offices scattered throughout the nation.

Dr. J. Robert Oppenheimer, the distinguished physicist from the University of California, had set up the key establishment in the whole process at Los Alamos, New Mexico. More than any other one man, Oppenheimer is to be credited with the achievement of the completed bomb.

My own knowledge of these developments had come about only after I became President, when Secretary Stimson had given me the full story. He had told me at that time that the project was nearing completion and that a bomb could be expected within another four months. It was at his suggestion, too, that I had then set up a committee of top men and had asked them to study with great care the implications the new weapon might have for us. . . .

This committee was assisted by a group of scientists . . . [that included] Dr. Oppenheimer, Dr. Arthur H. Compton, Dr. E. O. Lawrence, and the Italian-born Dr. Enrico Fermi. . . .

It was their recommendation that the bomb be used against the enemy as soon as it could be done. They recommended further that it should be used without specific warning and against a target that would clearly show its devastating strength. . . . It was their conclusion *that no technical demonstration they might propose, such as over a deserted island, would be likely to bring the war to an end. . . .*

The final decision of where and when to use the atomic bomb was up to me. Let there be no mistake about it. I regarded the bomb as a military weapon and never had any doubt that it should be used. The top military advisors to the President recommended its use, and when I talked to Churchill he unhesitatingly told me that he favored the use of the atomic bomb if it might aid to end the war.

*In deciding to use this bomb I wanted to make sure that it would be used as a weapon of war in the manner **prescribed** by the laws of war. That meant that I wanted it dropped on a military target. I had told Stimson that the bomb should be dropped as nearly as possible upon a war production center of prime military importance. . . .*

Four cities were finally recommended as targets: Hiroshima, Kokura, Niigata, and Nagasaki. They were listed in that order as targets for the first attack. . . .

On July 28 Radio Tokyo announced that the Japanese government would continue to fight. . . . There was no alternative now. The bomb was scheduled to be dropped after August 3 unless Japan surrendered before that day.

On August 6, the fourth day of the journey home from Potsdam, came the historic news that shook the world. . . . (Truman, Memoirs, *pp. 415-21)*

Prescribed: Exactly as ordered.

What happened next . . .

On July 26, 1945, the Allies issued the Potsdam Declaration, which gave the Japanese a choice of unconditional surrender or "prompt and utter destruction." (See Harry S. Truman entry in chapter four for more information about the Potsdam Declaration.) No specific mention was made of America's plan to use an atomic weapon in the war against Japan. The Japanese refused to surrender.

On August 6, 1945 at 8:16 A.M., the United States bombed the Japanese city of Hiroshima. (See Rodney Barker entry in chapter three for more information about the effects

Letters from Albert Einstein to Franklin Roosevelt

Back in the late 1930s Hungarian-born physicist Leo Szilard (1898-1964) immigrated to the United States and began working with Enrico Fermi on atom-splitting research and experimentation. Szilard was particularly worried that the Germans would develop and use an atomic bomb to achieve world domination. Even before the United States entered World War II, Szilard believed that President Franklin Roosevelt should be informed about the potential uses of nuclear power. He convinced German-born physicist Albert Einstein (1879-1955) to get involved.

Einstein and Szilard met on Long Island, New York, in the summer of 1939. Einstein, the most famous scientist in the world at the time, agreed to warn Roosevelt about Germany's alleged work on the bomb. After discussing the primary points that should be included in the initial letter, Einstein dictated his thoughts.

Szilard later translated Einstein's German, and Einstein added his signature. (Some sources suggest that Szilard was the real author of the letters.)

The first of four letters—dated August 2, 1939—reached Roosevelt in October. It begins: "Some recent work by E. Fermi and L. Szilard . . . leads me to expect that the element uranium may be turned into a new and important source of energy in the immediate future." The letter goes on to suggest that (1) this energy could power a new kind of bomb for use in warfare; (2) the U.S. government should stay current on the latest developments in nuclear energy; and (3) the United States should fund nuclear experiments. America's commitment to nuclear research did not begin in earnest, however, until December of 1942. Later in his life, Einstein is said to have regretted his role in pushing for the development of nuclear weapons.

of the bombing of Hiroshima.) Two days later the Soviet Union declared war on Japan. By this time it was clear that the Japanese had lost the war, but still they refused to give up the fight. On August 9 a "Fat Man" bomb—twice as powerful as "Little Boy"—was dropped on Nagasaki. A few days later Japan surrendered, ending World War II.

In a collection of his writings titled *Where the Buck Stops*, Truman noted: "I gave the final order, saying I had no qualms 'if millions of lives could be saved.' I meant both American and Japanese lives. . . . I did what I thought was right."

Did you know . . .

- Harry Truman considered his job as president of the United States "the greatest honor and the most awful responsibility" anyone could ever have.

- Three years after the war Truman surprised America when he was elected to the office of president in his own right. Chicago's *Daily Tribune* reported Truman's loss to his opponent, Republican candidate Thomas Dewey, in its November 3, 1948 edition. (The infamous headline read "Dewey Defeats Truman.") But Truman actually won the 1948 election by about two million votes.

- In *The Autobiography of Harry S. Truman,* edited by Robert H. Ferrell, Truman wrote: "I have been reading a book about me. . . . [It] is supposed to be an educational one for young people. It contains more misstatements and false quotations than it contains facts and true statements." Truman penned several autobiographical manuscripts—later pieced together by Ferrell—to clear up all the "misinformation" that had been published about him in his lifetime.

For More Information

Books

Miller, Merle. *Plain Speaking: An Oral Biography of Harry S. Truman.* New York: Berkley Publishing, 1974.

Wheeler, Keith, and the editors of Time-Life Books. *The Fall of Japan.* "Time-Life Books World War II Series." Alexandria, VA: Time-Life Books, 1983.

Periodicals

Newsweek, Special Report: "Hiroshima: August 6, 1945," July 24, 1995.

Videos

Hiroshima and Nagasaki: Was Truman's Decision to Use the Bomb Justified? Zengar Video, 1989.

Web Sites

The Hiroshima Project. [Online] http://err.org/akke/HiroshimaProject/GuidedTour/Events/Usa/ManhattanProject/index.html (accessed on September 6, 1999).

A-Bomb WWW Museum [Online] http://www.csi.ad.jp/ABOMB/ index.html (accessed on September 6, 1999).

Sources

Beyer, Don E. *The Manhattan Project: America Makes the First Atomic Bomb.* New York: F. Watts, 1991.

Black, Wallace B., and Jean F. Blashfield. *Hiroshima and the Atomic Bomb.* "World War II 50th Anniversary Series." New York: Crestwood House, 1993.

Dolan, Edward F. *America in World War II: 1945.* Brookfield, CT: Millbrook Press, 1994.

Feinberg, Barbara Silberdick. *Hiroshima and Nagasaki.* "Cornerstones of Freedom Series." Chicago: Children's Press, 1995.

Hargrove, Jim. *Harry S. Truman: Thirty-third President of the United States.* "Encyclopedia of Presidents Series." Chicago: Children's Press, 1987.

Leavell, J. Perry, Jr. *World Leaders Past and Present: Harry S. Truman.* New York: Chelsea House, 1988.

Seddon, Tom. *Atom Bomb.* New York: W.H. Freeman, 1995.

Truman, Harry S. *Memoirs by Harry S. Truman* Volume 1: *Year of Decisions.* Garden City, NY: Doubleday, 1955.

Truman, Harry S. *The Autobiography of Harry S. Truman.* Edited by Robert H. Ferrell. Boulder: Colorado Associated University Press, 1980.

Truman, Harry S. *Where the Buck Stops: The Personal and Private Writings of Harry S. Truman.* Edited by Margaret Truman. New York: Warner, 1989.

Rodney Barker

Excerpt from The Hiroshima Maidens:
A Story of Courage, Compassion, and Survival
Published in 1985

In May 1945 the war in Europe came to a close, thus freeing up American, British, and Soviet forces, collectively known as the Allies, for the battle against Japan. At that time, naval blockades were already strangling Japanese ports. In addition, the United States had captured key islands in the Pacific and established air bases on them. (See Eugene B. Sledge entry in chapter four for more information about the war in the Pacific.) Air assaults were launched from these bases throughout the spring of 1945, crushing the Japanese military and crippling key cities on the home islands (the chain of four islands making up the heart of Japan). An invasion of the main island—first of Kyushu (pronounced "key-OO-shoe"), then northward to the capital city of Tokyo on Honshu—was tentatively scheduled for late 1945 and early 1946, but the Allies knew that the steadfast Japanese would fight harder than ever to defend the home islands.

According to military estimates, about five hundred thousand American soldiers would be lost in the invasion. U.S. president Harry S. Truman had repeatedly called for the "unconditional surrender" of Japan, but the Japanese simply

"Hiroko raised her arm and pointed, and at that very instant the air seemed to catch fire. There was a searing white dazzle that prickled hotly and she had time only to think she had been shot before she blacked out."

The United States planned an invasion of Japan at the southern island of Kyushu for November 1945.

would not agree to surrender on such terms. Their devotion to their emperor and their commitment to the honor of the Japanese nation would not allow them to unconditionally surrender.

The Potsdam Declaration, a statement released by the leaders of the Allied nations on July 26, 1945, demanded the "unconditional surrender of all Japanese armed forces." According to the declaration, failure to surrender would result in the "the prompt and utter destruction" of Japan. The Japanese did not know that a new weapon—an atomic weapon— would be used against them to hasten that surrender.

Hiroshima (pronounced "hih-ROH-shih-muh" or "HEAR-oh-SHEE-muh"), located on the main Japanese island of Honshu, and Nagasaki (pronounced "nah-guh-SAH-key"), on the island of Kyushu, were the targets of the first atomic bombs. Early on the morning of August 6, 1945, a B-29 bomber called the *Enola Gay* took off from the U.S. air base on the tiny

Colonel Paul Tibbets, commander of the *Enola Gay*, the plane that dropped the atomic bomb on Hiroshima. *(Reproduced by permission of Corbis/Bettmann)*

South Pacific island of Tinian, nearly 1,500 miles southeast of Japan. Inside the bomber was a ten-foot long, eight-thousand—pound atomic bomb nicknamed "Little Boy."

It was a five-hour trip by air to the B-29's destination-the city of Hiroshima. Lieutenant Colonel Paul W. Tibbets piloted the *Enola Gay*. Two bombers flew behind him.

The people of Hiroshima were not alarmed by the sight of B-29 bombers flying over the city's business district. Since U.S. forces had established air bases on conquered islands in the Pacific, fly-overs had become a routine occurrence. But no one expected the horror that was about to be unleashed. The atomic bomb was dropped from the *Enola Gay* a little after 8:15 A.M. and exploded less than a minute later about 1,850 feet over Hiroshima.

The bomber crew wore special glasses to protect their eyes from the burst of light that came with the explosion of the bomb. Witnesses in the air reported seeing a flash, hearing a rumble from the blast, and feeling a strong jolt. A huge fireball enveloped Hiroshima, followed by a rising mushroom cloud of smoke. Later, black rain fell on the city from heavy dark clouds.

On the ground, unimaginable heat and flames melted everything in sight. Thousands of buildings collapsed into heaps of rubble. Uncovered flesh was immediately charred and blistered by the high temperatures.

The tragedy at Hiroshima killed between seventy thousand and eighty thousand people instantly. Over the next five years, thousands more people (about half the city's population) would die from the aftereffects of the bombing. The Japanese use the term *hibakusha* (pronounced "hih-buh-KOO-shuh") to refer to survivors of the atomic bombs dropped at the end of World War II.

Things to remember while reading the excerpt from *The Hiroshima Maidens:*

- The United States was the first country to develop and use a nuclear weapon. The bombing of Hiroshima, therefore, marked the beginning of the Nuclear Age.

- The Hiroshima Maidens were twenty-five young women who were injured in the Hiroshima bombing. They were bonded by their common experiences.

- In the spring of 1955, as part of a massive humanitarian effort, the Maidens were flown to the United States for plastic surgery at New York's Mount Sinai Hospital.

- While in the United States, the Hiroshima Maidens stayed at the homes of American host families. Rodney Barker, author of *The Hiroshima Maidens: A Story of Courage, Compassion, and Survival* and a member of one of the host families, was nine years old when two of the Maidens came to stay at his house.

- In 1979 Barker received a travel grant to research and write about postwar Hiroshima. His reports were published in the *Denver Post*. Background material from his visit to Japan, along with recorded interviews conducted in the

United States and Japan between 1979 and 1984, provided the foundation for his book, *The Hiroshima Maidens*.

- The following excerpt recounts the experiences of two girls—Hiroko Tasaka and Shigeko Niimoto—on the morning of August 6, 1945.

Excerpt from The Hiroshima Maidens

*The sky was blue that Monday morning, but as Hiroko Tasaka dashed out the door of her grandparents' home in the suburban outskirts of Hiroshima, she could feel the humidity like a fever. . . . It was early, but already the streets were **teeming** with soldiers, laborers, students. . . .*

*This was the first day the students from the all-girls Hiroshima Commercial High School had been summoned to assist **demolition** crews with the house-clearing program. . . . Today they were to clear the debris of dismantled houses, moving stones to one spot along the street, boards to another, where they would be picked up later and carted to a dump site somewhere outside the city. Donning a white hiking cap to shade her face and white gloves to protect her hands, Hiroko began the day's work.*

Perhaps fifteen minutes passed and she was struggling with a rock from the house foundation when a classmate beside her called out, "Hiroko, look. B-chan." In those days that was how they referred to B-29s, as though they were little pets.

Hiroko stopped working and looked up. She thought it made a lovely site, gleaming in the sunlight. . . .

"Where?" another girl asked. "I can't see it."

*Hiroko raised her arm and pointed, and at that very instant the air seemed to catch fire. There was a **searing** white dazzle that prickled hotly and she had time only to think she had been shot before she blacked out.*

When her senses returned, she was lying on her back in the middle of an unfamiliar darkness. Not a single star shone and no light could be seen. She rose shakily to her feet. . . . It was impossible to see

Teeming: Overflowing.

Demolition: Wrecking; tearing down.

Searing: Burning; scorching.

more than a few feet in any direction. . . . In just a few steps she thought she could see more clearly, and a short distance further she broke out into the daylight. In front of her the Kyobashi River shimmered, and without hesitating she slid down the embankment and plunged into the cool current.

*. . . . Hiroko looked around and saw that scores of other people had sought shelter in the river. The tattered remains of their uniforms identified practically all of them as schoolmates, but it was impossible to distinguish individuals because every face was swollen to **a piteous likeness**. That led her to examine herself and she was startled to discover that her half-sleeved blouse was scorched and, even though she felt no pain, the skin on her bare arms had split open, exposing the pink tissue underneath.*

No one knew what had happened. After an excited exchange, however, it was decided a bomb must have exploded directly on the work site. Just then a woman whose hair was singed, wearing rags that smoked as if they were about to burst into flames, rushed up to the riverbank crying, "The city is no longer safe. We must try to get back to school." . . .

*As a group they scrambled out of the water, trotted across Hijiyama Bridge, and proceeded down the road that wound around the base of Hijiyama. . . . When the path ahead was obstructed by flames and further progress was impossible, the group abandoned the pavement and charged the slopes of Hijiyama. . . . There was no path to follow and the **scrub oak bushes** dotting the hillside were igniting with a whoosh, so everyone went in different directions. In her quest for the safety of higher ground, Hiroko took a route that went straight up, though more than once the loose rock underfoot gave way, carrying her backward on a clattering landslide.*

*It took her almost an hour before she reached a clearing near the summit. . . . In a daze she sat down on a rock and watched others come up from below. As she saw that every single face was puffy and bloodsmeared, her hand went automatically to her own face and she wondered if hers might be the same. It was getting hard for her to keep her eyes open. In front of her a woman was working her way up an **outcropping**, and when she made it over the top Hiroko called to her, "Excuse me, but would you tell me what my face looks like?"*

With hardly a glance the woman responded, "We all look the same," and passed on.

. . . An authoritative voice call[ed] all who could still walk to proceed to the station where a rescue train was due. [Hiroko] was rapidly

A piteous likeness: Barely recognizable; looking horribly distorted.

Scrub oak bushes: Small shrubs.

Outcropping: Projecting rock.

Depot: Building for railroad passengers.

losing her vision and knew soon she would be blinded by the swelling. As it was, she found the **depot** by clutching the clothes of those walking in front of her.

As the hours passed, direct exposure to the sun turned up the heat of her burns, and just when Hiroko was beginning to give up hope that the trains were still running, someone shouted, "Here it comes." As no one wanted to be left behind, people swarmed over the engine and climbed through the windows before the wheels rolled to

In 1955, as part of a massive humanitarian effort, the Hiroshima Maidens were flown to the United States for plastic surgery at New York's Mount Sinai Hospital. *(Reproduced by permission of the Corbis/Bettmann)*

The Human Cost: Rodney Barker |

Physical Effects of the Bomb on Its Victims

The splitting of uranium atoms causes an enormous release of energy. Accompanying this burst of energy are invisible waves or rays that cause deadly radiation sickness. In Hiroshima and Nagasaki, radiation poisoning affected people as far as a mile and a half away from the explosions.

The heat and fire from the exploding bombs caused deep, painful burns on the faces and bodies of thousands of people. As their wounds healed, many victims were left severely disfigured by the formation of scar tissue. In most cases, however, the effects of radiation did not become apparent until months later. Symptoms of radiation sickness among *hibakusha* included weakness, hair loss, purplish bruiselike spots on the skin, sores in and on the mouth, bleeding gums, vomiting, diarrhea, and little resistance to infection (a low white blood cell count). A higher than expected incidence of various cancers has also been reported in atomic bomb survivors.

Mortification: Shame; humiliation; horror.

Air-raid hood: Covering worn to protect the heads of people on the ground during an attack by armed airplanes.

a stop. Hiroko tried to stand up, but to her **mortification** her legs gave out each time and she was unable to crawl the last part of the way across the platform before the train pulled slowly away.

. . . .

Shigeko Niimoto was bent over trying to untie the **air-raid hood** she had left on after an earlier alarm when she heard her Middle School classmate say, "Look, Niimoto-**san**. Something's dropped from that plane." She stopped what she was doing and tilted her head back. Using her hands as a visor to shade the sun, she looked up just in time to witness an explosion of light, white and blinding. Screaming, she covered her face with both hands and dropped to her knees. The last thing she remembered was a violent blast of wind slamming her sideways.

. . . . Her mind was fuzzy and everything around her blurred. As she got to her feet she peered into a thick, shifting mist through which she saw flickering fires and forms. . . . She was unable to make out anything distinctly until the floating mists parted to reveal a frightening procession of figures that looked to her like **cadavers** making an **exodus** from their graves. They moved slowly, almost dreamily, without making a sound. They held their hands out in front of their chests like sleepwalkers. At first she thought they were wrapped in wisps of smoke, but as her vision increased she saw it was their skin peeling from their bodies. She drew a deep breath, holding it in. Something terrible had gone wrong and she wanted no part of it.

"Niimoto-san. Niimoto-san."

At the sound of her name being called, she turned. One of the nightmarish figures was moving toward her. Instinctively she **recoiled.** "Who are you?"

Women tending a child who was wounded in the atomic bomb blast in Hiroshima.
(Reproduced by permission of the Corbis Corporation [Bellevue])

"Araki. Sachiko Araki."

To Shigeko's astonishment, it was her best friend. "Oh, Sachiko, what happened?"

Having seen the way she was looked at, her friend asked, "Do I look that bad?"

"No," Shigeko lied, "it's just slight." Then, noticing how Araki-san's eyes were fixed on her, she asked, "How about me?"

"Just slight too."

Without any discussion of what might have happened, Shigeko found herself pulled by the arm to a street not far away where her friend's mother was trapped under the wreckage of their completely collapsed home. The roof had come down on top of the woman and only her head stuck out. Shigeko stood **dumbfounded** for a moment, wondering what she was supposed to do, before joining Araki-san, who was frantically pushing splintered timbers and shattered tiles aside.

But there was a mound of debris to move and not much time. The house next door had erupted in fire and the heat grew more intense

San: A Japanese suffix used to signify the polite form of a name.

Cadavers: Dead bodies.

Exodus: Exit; departure.

Recoiled: Pulled back in fear or shock.

Dumbfounded: Confused; puzzled.

by the minute. Araki-san's mother was the first to admit it was useless. "There's nothing that can be done for mother, dear," she said in a surprisingly calm voice. "Go and find father."

When Araki-san [said that] she could not bear to desert her mother, [that] they would die together, she was ordered away. "Do as I say. Hurry. Right now."

*As they backed away the house became a raging **funeral pyre**. "Good-bye," [Shigeko's] friend cried. "Good-bye, mother." The last they saw of Araki-san's mother [was] her face float[ing] in flames but she was still smiling. (Barker, pp. 18-25)*

Funeral pyre: A pile of wood for burning a dead body.

What happened next . . .

Three days after "Little Boy" was dropped on Hiroshima, a B-29 bomber named *Bock's Car* dropped a plutonium-powered "Fat Man" bomb on the city of Nagasaki, killing forty thousand more Japanese. Thousands were injured. Ironically, the bomb fell directly over a Roman Catholic cathedral. On August 15, 1945—V-J Day (Victory over Japan Day)—the Japanese surrendered to the Allies and World War II came to a close.

"It always bothered [Hiroko]," noted Barker, "that in the American version [of the bomb story] the bomb was dropped, the war was over, and that was it, while for her and so many others that was just the beginning." People affected by the bomb—*hibakusha*—had to deal with tremendous physical and psychological stresses. Their injuries made them outcasts. They endured discrimination in the workplace and were not considered "marriageable" in Japan. The bottom half of Hiroko's face was badly burned, and her arms were frozen at an angle—bent by scar tissue. Shigeko suffered severe burns to her face.

Even after their surgeries, the girls faced rejection in Japan. Results varied, but overall the Maidens' faces did not— and never would—look the same as they had before the bombing. "They looked much better," explained Barker, "but in a number of cases the disfiguring marks were still bad enough to attract attention."

Hiroko underwent twenty-seven operations—fourteen in Japan and thirteen in the States—became a dressmaker, and opened her own shop in Hiroshima. Later, she gave up her career to accept the marriage proposal of an American man who had long been captivated by her bravery and inner beauty. The adjustment to her new life in the United States was difficult for Hiroko, and her marriage was, at times, quite rocky. Language proved to be the main barrier in the couple's path—she knew very little English, and he did not speak Japanese. After his retirement, though, Hiroko's husband agreed to go to Japan with her.

Shigeko spent six months in Japan after her surgeries, then returned to the United States. She was taken in by *Saturday Review* editor and humanitarian Norman Cousins and his family. (Cousins had organized the Hiroshima Maidens project.) Shigeko had a son in 1962 and later worked with the physically disabled as a home-care therapist.

Destruction in Nagasaki after the bomb. *(© Archive Photos, Inc. Reproduced by permission)*

⬙ Debate Over Use of the Bomb

More than a half-century after atomic bombs were dropped over Hiroshima and Nagasaki, intense debate still rages over their use.

Opponents of the use of nuclear weapons on Japan maintain that the Allies' demand for unconditional surrender was too harsh. (See Harry S. Truman entries in chapters three and four.) Some historians feel that the Japanese would have surrendered prior to the bombings if they had been assured that their emperor would be retained in a postwar world. At the very least, say critics, a detailed warning should have been issued to Japan—a warning that the bomb would be dropped if full surrender had not been made by a certain date. Others suggest that a display or demonstration of the power of the bomb in an unpopulated area might have convinced the Japanese to surrender.

Defenders of the bomb point to Japan's surprise attack on Pearl Harbor, their cruel treatment of Allied prisoners of war throughout World War II, and their alarming use of fanatical suicide bombers (*kamikazes*) against Allied ships as justification for bombing without warning.

In the final analysis, most observers agree on one thing: that the primary reason the bomb was dropped on Hiroshima was to end the war as quickly as possible. In his official announcement of the bombing, U.S. president Harry S. Truman stated: "It was to spare the Japanese people from utter destruction that the ultimatum of July 26 was issued at Potsdam. Their leaders promptly rejected that ultimatum. If they do not now accept our terms, they may expect a rain of ruin from the air, the like of which has never been seen on this earth." The bombing of Nagasaki took place three days later.

Did you know . . .

- The United States became involved in nuclear weapons research because of fears that Hitler's Germany would develop and use the bomb during World War II.

- Final assembly of the bomb that was dropped on Hiroshima took place after the *Enola Gay* (the B-29 that carried it) had taken flight. This safety precaution eliminated the possibility of the bomb exploding on or over the U.S. base at Tinian.

- When Truman, British prime minister Winston Churchill, and Soviet leader Joseph Stalin met for the Potsdam Conference in July of 1945, spies for the Soviet Union had already handed over the secret plans for the atomic bomb to the Soviet government. The postwar years were marked by a feverish arms race between the United States and the Soviet Union.

- The Hiroshima Peace Memorial was erected around the remains of the city's Museum of Science and Industry, a huge concrete structure left gutted but still standing after the atomic blast. The peace monument is inscribed with the words, "Repose ye in peace, for the error shall never be repeated." Each year a commemorative service is held at the site.

- The Federation of American Scientists and the Atomic Energy Commission were both organized in the postwar years to promote the regulation of nuclear weaponry worldwide.

Further Reading

Books

Sekimori, Gaynor. *Hibakusha: Survivors of Hiroshima and Nagasaki.* Boston: Charles E. Tuttle, 1986.

Videos

Hiroshima Witness. Produced by the Hiroshima Peace Cultural Center and NHK (the public broadcasting company of Japan), 1986.

Web Sites

Voice of Hibakusha. [Online] http://129.171.129.67/mf/hibakusha/index. html (accessed on September 6, 1999).

Sources

Barker, Rodney. *The Hiroshima Maidens: A Story of Courage, Compassion, and Survival.* New York: Viking, 1985.

"Birth of an Atomic 'Little Boy.'" *Newsweek,* March 8, 1999, p. 50.

Dolan, Edward F. *America in World War II: 1945.* Brookfield, CT: Millbrook Press, 1994.

Feinberg, Barbara Silberdick. *Hiroshima and Nagasaki.* "Cornerstones of Freedom Series." Chicago: Children's Press, 1995.

Feis, Herbert. *The Atomic Bomb and the End of World War II.* Princeton, NJ: Princeton University Press, 1966. Originally published as *Japan Subdued,* 1961.

Maruki, Toshi. *Hiroshima No Pika.* New York: Lothrop, Lee & Shepard, 1982.

Morimoto, Junko. *My Hiroshima.* New York: Viking, 1990.

Seddon, Tom. *Atom Bomb.* New York: W.H. Freeman, 1995.

"Text of Statement by Truman on Development of Atomic Bomb." *New York Times,* August 7, 1945, p. 4.

Ernie Pyle

"Notes from a Battered Country"

"The Death of Captain Waskow"

"I Thought It Was the End"

"Waiting for Tomorrow"

"On Victory in Europe"

**Excerpts from *Ernie's War: The Best of Ernie Pyle's World War II Dispatches*
Written by Ernie Pyle between 1943 and 1945
Collected and published in book form, 1986**

The battles of World War II (1939-45) spread beyond Europe and Asia to the continent of Africa when Italian forces invaded the northeast African country of Egypt in September of 1940. The northern tip of Africa is separated from Italy by the Mediterranean Sea and Italy wanted to expand its territory into North Africa. Italy's ally Germany landed troops in North Africa in February, 1941. By 1942 the northwest African regions of Morocco, Algeria, and Tunisia had been invaded by German and Italian—or Axis—forces.

In late 1942 and early 1943 the Allied powers (the Allied troops fighting in this region were from Great Britain, the Dominion of Canada, and the United States) succeeded in pushing the German and Italian troops out of northern Africa. (The term "Dominion" refers to the self-governing nations of the British Commonwealth, namely Canada, Australia, New Zealand, and South Africa. "Commonwealth" refers to the association of independent nations that were formerly under British control. The Allies were the nations fighting against Germany, Italy, and Japan during World War II. The major Allied countries included Great Britain, the United States, the Soviet Union, France, and China.)

"Along the road for twenty or thirty miles behind the fighting front, you pass through one demolished town after another. Most of the inhabitants take to the hills after the first shelling. . . . Some go to live in caves; some go to relatives in the country. A few in every town refuse to leave no matter what happens...."

From Africa the Allies moved northward to the island of Sicily, which lies off the southern coast of Italy in the Mediterranean Sea. Their goal was to defeat Italian forces on the island and then launch an invasion of the Italian mainland. The attack on Sicily began July 10, 1943 and lasted five weeks. After the Italians surrendered, German forces continued to defend Italy against the Allies.

Throughout September, American and British troops—joined this time by the French—advanced into southern Italy, pushing the German forces northward. The Luftwaffe (German air force) did extensive damage to Allied warships at the southerly seaports of Salerno and Bari, and after intense fighting German ground troops stopped the Allies at Cassino, a mountainous town in central Italy that served as a key position in Germany's line of defense. By launching an invasion at Anzio (a harbor in the Mediterranean Sea, located about fifty miles south of Rome), the Allies were able to lure the Germans away from Cassino. The Battle of Anzio stretched through the winter of 1944.

American journalist Ernie Pyle witnessed the fighting at Anzio firsthand. From the end of 1940 to early 1945 his writing assignments took him to England, Africa, Sicily, Italy, France, and tiny islands in the Pacific. Pyle went wherever the action was—accompanying soldiers in combat around the globe—and then composed vivid, penetrating accounts of the tragedy of war as it was being fought. His columns brought the war home to Americans.

Pyle's last dispatches (or news items) were filed from the Pacific front in early 1945. Capturing the islands of Iwo Jima and Okinawa was, at that time, considered crucial to an Allied victory in the Pacific. Both locations were viewed as prime launching points for air invasions of the Japanese home islands. (Note that a massive invasion of the Japanese mainland never took place. The Japanese surrendered to the Allies after atomic bombs were dropped on the cities of Hiroshima and Nagasaki. See Harry S. Truman entry in chapter 3.)

The Japanese stationed their fighter planes on the heavily fortified island of Iwo Jima, located 600 miles from the capital city of Tokyo on Honshu (one of Japan's four main islands). The U.S. Marine invasion of Iwo Jima was scheduled for February 19, 1945. For ten straight weeks before that, U.S. Navy war-

U.S. Marines raising the American flag on Mount Suribachi on Iwo Jima.
(Reproduced by permission of the National Archives and Records Administration)

ships and planes bombarded the tiny, barren island. Then, during the early morning hours of February 19, a two-mile-long stretch of beach was bombarded one last time in preparation for the 9:00 A.M. marine landing. Heavily armed Japanese forces fought back from concealed locations carved into the craggy rock of Mount Suribachi, situated high above the beaches. The first day of fighting left well over five hundred marines dead, but the Americans continued their slow advance inland. On February 23 a small force of marines managed to climb to the top of Mount Suribachi and raise the American flag.

The fierce battle for Iwo Jima lasted another month. When it was over, more than twenty thousand Japanese soldiers were dead; nearly seven thousand Americans had been killed and another twenty thousand were wounded.

Allied B-29 bombers attacked Tokyo early in March of 1945. At the end of the month U.S. forces began the long and bloody invasion of Okinawa (one of the Ryukyu—pro-

![Important Names icon]

Important Names

Bold, fiery, and controversial—these are just a few of the words frequently used to describe two key leaders of the Allied forces: George S. Patton (1885-1945) and Sir Bernard Law Montgomery (1887-1976). U.S. General George Patton, nicknamed "Old Blood and Guts," commanded the U.S. 7th Army in its 1943 attack on Sicily. British Field Marshal Montgomery, better known as "Monty," led forces in Sicily and Italy. Both Patton and Montgomery played important roles in the Allied invasions of French North Africa (1942) and northern France (1944; see Veterans of D-Day entry).

nounced "ree-YOU-kyew"—Islands, located about 350 miles south of the Japanese main islands). By this time the Japanese navy had been virtually shattered, so Japanese military leaders sent out an enormous force of *kamikaze* fighters (pronounced "kahm-ih-KAH-zee"; translated as "divine wind") to attack enemy forces. (Kamikazes were suicide bombers—Japanese pilots who purposely crashed their planes into Allied ships.)

The three-month-long air and land battle for Okinawa proved to be the most devastating campaign carried out in the Pacific. One in three U.S. Marines who fought on Okinawa were either killed or wounded, and thousands of soldiers suffered psychological as well as physical wounds. By late June of 1945, when the island was completely conquered by the Allies, about 130,000 Japanese had been killed.

Things to remember while reading the excerpts from *Ernie's War: The Best of Ernie Pyle's World War II Dispatches*:

- Journalist Ernie Pyle was an eyewitness to the horrors of war on three continents: Europe, Africa, and Asia.

- Pyle's dispatches are noted for their insight and honesty. Literary critics often refer to his writing style as "spare" because he used simple, direct, repetitive language to convey his ideas and impressions.

- Pyle's moving account of the death of Captain Henry T. Waskow is generally considered his best piece. (See second Pyle excerpt, titled "The Death of Captain Waskow.")

- The piece titled "On Victory in Europe" was found on Pyle's body after his death on the Pacific island of Ie Shima (pronounced "ee-SHEE-muh").

"Notes from a Battered Country"

IN ITALY, December 28, 1943—*The little towns of Italy that have been in the path of this war from Salerno northward are nothing more than great rubble heaps. There is hardly enough left of most of them to form a framework for rebuilding.*

*When the Germans occupied the towns, we rained **artillery** on them for days and weeks at a time. Then after we captured a town, the Germans would **shell** it heavily. **They** got it from both sides.*

*Along the road for twenty or thirty miles behind the fighting **front**, you pass through one demolished town after another. Most of the inhabitants take to the hills after the first shelling. . . . Some go to live in caves; some go to relatives in the country. A few in every town refuse to leave no matter what happens, and many of them have been killed by the shelling and bombing from both sides.*

*A countryside is harder to **disfigure** than a town. You have to look closely, and study in detail, to find the **carnage wrought upon** the green fields and the rocky hillside. It is there, but it is temporary—like a skinned finger—and time and the rains will heal it. Another year and the countryside will cover its own scars.*

*If you wander on foot and look closely you will see the signs—the limb of an olive tree broken off, six swollen dead horses in the corner of a field, a strawstack burned down, a chestnut tree blown clear out with its roots by a German bomb, . . . empty gun pits, and countless **foxholes**, and rubbish-heap stacks of empty **C-ration** cans, and now and then the lone grave of a German soldier.*

These are all there, clear across the country, and yet they are hard to see unless you look closely. A countryside is big, and nature helps fight for it.

"The Death of Captain Waskow"

AT THE FRONT LINES IN ITALY, January 10, 1944—*In this war I have known a lot of officers who were loved and respected by the soldiers under them. But never have I crossed the trail of any man as beloved as Capt. Henry T. Waskow of Belton, Texas.*

Artillery: Missiles.

Shell: Bombard. When used as a noun, refers to fragmented metal casings left after heavy shooting.

They: The Italian towns and the people who lived in them.

Front: Battle zone.

Disfigure: Visibly damage, impair, or ruin.

Carnage wrought upon: The physical marks left on the land from the fighting.

Foxholes: Pits that provide cover from enemy fire.

C-ration: Canned food consumed by U.S. Army soldiers in the field.

Ernie Pyle, seated, second
from right in front of the
tank, with members of the
U.S. Fifth Army in Anzio,
Italy. *(Reproduced by
permission of the Corbis
Corporation [Bellevue])*

*Capt. Waskow was a **company** commander in the 36th Division.
He had led his company since long before it left the [United] States.
He was very young, only in his middle twenties, but he carried in him
a sincerity and gentleness that made people want to be guided by
him.*

"After my own father, he came next," a sergeant told me.

*"He always looked after us," a soldier said. "He'd go to bat for us
every time." . . .*

*I was at the foot of the mule trail the night they brought Capt.
Waskow's body down. The moon was nearly full at the time, and
you could see far up the trail, and even part way across the valley
below. . . .*

*Dead men had been coming down the mountain all evening,
lashed onto the backs of mules. They came lying belly-down across
the wooden pack-saddles, their heads hanging down on the left side
of the mule, their stiffened legs sticking out awkwardly from the other
side, bobbing up and down as the mule walked. . . .*

Company: A unit of soldiers.

The first one came early in the morning. They slid him down from the mule and stood him on his feet for a moment, while they got a new grip. In the half light he might have been merely a sick man standing there, leaning on the others. Then they laid him on the ground in the shadow of the low stone wall alongside the road.

I don't know who that first one was. You feel small in the presence of dead men, and ashamed at being alive, and you don't ask silly questions.

We left him there beside the road, that first one, and we all went back into the cowshed and sat on water cans or lay on the straw, waiting for the next batch of mules.

Somebody said the dead soldier had been dead for four days, and then nobody said anything more about it. We talked soldier talk for an hour or more. The dead man lay all alone outside in the shadow of the low stone wall.

Then a soldier came into the cowshed and said there were some more bodies outside. We went out into the road. Four mules stood there, in the moonlight, in the road where the trail came down off the mountain. The soldiers who led them stood there waiting. "This one is Captain Waskow," one of them said quietly.

Two men unlashed his body from the mule and lifted it off and laid it in the shadow beside the low stone wall. Other men took the other bodies off. Finally there were five lying end to end in a long row, alongside the road. You don't cover up dead men in the combat zone. They just lie there in the shadows until somebody else comes after them.

*The unburdened mules moved off to their olive orchard. The men in the road seemed reluctant to leave. They stood around, and gradually one by one I could sense them moving closer to Capt. Waskow's body. Not so much to look, I think, as to say something **in finality** to him, and to themselves. I stood close by and I could hear.*

Ernie Pyle

Indiana-born journalist Ernest Taylor Pyle (1900-1945), who wrote under the name Ernie Pyle, was one of the best known and most respected correspondents of World War II. Early on he was recognized for his keen-eyed reporting, and before the war he penned a daily column that appeared in about two hundred newspapers throughout the United States. Pyle covered the war as it unfolded in England, North Africa, Sicily, Italy, France, and the Pacific. In 1944 he was awarded the prestigious Pulitzer Prize for reporting. The next year, while traveling with four soldiers on the tiny island of Ie Shima (located in the Pacific just west of Okinawa), he was struck in the head by a Japanese sniper's bullet. Pyle died instantly and was later buried on the island in a handmade wooden coffin.

In finality: At this final and ultimate point.

American troops file down a mountainside in Sicily, an island off the southern tip of Italy. The Allied attack on Sicily began July 10, 1943. Their goal was to defeat Italian forces on the island and then launch an invasion of the Italian mainland.
(Reproduced by permission of AP/Wide World Photos, Inc.)

One soldier came and looked down, and he said out loud, "God damn it." That's all he said, and then he walked away. Another one came. He said, "God damn it to hell anyway." He looked down for a few last moments, and then he turned and left.

Another man came; I think he was an officer. It was hard to tell . . . in the half light, for [everyone was] bearded and grimy dirty. The man looked down into the dead captain's face, and then he spoke directly to him, as though he were alive. He said: "I'm sorry , old man."

Then a soldier came and stood beside the officer, and bent over, and he too spoke to his dead captain, not in a whisper but awfully tenderly, and he said:

"I sure am sorry, sir."

Then the first man squatted down, and he reached down and took the dead hand, and he sat there for a full five minutes, holding the dead hand in his own and looking intently into the dead face, and he never uttered a sound all the time he sat there.

And finally he put the hand down, and then reached up and gently straightened the points of the captain's shirt collar, and then he sort of rearranged the tattered edges of his uniform around the wound. And then he got up and walked away down the road in the moonlight, all alone. . . .

"I Thought It Was the End"

WITH THE FIFTH ARMY BEACHHEAD FORCES IN ITALY, March 20, 1944—*We **correspondents** stay in a **villa** run by the 5th Army's Public Relations Section. . . .*

*The house is on the waterfront. The current sometimes washes over our back steps. The house is a huge, rambling affair with four stories down on the beach and then another complete section of three stories just above it in the **bluff**, all connected by a series of interior stairways.*

*For weeks long-range artillery shells had been hitting in the water or on shore within a couple of hundred yards of us. **Raiders** came over nightly, yet . . . this villa . . . seemed to be charmed. . . .*

*. . . [T]he part of the house down by the water [was] considered safer because it was lower down. But I had been sleeping alone in the room in the top part because it was a lighter place to work in the daytime. We called it "Shell Alley" up there because the **Anzio-bound** shells seemed to come in a groove right past our **eaves** day and night.*

On this certain morning I had awakened early and was just lying there for a few minutes before getting up. It was just seven and the sun was out bright.

Suddenly the anti-aircraft guns let loose. Ordinarily I don't get out of bed during a raid, but I did get up this one morning. . . .

I had just reached the window when a terrible blast swirled me around and threw me into the middle of my room. . . .

The half of the window that was shut was ripped out and hurled across the room. The glass was blown into thousands of little pieces. Why the splinters or the window frame itself didn't hit me I don't know.

From the moment of the first blast until it was over probably not more than fifteen seconds passed. Those fifteen seconds were so fast and confusing that I truly can't say what took place, and the other correspondents reported the same.

*There was **debris** flying back and forth all over the room. One gigantic explosion came after another. . . .*

Correspondents: Reporters.

Villa: Large country home on a big piece of land.

Bluff: Cliff.

Raiders: In this case, the Germans.

Anzio-bound: Headed for the seaport of Anzio, located near the capital city of Rome in central Italy.

Eaves: The section of a roof that hangs over an outside wall.

Debris: Broken rock, brick, and pieces of wall.

I jumped into one corner of the room and squatted down and sat **cowered** *there. I definitely thought it was the end. Outside of that I don't remember what my emotions were.*

Suddenly one whole wall of my room flew in, burying the bed where I'd been a few seconds before under hundreds of pounds of brick, stone and **mortar**. . . .

Then the wooden doors were ripped off their hinges and crashed into the room. . . . The French doors leading to the balcony blew out and one of my chairs was upended through the open door. . . .

Finally the terrible nearby explosions ceased and gradually the **ack-ack** *died down and at last I began to have some feeling of relief that it was over and I was still alive. But I stayed crouched in the corner until the last shot was fired.*

. . . When our bombing was over, my room was in a shambles. It was the sort of thing you see only in the movies.

More than half the room was knee-deep with broken brick and tiles and mortar. The other half was a disarray all covered with plaster dust and broken glass. My typewriter was full of mortar and broken glass, but was not damaged.

My pants had been lying on the chair that went through the door, so I dug them out from under the debris, put them on and started down to the other half of the house.

Down below everything was a mess. The ceilings had come down upon men still in bed. Some beds were a foot deep in debris. That nobody was killed was a pure miracle. . . .

The boys *couldn't believe it when they saw me coming in. Wick Fowler of the* Dallas News *had thought the bombs had made direct hits on the upper part of the house. He had just said to George Tucker of the Associated Press, "Well, they got Ernie."*

But after they saw I was all right they began to laugh and called me "Old Indestructible." I guess I was the luckiest man in the house, at that, although **Old Dame Fortune** *was certainly riding with all of us that morning.*

"Waiting for Tomorrow"

OFF THE OKINAWA BEACHHEAD, April 3, 1945—This is the last column before the invasion. It is written aboard a troop transport the evening before we storm onto Okinawa. . . .

Cowered: Crouched down in fear.

Mortar: Building material used to hold bricks together or for plastering walls

Ack-ack: Antiaircraft fire.

The boys: The other correspondents living in the villa.

Old Dame Fortune: Another name for "Lady Luck."

A wounded soldier being lifted out of the tank that brought him back from the front lines in Okinawa. The fighting there was extremely brutal with both sides suffering heavy casualties. *(Reproduced by permission of the Corbis Corporation [Bellevue])*

. . . We will take Okinawa. Nobody has any doubt about that. But we know we will have to pay for it. Some on this ship will not be alive twenty-four hours from now.

April 16, 1945—We camped one night on a little hillside that led up to a bluff overlooking a small river. The bluff dropped straight down for a long way. Up there on top of the bluff it was just like a little park.

Japan, the Ryukyu Islands (south of the main islands), and Okinawa.

The bluff was terraced, although it wasn't farmed. The grass on it was soft and green. And those small, straight-limbed pine trees were dotted all over it.

Looking down from the bluff, the river made a turn and across it was an old stone bridge. At the end of the bridge was a village—or what had been a village.

It was now just a jumble of ashes and sagging **thatched** roofs from our **bombardment**. In every direction little valleys led away from the turn in the river.

It was as pretty and gentle a sight as you ever saw. It had the softness of **antiquity** about it and the miniature charm and **daintiness** that we see in Japanese **prints**. And the sad, **uncanny** silence that follows the **bedlam** of war.

A bright sun made the morning hot and a refreshing little breeze sang through the pine trees. There wasn't a shot nor a warlike sound within hearing. I sat on the bluff for a long time, just looking. It all seemed so quiet and peaceful. I noticed a lot of the Marines sitting and just looking, too.

Thatched: Grass-covered.

Bombardment: Assault or attack with bombs.

Antiquity: Ancient times.

Daintiness: Small and delicate; not at all rough.

Prints: Reproductions of original works of art.

Uncanny: Eerie; strange.

Bedlam: Confusion; turmoil; chaos.

"On Victory in Europe"

*And so it is over. The **catastrophe** on one side of the world has run its course. The day that it had so long seemed would never come has come at last.*

I suppose emotions here in the Pacific are the same as they were among the Allies all over the world. First a shouting of the good news. . . .

*And then an unspoken sense of gigantic relief-and then a hope that **the collapse in Europe** would hasten the end in the Pacific. . . .*

*This is written on a little ship lying off the coast of the Island of Okinawa, just south of Japan, on the other side of the world from **Ardennes**. . . .*

***To me the European war is old**, and the Pacific war is new.*

. . . In the joyousness of high spirits it is easy for us to forget the dead. . . .

But there are many of the living who have had burned into their brains forever the unnatural sight of cold dead men scattered over the hillsides and in the ditches along the high rows of hedge throughout the world.

Dead men by mass production—in one country after another—month after month and year after year. Dead men in winter and dead men in summer.

*Dead men in such familiar **promiscuity** that they become **monotonous**.*

*Dead men in such **monstrous infinity** that you come almost to hate them.*

These are the things that you at home need not even try to understand. To you at home they are columns of figures, or he is a near one who went away and just didn't come back. You didn't see him lying so grotesque and pasty beside the gravel road in France.

We saw him, saw him by the multiple thousands. That's the difference. . . . (Pyle, pp. 184-85, 195-97, 238-40, 402, 411, 418-19)

Catastrophe: Violent, tragic event.

The collapse in Europe: The surrender of German forces in Europe, marking the end of the war there.

Ardennes: (Pronounced "ar-DENN") A large forested area in southeastern Belgium. It was the site of the 1944-1945 campaign known as the Battle of the Bulge.

To me the European war is old: Pyle spent two and a half years covering the European front, but he was only in the Pacific for four months before his death.

Promiscuity: Casualness; crudeness.

Monotonous: The same.

Monstrous infinity: Overwhelming or unnatural numbers.

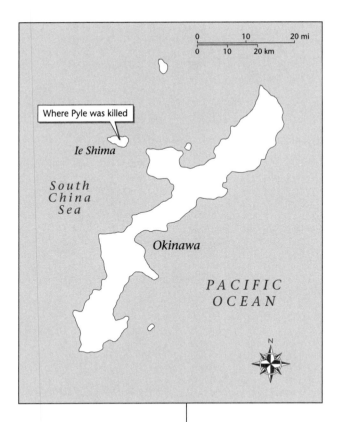

Scale:
0 — 10 — 20 mi
0 — 10 — 20 km

Where Pyle was killed

Ie Shima

South China Sea

Okinawa

PACIFIC OCEAN

N

Okinawa and Ie Shima, where Ernie Pyle was killed.

What happened next . . .

Bitter fighting in Italy continued after Pyle left in April of 1944. The main goal of the American and British armies was to capture the Italian capital of Rome. Backed by French, French-African, and Polish troops, they attacked all German positions from Cassino out to the Mediterranean Sea. At the same time, the Allied troops on the beaches of Anzio broke their deadlock with the Germans and managed to overpower them. With the combined strength of Britain's Royal Air Force (RAF) and the U.S. Army Air Force paving the way for them, American and British ground troops were able to take Rome in June 1944 and then advance northward into the city of Bologna.

Pyle was in France a day after the Allied invasion of Normandy (June 6, 1944; see Veterans of D-Day entry in chapter 4). Later, after returning to the States for a short time, he reluctantly set out for the Pacific, fearful that he wouldn't survive the war. "You begin to feel that you can't go on forever without being hit," he noted in one interview. "I feel that I've used up all my chances. And I hate it." Pyle was killed on April 18, 1945. (See box on p. 149.) The war in Europe ended three weeks later.

Did you know . . .

- Before the Second World War began, World War I (1914-18) was known simply as the "World War." The two wars did not receive the names World War I and World War II until after the second war ended in 1945.

- The 1945 feature film *G.I. Joe* was based on Pyle's experiences with American soldiers in Italy.

- Before Pyle left home for the Pacific, his wife, Jerry, begged him to reconsider. Like Pyle, she feared that he had "used up all [his] chances" and would be killed while on assignment. Pyle readily admitted that he wanted to stay home but felt that if he didn't go he'd "work up a guilty feeling that would haunt [him]." He concluded: "There's just nothing else I can do."

For More Information
Books

Marling, Karal Ann, and John Wetenhall. *Iwo Jima: Monuments, Memories, and the American Hero*. Cambridge, MA: Harvard University Press, 1991.

Miller, Lee G. *The Story of Ernie Pyle*. Originally published in 1950. Reprinted. Westport, CT: Greenwood, 1970.

Tobin, James. *Ernie Pyle's War: America's Eyewitness to World War II*. New York: Simon & Schuster, 1997.

Videos

The War Chronicles: World War II. Volume 2: *The Beachhead at Anzio*. Volume 5: *Island Hopping: The Road Back* and *Jungle Warfare: New Guinea to Burma*. Produced by Lou Reda Productions. A&E Home Video Presents History Channel Video/New Video, 1995.

Web Sites

AITLC Guide to Ernie Pyle. [Online] http://tlc.ai.org/pyleindx.htm (accessed on September 6, 1999).

Sources

Black, Wallace B., and Jean F. Blashfield. *Invasion of Italy*. "World War II 50th Anniversary Series." New York: Crestwood House, 1992.

Black, Wallace B. *Island Hopping in the Pacific*. "World War II 50th Anniversary Series." New York: Crestwood House, 1992.

Black, Wallace B. *Iwo Jima and Okinawa*. "World War II 50th Anniversary Series." New York: Crestwood House, 1993.

Dolan, Edward F. *America in World War II: 1944*. Brookfield, CT: Millbrook Press, 1993.

Dolan, Edward F. *America in World War II: 1945*. Brookfield, CT: Millbrook Press, 1994.

Pyle, Ernie. *Ernie's War: The Best of Ernie Pyle's World War II Dispatches*. Edited with a biographical essay by David Nichols. Foreword by Studs Terkel. Originally published in 1986. New York: Touchstone, 1987.

Skipper, G.C. *Invasion of Sicily*. "World at War Series." Chicago: Children's Press, 1981.

World War II Nurses

Excerpt from **No Time for Fear: Voices of American Military Nurses in World War II**

Edited by Diane Burke Fessler
Published in 1996

During World War II (1939-45) nearly sixty thousand American nurses served in the Army Nurse Corps (ANC). Whether stationed in Europe or in the Pacific, they risked their lives daily, working on or near the front lines; on land, sea, and air transport vehicles; and in field hospitals.

As caretakers of wounded soldiers fresh from the battlefield, wartime nurses dealt with every sort of injury imaginable—from gaping chest wounds and massive hemorrhages to amputations and severe burns. One of the most difficult aspects of their job, though, was helping soldiers handle the psychological damage brought on by brutal combat experiences. Brave World War II nurses, doctors, and medics (enlisted men who served as orderlies) remained strong in the face of death. Although vulnerable to attack by enemy forces, they shunned the danger and set aside their own fears to stay with the patients who needed them.

"My strongest memory is how many times a patient would say, 'Get to me when you can. He needs you more than I do.' I've never taken care of patients like that since."

Myrtle Brethouwer Hoftiezer,
U.S. Army

Army nurses wade ashore in Naples, Italy.
(Reproduced by permission of the Corbis/Hulton-Deutsch Collection)

Things to remember while reading excerpts from *No Time for Fear: Voices of American Military Nurses in World War II*:

- Wartime nurses and doctors worked in overcrowded makeshift hospitals, under less-than-sanitary conditions, often without adequate supplies, and sometimes even without running water or electricity.

- World War II nurses tended to hundreds of patients each day, working on their feet—with little or no rest—as many as eighty-four hours in a week.

- Soldiers were disabled not only by wounds but by the effects of debilitating diseases, including malaria (a potentially fatal disease transmitted by infected mosquitoes), beriberi (a serious nutritional disorder caused by inadequate intake of Vitamin B1) and dengue fever (a tropical fever also transmitted by mosquitoes).

- Some American nurses were in charge of caring for injured enemy forces at prisoner of war (POW) camps. These nurses had to set aside all feelings of intolerance, prejudice, and anger in order to care for the ailing members of the German military.

- Nurses treated the troops with equal measures of compassion, courage, and humor. They aided their patients by building morale and helped to heal overburdened minds as well as broken bodies. Many soldiers were inspired by the example of the hardworking nurses who cared for them. If the nurses could take the daily horrors of war, then the troops felt they could do the same.

Excerpt from No Time for Fear: Voices of American Military Nurses in World War II

Agnes Shurr, U.S. Navy

USS *Solace*

Soon after the attack on Pearl Harbor the [hospital ship] Solace *went to the South Pacific, and when we were at an island called* **Tongatabu,** *an enormous number of warships appeared in the harbor. Everyone knew they were gathering for something, but we nurses were never told what. That was when the battles of the Coral Sea and Midway [see Franklin D. Roosevelt entry in chapter one] were being planned early in the war. We went on to* **Noumea, New Caledonia.**

We took on casualties from the Coral Sea battle and from Guadalcanal and that area. Casualties were terribly high. We treated them and took them to hospitals in New Zealand; we made several trips like that. Sometimes we transferred patients from our ship to another at sea.

*The time I was most frightened, we were traveling "**blackout**" with blackout curtains and red lights inside that allowed us to see. Hospital ships usually traveled alone, and at night turned lights on. This time our commanding officer felt that if we were lighted up, the Japanese would see the warships. We were fired on in the middle of*

Tongatabu: (Often spelled "Tongatapu"; pronounced "ton-guh-TAH-pooh") A 100-square-mile island in the southwest central Pacific Ocean.

Noumea, New Caledonia: Capital town of the New Caledonia island group, which is located in the southwest Pacific, to the east of Australia. The islands were the sites of Allied military bases during World War II.

"Blackout": Darkness (mandatory "lights out") enforced during wartime to discourage enemy air raids.

the night, and it hit not far from where I was sleeping. I woke up to the sound of the explosion and the "call to stations." Earlier that day we took on a large load of casualties. My ward had **litter** patients so I prepared them to abandon ship. We waited, and I was sure we were going down. How could anyone fire on us, unless they intended to sink us? After a period of time, the all-clear sounded, and we were never told what happened. In those days everything was secret, and we accepted it.

It wasn't until 1991, when a book was published by one of our hospital men, that I found out the firing was from a **"friendly"** ship. The book, The USS Solace Was There, states that a U.S. ship asked for identification, then fired across our bow but hit us instead. Our lights were turned on, and it was all over.

Margaret Richey Raffa , U.S. Army Air Force

801st Medical Air Evacuation Squadron

We were the first flight nurse squadron to go to the Pacific, landing in New Caledonia in February 1943. We enjoyed the temperature and flowers, which are equally beautiful there all year, but conditions were very primitive. The river behind our tents was our washing machine, and we hung clothes to dry from trees. There were twenty-four nurses, and millions of mosquitoes, all living in one tent. One night during the first week, the tent blew down during a **typhoon**, and our foot lockers almost floated away.

C-47s [acting as medical evacuation planes] flew to the front with cargo and ammunition, and the nurses rode on top of the cargo. We often had troops going to the forward areas, which was sad for us. They would get into long discussions, feeling that they would probably never come back. The worst part is, some of them didn't.

When we went to Guadalcanal, the plane wouldn't fly directly over the island but flew along the beach, staying low to avoid being spotted by the Japanese. This was emotionally trying for us, not knowing what the landing field would be like. There were no ambulances. The most seriously wounded patients would be on litters, with other wounded in different vehicles. We took off quickly because the Japanese were **strafing** the field. Our casualties were still in rather bad shape, having had only first aid treatment. They had **shrapnel** and bullet wounds and injuries from hand grenades, often of the chest,

Litter: Stretcher.

"Friendly": A reference to "friendly fire," an accidental attack on one's own forces.

Typhoon: A tropical storm characterized by high winds and heavy rains.

Strafing: Firing at (with machine guns) in a long line and at close range.

Shrapnel: Fragments of an exploded bomb or shell.

Shock: Insufficient circulation of the blood caused by serious trauma. When shock sets in, the brain and other organs are deprived of the blood supply they need to function.

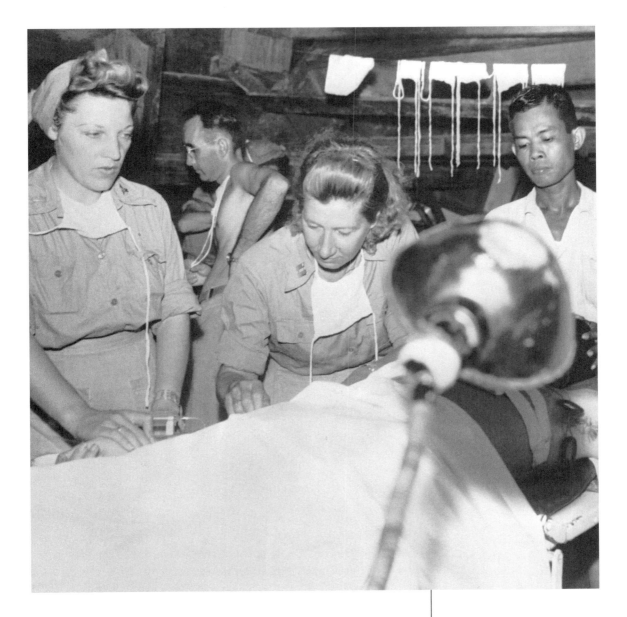

*abdomen, or head. It presented quite a problem, since there were no doctors on board, and we had to rely on our own initiative. We always had to be alert for symptoms of **shock** and hemorrhage, and from the time we took off until we landed, we had our hands full with these mutilated bodies. One nurse might have twenty-four patients, most of them on litters, for a five hour flight, and in those days we didn't have the [help of] enlisted medical technicians. We felt a tremendous*

Army nurses attending a wounded soldier. Nurses often had to work in unsanitary and difficult circumstances.
(Reproduced by permission of Corbis/Bettmann)

responsibility.

*Some patients were taken to the hospital in **New Hebrides** and later evacuated back to the States, but there were general hospitals in New Caledonia where these patients received good enough care to be returned to duty. We took boys back up to the front lines a month or two after we'd brought them out wounded.*

The problems were constant. For instance, after we reached [an altitude of] 8,000 feet there was a lack of oxygen, and often we climbed to 10,000 feet because of weather conditions. Then we had to give oxygen to patients continuously. Small oxygen tanks were all we had room for, and patients shared them. We did use alcohol on the tanks between patients, but it wasn't very sanitary. A lot of the planes didn't have heaters, and at 10,000 feet, even in the South Pacific, it was cold.

*Sometimes we had to make forced landings because of maintenance or weather or fuel shortages, and this caused big problems for the commanding officers of the airstrips where we landed. Most of the time these fields were under attack by the Japanese, and we'd often have to head for **foxholes**, with the war being fought right above us. One time I was going to stand at the edge of a foxhole to watch as they went after a Japanese plane. A **GI** decided to head for the same place and hit my feet, knocking me over. I decided to stay down after that.*

Evangeline Bakke Fairall, U.S. Army

250th Station Hospital

I didn't think I'd ever know what it was to be warm after we landed in Liverpool, England, in January 1944. It was night and pouring rain, and we marched in formation carrying our heavy packs to the train. We stood for what seemed like hours while the rain beat a tattoo on our helmets, like rain on a tin roof. The American Red Cross greeted us with doughnuts, hot coffee, and gum after we boarded the train. It was wonderful, for all we'd had to eat was breakfast that day.

Blackouts were always in effect, so we had to do a lot in complete darkness, often without the aid of even a flashlight to show the way. Utter, pitch-black darkness descended about 4:30 P.M. and lasted until 8:30 A.M. Because of air raids, the blackout system was so complete that you never saw even a crack of light when a door was opened. Almost everyone had black and blue marks on their knees

New Hebrides: (Pronounced "HEH-bruh-deez") Group of islands in the southwest Pacific Ocean, near New Caledonia. Site of major Allied naval base during World War II. Since achieving independence in 1980, the island group has been called Vanuatu.

Foxholes: Pits that provide cover from enemy fire.

GI: Reference to U.S. soldiers, taken from the abbreviation for "government issue."

from bumping into signs, posts, and fences.

We soon learned to dread air alerts but had no desire to ignore them. Many a night, and often on **consecutive** nights, we climbed out of bed, put our trench coats over pajamas, went to the wards to be with the patients, and remained there until the "all clear" came. I remember getting patients up and putting them under each bed. It could be an hour or two hours later before we could return to our tents, cold and hungry. The tents were so cold, and heavy rains kept everything damp. We kept clothes under the pillow at night to keep them dry. The **latrine** and showers were up a hill, and we had to walk there out in the open, day or night.

We knew D day was coming but weren't supposed to talk about it, even among ourselves in our tents. I'll never forget the morning of D day. Very early we heard thousands of planes going overhead, toward **the Continent**; just thousands. As the day went on, they were coming back, and we knew fewer were returning. Everyone was quiet.

When we heard our first convoy of battle patients was coming, we were very excited, because we could finally get to do the work we had come to do. We couldn't do enough for that first group of one hundred patients. Then, as more came, the number soon jumped to over a thousand. My first battle patient had a bullet wound in the spine and was paralyzed from the neck down. I'll never forget that first patient.

This went on for several weeks, and everyone was busy. Then we were told we were to be a rehabilitation hospital, caring only for **convalescent** patients, getting them in shape physically and mentally to return to combat. Our spirits went down with a thud, but we gradually adjusted to the change.

About three months later our status changed again, and we received new battle casualties. We worked like beavers, never enough nurses to go around. One nurse might have responsibility for nearly two hundred very sick patients, spread over an area of approximately two city blocks. With the aid of competent **wardmen**, we managed to

Deaths in World War II by Country

Country	Number of Deaths
Soviet Union	20,600,000
China	10,000,000
Germany	6,850,000
Poland	6,123,000
Japan	2,000,000
France	810,000
United States	500,000
Italy	410,000
Great Britain	388,000

Numbers taken from "The History Place: Statistics of World War II, including the European and Pacific Theaters." [Online] Available http://www.history place.com/worldwar2/timeline/statistics.htm.

Consecutive: One after another.

Latrine: Toilet.

The Continent: Europe.

Convalescent: Patients who would eventually recover their health and strength.

Wardmen: Men in charge of monitoring certain sections of the field hospitals.

get along.

We had every type of case, and sometimes those sick, sick patients kept our morale up more than we did their's. They came to us in many ways, sometimes by plane straight from the front. Just before Christmas 1944, we were busier than ever, and I remember one patient telling me, "I was crawling out of my foxhole about 3:30 this afternoon, and here I am." It was about 7:30 in the evening when we were talking, and we were a long way from the combat area.

*The number of **orthopedic** patients was astounding, running well over four hundred. Ward after ward was filled with fractures, almost everyone up in **traction**, with rarely an **ambulatory** patient in these wards.*

One nurse who was inspecting our hospital really lifted my spirits. She had seen several of these wards with nothing but patients in traction, the nurses wearing raincoats over their uniforms for warmth, and pantlegs wet well above the knees from the heavy, drenching rain. This nurse was amazed that we could care for patients in that situation. I asked, "Have you seen the General Hospital down the road?" It was made of brick, while we were a tent hospital. They had covered ramps between buildings, and we had to walk through the rain and mud to carry supplies and food to each tent. She said, "I've been there several times, but I like this place. You have to have what it takes to work here."

Myrtle Brethouwer Hoftiezer, U.S. Army

166th General Hospital

[Fall 1944] After training at Camp McCoy [in Wisconsin], we had more to go through at Camp Kilmer where we learned to use the gas masks, were put through an obstacle course, and more marching. I remember the GIs yelling and whistling from every barracks window as we went through the mud and did pushups.

One of my first memories of Europe was the public toilet we had to use in England. We were at the dock, waiting to cross the English Channel, and while I was seated in the "privy," a young man came in and sat next to me. When I told the other nurses about it, they asked what I did. "I passed him the paper," I told them. . . .

Orthopedic: Relating to bone injuries.

Traction: A pulling force (usually weights) exerted on a broken bone during the healing process.

Ambulatory: Able to walk.

It rained and rained at the beginning of our stay in France, and we often had to move the cots we slept in to higher ground to stay dry. We ate outside from our mess kits, often in the rain. Our first hot meal was Cream-of-Wheat, which tastes wonderful in a muddy field in France. We wore the ugly, olive drab underwear for a month without being able to wash it. Our bathtub was a helmet, and the latrine was a dug-out trench with a canvas screen around it, open to the sky and the pilots who flew overhead.

Everyone was excited when we were finally told to make beds and get ready for a trainload of patients. After all, we hadn't come to France to enjoy the winter climate. My strongest memory is how many times a patient would say, "Get to me when you can. He needs you more than I do." I've never taken care of patients like that since. (Fessler, pp. 29-32, 151-53, 204, 210-11)

Army nurses at a field hospital in France.
(Reproduced by permission of the National Archives and Records Administration)

These African American army nurses stationed in Australia were among the small number of black women allowed to join the Army Nurse Corps.
(Photograph by Frank Prist Jr. Reproduced by permission of Corbis)

What happened next . . .

In the post-World War II years, nursing came to be viewed as a serious profession. According to Judith A. Bellafaire in *The Army Nurse Corps,* the war "forever changed the face" of the nursing field.

Did you know . . .

- The U.S. government covered all educational expenses for student nurses between 1943 and 1948.

- Sixteen nurses were killed during World War II as a result of enemy action.

- Sixty-seven World War II nurses served time as prisoners of war.

- Sixteen hundred nurses were decorated for meritorious service, meaning they received awards or honors from the U.S. military for outstanding conduct while serving in the ANC.

- Segregation in the U.S. military limited the number of black nurses allowed in the ANC. At war's end, less than five hundred of the fifty thousand nurses in the ANC were black.

For More Information

Books

Archard, Theresa. *G.I. Nightingale: The Story of an American Army Nurse.* New York: W.W. Norton, 1945.

Gruhzit-Hoyt, Olga. *They Also Served: American Women in World War II.* Secaucus, NJ: Birch Lane Press, 1995.

Hardison, Irene. *A Nightingale in the Jungle.* Philadelphia: Dorrance, 1954.

Tomblin, Barbara Brooks. *G.I. Nightingales: The Army Nurse Corps in World War II.* Lexington: University Press of Kentucky, 1996.

Wandry, June. *Bedpan Commando: The Story of a Combat Nurse during World War II.* Elmore, OH: Elmore Publishing, 1989.

Web Sites

Army Nurse Corps History. [Online] http://www.army.mil/cmh-pg/anc/anchhome.html (accessed on September 7, 1999).

Sources

Ambrose, Stephen E. *Citizen Soldiers: The U.S. Army from the Normandy Beaches to the Bulge to the Surrender of Germany* New York: Touchstone, 1998.

Bellafaire, Judith A. *The Army Nurse Corps.* U.S. Army Center of Military History: CMH Pub 72-14.

Brokaw, Tom. *The Greatest Generation.* New York: Random House, 1998.

Fessler, Diane Burke. *No Time for Fear: Voices of American Military Nurses in World War II.* East Lansing: Michigan State University Press, 1996.

Goolrick, William K., Ogden Tanner, and the editors of Time-Life Books. *The Battle of the Bulge.* "Time-Life Books World War II Series." Alexandria, VA: Time-Life Books, 1979.

Breakthrough

Stephen E. Ambrose
...173

Stephen E. Ambrose
...187

E. B. Sledge
...197

Harry S. Truman
...211

The World War II invasion of Europe by British and American forces took place in mid-1944. The Allies (those nations fighting against the Germans during World War II) sought to free the German-occupied countries of Europe from German leader Adolf Hitler's grasp. Allied troops landed on the beaches of Normandy, France, on June 6, 1944—D-Day. *Voices of D-Day: The Story of the Allied Invasion Told by Those Who Were There*, edited by **Ronald J. Drez**, is a collection of survivors' accounts of the Normandy landing.

From Normandy, the Allies began their march eastward through France and Belgium toward Germany. In December 1944 the Germans launched a counterattack in the Ardennes Forest of southeastern Belgium, entangling Allied forces in a costly conflict known as the Battle of the Bulge. (The battle was so-named because the advancing German army created a "bulge" in the American line of defense.) Excerpts from *Citizen Soldiers: The U.S. Army from the Normandy Beaches to the Bulge to the Surrender of Germany*, edited by **Stephen Ambrose**, reveal how American troops were taken by surprise in the Ardennes but managed to recover their strength, rally their forces, and push the Germans out of Belgium by the end of December.

While the last leg of the European war was being fought in France, in Belgium, and finally in Germany, another war was being waged in the Pacific. The bitter realities of the war against the Japanese are depicted with honesty and simplicity in **Eugene B. Sledge's *With the Old Breed at Peleliu and Okinawa.*** Young Sledge and his fellow marines endured the incredible misery of Pacific island fighting between 1944 and 1945. The excerpt from *With the Old Breed* sheds light on the brutal but historically neglected battle for the island of Peleliu.

While Sledge and his comrades were clashing with the Japanese in the Pacific, the war in Europe was drawing to a close. With Soviet troops approaching from the east and American and British forces closing in from the west, the fate of Germany was sealed. Hitler committed suicide in his underground bunker on April 30, 1945. Germany surrendered to Allied forces a week later.

On May 8, 1945, when President **Harry S. Truman** spoke to the American people on the surrender of Germany, he claimed the war was only half won. His statement to the nation on the surrender of the Japanese—delivered less than four months later—came on the heels of his controversial decision to unleash the power of a nuclear weapon on the Japanese home islands.

Veterans of D-Day

Excerpt from Voices of D-Day: The Story of the Allied Invasion Told By Those Who Were There

Edited by Ronald J. Drez
Published in 1994

The Allied invasion of the beach in Normandy remains the largest and most difficult wartime invasion ever planned. (In World War II [1939-1945] the leading Allied Powers were all of the countries fighting against Germany, Italy, and Japan, led by the United States, Great Britain, and the Soviet Union.) France was heavily fortified (protected by mines and artillery) by the German military, and it had to be conquered before the Allies could advance into Germany. The beaches of Normandy, on France's northwestern coast, were chosen as the site for an amphibious (a combined land, sea, and air force) invasion of the European continent by British and American forces.

German forces in France were led by Field Marshal Erwin Rommel, known as the "Desert Fox" for his clever moves in North Africa earlier in the war. Under his command, German tank divisions in Africa had dealt the British one defeat after another. But by 1944 the Germans were feeling the effects of Allied air assaults on their factories, airfields, and oil refineries. The Royal Air Force (RAF) and U.S. Air Force crippled the Luftwaffe (German air force) prior to the invasion at Normandy, thus leaving the Germans more vulnerable to an inva-

"After we jumped into the water, it was every man for himself. I waded parallel to the beach with my squad because the heavy fire was directed towards the boats.... I saw Lieutenant Hilscher go down on his knees as a shell exploded. He fell into the hole caused by the explosion. He died there on the beach."

Warner Hamlett, Sergeant, Company F

sion. Although the German army had conquered most of Europe, it was already reeling from months of unsuccessful fighting in Italy and the Soviet Union.

German military leaders knew the Allies were organizing an invasion of German-occupied France, but they did not know when or where it would occur. Rumor spread that American General George S. Patton had assembled troops and was planning to cross the English Channel at Dover and land at the French seaport of Calais. The Germans increased their forces at Calais, but the actual landing spot would be farther to the southwest, along the Caen area in Normandy.

In spite of stormy weather, General Dwight D. Eisenhower, supreme commander of the Allied invasion force, ordered the launch of Operation Overlord on June 5, 1944. (Operation Overlord was the code name for the Allied invasion of Normandy; see box on Eisenhower on p. 182.) A force of American paratroopers (parachute troops) landed in France that night—the night before the actual land invasion. Their goal was to scout the terrain and guide the landing of later airborne divisions from Great Britain, Canada, and the United States. Heavy fire from the Germans on the ground forced the initial groups of paratroopers off course, but the multinational Allied invasion—headed by General Bernard Montgomery—went on as scheduled.

Some nine hundred planes flew over Normandy, dropping an estimated thirteen thousand paratroopers inland from the beaches. Their mission was to stall the Germans by destroying bridges, blocking roads, and disrupting communications. They also served as backup for the main invasion forces that would land on the beaches the morning of June 6, 1944—D-Day.

The invasion took place over a fifty-mile area and was divided into five beaches with the code names Sword, Juno, Gold, Omaha, and Utah. (Sword and Juno were attacked by British regiments, Gold was taken by the Canadian infantry, and Omaha and Utah were in the American sector.) The American, British, Canadian, and French soldiers who would fight on those beaches were crammed into five thousand Allied ships. Americans of the 29th Division landed at Omaha, which met with the heaviest resistance. Germans were stationed in the cliffs above Omaha Beach. They showered the landing force with shells and machine-gun fire. Some troops never made it

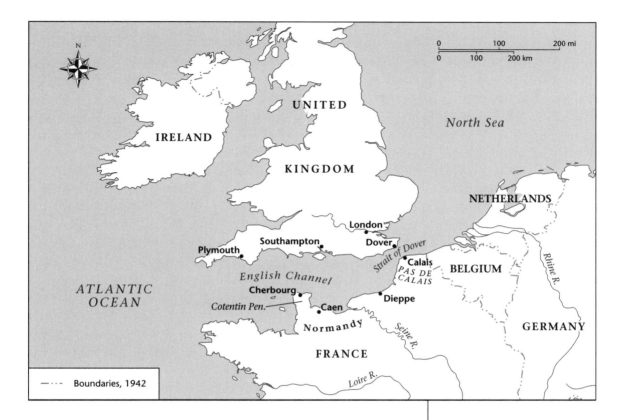

Boundaries, 1942

out of the landing craft. Others drowned in the turbulent waters of the English Channel. By the end of D-Day, there were twenty-five hundred Allied casualties on Omaha Beach alone.

Things to remember while reading the excerpt from *Voices of D-Day: The Story of the Allied Invasion Told By Those Who Were There*:

- The term "D-Day" refers to the date set for the start of an operation, in this case, the invasion of France by the Allies on June 6, 1944.

- The English Channel waters are well known for their unpredictable nature. Eisenhower gave the go-ahead for the start of the Normandy invasion in the midst of tumultuous weather. Forecasters predicted a short break in the stormy conditions for the sixth of June, and those predictions determined the exact date of the D-Day invasion.

The Allies planned to invade German-occupied France at Normandy. The Germans had thought the invasion would come at Pas de Calais, which was much closer to England and would have meant a shorter English Channel crossing.

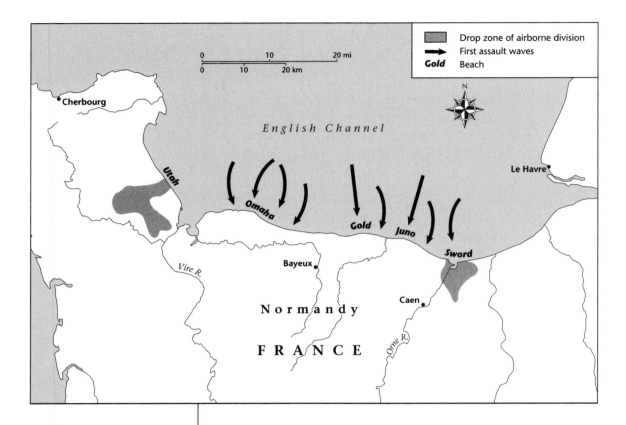

English Channel

Cherbourg

Le Havre

Utah

Omaha

Gold

Juno

Sword

Vire R.

Bayeux

Caen

N o r m a n d y

F R A N C E

Orne R.

Drop zone of airborne division
First assault waves
Gold Beach

0   10   20 mi
0   10   20 km

N

The beaches of Normandy were divided into five areas for the attack and given code names: Utah, Omaha, Gold, Juno, and Sword

- Field Marshal Rommel oversaw the construction of an elaborate defense system to guard the Normandy shore. The coast was lined with barbed wire, mines, armed concrete bunkers (underground chambers), huge wooden posts rigged with explosives, and an underwater network of sharp steel barriers. These fortifications were known as the Atlantic Wall.

- *Voices of D-Day: The Story of the Allied Invasion Told By Those Who Were There* describes the Normandy landing in vivid detail. The personal accounts of the soldiers who took part in the invasion were collected by editor Ronald J. Drez for a special D-Day Project of the University of New Orleans' Eisenhower Center.

- The accounts of Warner Hamlett and Harold Baumgarten are taken from the chapter titled "The 116th at Omaha Beach." Robert H. Miller and Warren Rulien's stories are taken from "Easy Red and the First Division." (Easy Red was a subsection of Omaha Beach.)

- The following excerpts reveal the young soldiers' fear and bravery amid the chaos and confusion of the Normandy landing. Note in particular the sense of loss felt by the speakers, knowing that every minute could be their last, watching comrades shot down on the beach, and grappling with the harsh reality of their objective: to kill or be killed.

Excerpt from Voices of D-Day

WARNER HAMLETT (Sergeant, Company F): . . . "After we jumped into the water, it was every man for himself. I waded **parallel** to the beach with my squad because the heavy fire was directed towards the boats. As I was going straight towards the beach, I saw Lieutenant Hilscher go down on his knees as a shell exploded. He fell into the hole caused by the explosion. He died there on the beach. . . .

"When I finally reached the edge of the water, I started to run towards the **seawall** under a deafening roar of explosions and bullets. I saw a hole about seventy-five feet away, so I ran and jumped in, landing on top of O. T. Grimes. As soon as I caught my breath, I dashed forward again, but had to stop between the obstacles in order to rest. The weight of wet clothes, sand, and equipment made it difficult to run. One . . . soldier . . . had run straight to the seawall and was motioning for us to come on. At the same time, he was yelling, 'Get off the beach!' Our only chance was to get off the beach as quick as possible, because there we were sitting ducks. While resting in between the obstacles, Private Gillingham fell beside me, white with fear. He seemed to be begging for help with his eyes. His look was that of a child asking what to do. I said, 'Gillingham, let's stay separated as much as we can, because the Germans will fire at two quicker than one.' He remained silent and then I heard a shell coming and dove into the sand face down. **Shrapnel** rose over my head and hit all around me. It took Gillingham's chin off, including the bone, except for a small piece of flesh. He tried to hold his chin in place as he ran towards the seawall. He made it to the wall, where Will Hawks and I gave him his **morphine** shot. He stayed with me for approximately thirty minutes until he died. The entire time, he remained conscious and aware that he was dying.

Parallel: Extending in the same direction but never touching; in the same direction as.

Seawall: Raised structure that holds back water and protects the shore from the force of waves.

Shrapnel: Fragments of an exploded bomb or shell.

Morphine: Painkiller.

A landing craft loaded with soldiers heads for the Normandy coast. Many soldiers got seasick from the rough ride across the English Channel. *(Reproduced by permission of Corbis/The Mariner's Museum)*

Pillboxes: A roofed concrete compartment for machine guns and antitank weapons.

"We were supposed to wait at the seawall until wire cutters could cut the tremendous web of wire that the Germans had placed on top of it. During this time, Lieutenant Wise of F Company was directing his team behind the seawall, when a bullet hit him in the forehead. He continued to instruct his men until he sat down and held his head in the palm of his hand before falling over dead.

"We waited at the seawall until [it was] time to cross over the path cleared by the wire cutters. As we crossed the seawall, Germans in **pillboxes** fired upon each man as he dashed forward. After we crossed, the ground provided more protection, with small bushes and gullies. We took time to reorganize and planned to knock out the pillbox. First we tried direct attack using TNT on the end of long poles, but this was impossible because the Germans could shoot the men down as soon as they saw them coming through the barbed wire strung in front of the pillboxes. We then decided to run between the pillboxes and enter the trenches that connected them. These trenches had been dug by the Germans and gave them mobility and a means of escape. We entered the trenches, slipped behind the pillboxes, and threw grenades into them. After the explosion, we ran into the boxes to kill any that survived the grenade. Rows of pillboxes stood between us and the top of the cliff. Slowly, one by one, we advanced. . . . "

HAROLD BAUMGARTEN (Company B): . . . "Shells were continually landing all about me, in a definite pattern, and when I raised my head up to curse the Germans in the pillbox on our right flank . . . one of the shell fragments from an **88** exploded twenty yards in front of me and hit me in my left cheek. It felt like being hit with a baseball bat, only the results were much worse. My upper jaw was shattered; the left cheek was blown open, and my upper lip was cut in half. The roof of my mouth was cut up, and teeth and gums were laying all over inside. Blood poured freely from the gaping wound. The same 88-millimeter shell that hit me in the left side of my face hit Sergeant Hoback, of Company A, **flush** in the face, and he went under. I washed my face out in the six-inch cold, dirty [English] Channel water, and managed somehow not to pass out. I got rid of most of my equipment.

"The water was rising about an inch a minute, as the tide was coming in, so I had to get moving or drown. I had to reach a fifteen-foot seawall, which appeared to be two hundred yards in front of me, and I crawled forward, trying to take cover behind bodies and water obstacles made of steel. I got another rifle along the way as the Germans were zeroing in on me. I continued forward in a dead-man's float with each wave of the incoming tide.

"Finally, I came to dry sand, and there was another hundred yards to go, and I started across the sand, crawling very fast. . . . I reached the stone wall without further injury. . . .

"At the wall, I met a fellow from Company B from my boat team named Dominick Surrow, a boy from Georgia about my age, a rugged fellow, who looked at my face and said, 'Stay here, I'm going to run down the beach and get help.' He got killed.

"I watched him being washed around by the incoming water, and I saw the bodies of my buddies who had tried in vain to clear the beach. It looked like the beach was littered with the refuse of a wrecked ship that were the dead bodies of what once was the proud, tough . . . well-trained combat **infantrymen** of the 1st **Battalion** of the 116th Infantry."

ROBERT H. MILLER (Corporal, 149th Engineer Combat Battalion): "I was in Company B. Our Beach was the Easy Red Beach, which was situated right in front of **Saint-Laurent-sur-Mer.**

88: 88-millimeter shell.

Flush: Squarely; exactly; straight into.

Infantrymen: Soldiers fighting on foot.

Battalion: A large body of troops.

Saint-Laurent-sur-Mer: A beach that lies along the Bay of Seine, which is located on the northern coast of Normandy in northwestern France. (It was a portion of Omaha Beach.) The Bay of Seine is part of the English Channel, and separates England from France.

American soldiers leaving the ramp of a coast guard landing boat during the invasion of Normandy.
(Photograph by Robert F. Sergeant. Reproduced by permission of the National Archives and Records Administration)

Half-track: A military vehicle with wheels in the front and tanklike tracks in the back.

"A jeep was the first off the craft, and it went down and dropped clear underwater but made it in, since it was waterproofed and the exhaust pipe was extended well above the jeep itself, up above the waterline. The trucks came off and they made it in as well. The men started unloading at that point, and I jumped off the end of the ramp and went underwater completely, over my head. I ejected all of my equipment underwater and jumped as well as I could underwater and finally reached the waterline. . . . [I] got my head above water and started swimming in. That was a tough swim. The wet, heavy clothes were weighing me down. . . . My body felt like it weighed five hundred pounds, and I was very tired.

"I heard a number of screams behind me and many of the men drowned trying to make their way in to the beach. . . . I got about ten feet up the beach when I saw just a big white ball of nothingness, and the next thing I knew I was flat on my back looking up at the sky. My first thought was that my legs were blown off because I had tried to move them and nothing happened. . . . For some reason I just couldn't move. . . .

"Shortly, the medics came down behind a **half-track** and picked me up, and it was there that they gave me a shot of morphine. I woke up at the first-aid station on the beach, and the doctors were going over me and the nurse cutting off clothing and that sort of thing. I passed out shortly again. The next time I woke up I was loaded on an **LST,** and the navy aide was talking to me and asking what he could do for me . . . and I could hear ack-ack guns, the antiaircraft guns, going off up on deck.

"I passed out again and woke up on an **LCVP,** and we were headed toward the dock of some town in England. A colonel was next to me with a head wound, and he was just screaming terribly, and there were wounded laying all over the LCVP. The consequences of my injury was that I became a paraplegic and lost the use of my legs entirely."

WARREN RULIEN (16th Infantry): "Eight rope nets had been hung over the side of the ship and we began climbing down into the landing crafts. This wasn't an easy thing to do with all the equipment you had on and the rifle. Waves from the English Channel would separate the landing craft from the side of the ship and then it would crash back against the hull. I got down near the bottom of the net and had to time my jump into the landing craft.

"I felt so rotten from the seasickness that I was half enthusiastic about hitting the shore just to get off that landing craft. As we got nearer to the shore, bullets began hitting the sides but could not penetrate. . . . We ducked down low. It wasn't long after we stopped when the front of the landing craft was lowered. For a few seconds, everything seemed quiet and nobody moved. The image that flashed through my mind was 'They can shoot us through the front of the craft.'

"Someone shouted, 'Let's go!' We began pouring out of the craft, and as I stepped off of the ramp, I dropped into water up to my chest and I lost my rifle and began wading in to shore.

As supreme commander of the Allied forces in Europe, Dwight D. Eisenhower launched Operation Overlord, which took place on June 6, 1944. *(Reproduced by permission of the National Archives and Records Administration)*

LST: Landing ship, tank; amphibious (land and water) ships that can drive onto a beach to unload their cargo.

LCVP: Landing craft, vehicle and personnel; also called amphibian (land and water) tractors and assault amphibians.

Dwight David Eisenhower

Dwight David Eisenhower (1890-1969; nicknamed "Ike") was born October 14, 1890, in Denison, Texas. When he was just a baby, he moved with his family to Abilene, Kansas, a town once known as the end of the line on the Kansas-Pacific Railroad.

Money was tight, but a deep religious faith and strong family ties kept the Eisenhowers going. Young Ike and his five brothers worked together to help their mother with the household chores. The boys gardened, learned to do the laundry, and could cook a good meal on their own.

In his school days Eisenhower excelled in competitive sports. He also developed a keen interest in war history and mathematics. After graduating from the U.S.

Military Academy at West Point in 1915, Eisenhower served as a second lieutenant at Texas-based Fort Sam Houston. He married Mamie Doud the next year.

During the final phase of World War I (1914-18) Eisenhower instructed American troops in tank warfare. World War II (1939-45) erupted in Europe in 1939. As tensions escalated worldwide, the United States began gearing up for military involvement in the conflict. Eisenhower was promoted to the rank of brigadier general in 1941, directed Operation Torch (the code name for the invasion of North Africa) against the Germans in 1942 and 1943, then oversaw the assault on Italy. As supreme commander of the Allied forces in

"On both sides of me were many soldiers coming from other landing crafts, all wading in to shore. In front of me were steel rails driven into the bottom of the sea, which extended six feet out of the water, and on top were mines. By the time I got to the steel rails, the water was up to my waist. There were many dead soldiers floating around in the water, and bullets began hitting only a few feet in front of me, so I stepped behind one of the steel rails and squatted down. A young replacement about nineteen years old that was from my platoon shouted at me, 'Hey, Rulien, here I go!' and began running toward shore. He stepped onto the **sandbar**, and machine-gun fire opened up, and he dropped into the water on the other side.

"I took one of the bodies that was floating in the water and pushed it in front of me toward the shore. I had only gone a short distance when three or four soldiers began lining up behind me. I stood up and shouted, 'Don't bunch up!' and walked off, leaving them with the body. I got

Sandbar: A ridge of sand, especially along a coast, that is built up by the flow of waves.

Europe, he launched Operation Overlord (the secret Allied invasion of Normandy, France, which took place on June 6, 1944).

Eisenhower accepted Germany's surrender on May 8, 1945, the date that marked the end of World War II on the European front. Three years later he retired from the U.S. Army as a five-star general.

While serving for a few years as president of New York's Columbia University, Eisenhower began thinking about running for the office of U.S. president. He won election to the nation's highest office in 1952. The two-term president served during a tumultuous time in U.S. history: the Korean War (1950-1953) was in full swing, anti-Communist sentiment was strong in the United States, an arms race between the Soviet Union and the United States was escalating, and the civil rights movement was born. (Communism is a system of government in which the state controls the means of production and the distribution of goods. It clashes with the American ideal of capitalism, which is based on private ownership and a free market system.)

In 1961 Eisenhower and his wife retired to a farm near Gettysburg, Pennsylvania. The former president wrote several books and tried to stay out of the political limelight, favoring the role of avid golfer to that of political consultant. He died March 28, 1969, in Washington, D.C.

down as low as I could in the water until I reached the sandbar, and then I crossed it on my belly and kept moving forward until I reached the beach, where soldiers were bunched-up behind a sandbank.

*"Lying beside me, on his back, was a soldier who had been shot in the stomach. He held his hand over his stomach, moaning, but only for a short time; then he died. I picked up his rifle, threw back the bolt, and looked down the barrel to make sure that sand hadn't been jammed into the barrel. I put a **clip** of ammunition in and looked up the hill and saw German soldiers running along the crest. At that distance, they looked about two inches high and I began firing at them. On the shore, there were officers sitting there, stunned. Nobody was taking command. Landing crafts were continuing to bring waves of soldiers in, and they were bunching up on the beach.*

"Finally, out on the water, coming towards the shore, walking straight up with a staff of officers with him, I recognized Colonel Tay-

Clip: A device that holds bullets to be fed into the chamber of a gun.

Soldiers trying to get ashore at Omaha Beach. The posts seen sticking out of the water were part of the Germans' fortifications.
(Reproduced by permission of the Corbis Corporation [Bellevue])

lor, regimental commander. He stepped across the sandbar and bullets began hitting the water around him. He laid down on his stomach and started crawling towards shore, and when he got in, I heard him say to the officers, 'If we're going to die, let's die up there.' It seemed to take effect, because the officers began moving their men from that two yards of beach to reach their objective." (Drez, pp. 208-09, 216-17, 237-38, 253-54)

What happened next . . .

In all, 10,000 aircraft, 5,000 ships, and 155,000 soldiers landed at Normandy. Even though the losses at Omaha Beach were extremely heavy, the Allied invasion of Normandy was considered a success. Having established a foothold in France, the Allies began their march eastward toward Germany. (See

Stephen E. Ambrose entry in chapter four for more information on the Allied breakout from Normandy.)

Did you know . . .

- General Eisenhower had prepared a press statement in case the D-Day invasion failed. It read, in part: "I have withdrawn the troops. My decision to attack . . . was based on the best information available. The troops, the air and the Navy did all that bravery and devotion could do. If any blame or fault attaches to the attempt it is mine alone."

- The 1998 motion picture *Saving Private Ryan* is set against the Allied landing at Omaha Beach. Many of the real-life soldiers who invaded Normandy were in their late teens and early twenties—much younger than Tom Hanks and the other actors who portrayed them.

- A huge tank still sits on the sand of Normandy beach as a reminder of the horrible battle that took place there on June 6, 1944.

For More Information
Books

Ambrose, Stephen E. *D-Day, June 6, 1944.* New York: Simon & Schuster, 1994.

Eisenhower, Dwight D. *Crusade in Europe.* Garden City, NY: Doubleday, 1948.

Eisenhower, Dwight D. *At Ease: Stories I Tell to Friends.* Garden City, NY: Doubleday, 1967.

Hastings, Max. *Overlord: D-Day and the Battle for Normandy.* New York: Simon & Schuster, 1985. Reprinted, 1993.

Ryan, Cornelius. *The Longest Day.* Originally published in 1959. Reprinted. New York: Touchstone/Simon & Schuster, 1994.

Webster, David Kenyon. *Parachute Infantry: An American Paratrooper's Memoir of D-Day and the Fall of the Third Reich.* Introduction by Stephen E. Ambrose. Baton Rouge: Louisiana State University Press, 1994.

Videos

D-Day Remembered. "The American Experience." WGBH-TV (Boston)/Direct Cinema Limited, 1994.

Normandy: The Great Crusade. The Discovery Channel/Discovery Enterprises Group, 1993.

The War Chronicles: World War II. Volume 2: *D-Day . . . The Normandy Invasion.* Produced by Lou Reda Productions. A&E Home Video Presents History Channel Video/New Video, 1995.

Web Sites

The 50th Anniversary of the Invasion of Normandy. [Online] http://www.nando.net/sproject/dday/dday.html (accessed on September 6, 1999).

Britannica.com presents Normandy 1944. [Online] http://www.normandy.eb.com/normandy/ (accessed on September 6, 1999).

Sources

Dolan, Edward F. *America in World War II: 1944.* Brookfield, CT: Millbrook Press, 1993.

Drez, Ronald J., ed. *Voices of D-Day: The Story of the Allied Invasion Told By Those Who Were There.* Foreword by Stephen E. Ambrose. Originally published in 1994. Baton Rouge: Louisiana State University Press, 1996.

Hargrove, Jim. *Dwight D. Eisenhower: Thirty-fourth President of the United States.* "Encyclopedia of Presidents Series." Chicago: Children's Press, 1987.

Newsweek, March 8, 1999, pp. 48-9.

Sandberg, Peter Lars. *World Leaders Past and Present: Dwight D. Eisenhower.* New York: Chelsea House, 1986.

Stein, R. Conrad. *Cornerstones of Freedom: D-Day.* Chicago: Children's Press, 1977. Rev. ed., 1993.

Sweeney, James B. *Army Leaders of World War II.* New York: F. Watts, 1984.

Stephen E. Ambrose

Excerpt from Citizen Soldiers: The U.S. Army
from the Normandy Beaches to the Bulge
to the Surrender of Germany
Published in 1997

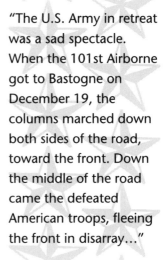

The Allies broke out of Normandy, France, on July 25, 1944. The Allied forces in France were made up of soldiers from Britain, Canada, France, and the United States. Their goal was to fight their way through France and Belgium and into Germany, eventually forcing the surrender of the German forces occupying most of Europe.

Allied forces made great strides throughout the summer of 1944. The French capital, Paris, was liberated from Germany's control on August 25. By December, the Allied advance on Germany was stopped in its tracks because supplies of gas, food, and ammunition were running short. The German army launched a counterattack against the Allies on December 16, 1944. More than 250,000 heavily armed German troops gathered to repel the Allies and capture the Belgian city of Antwerp; it was through this port city that Allied forces received their supplies.

The Germans directed their line of attack through the dense woods of the Ardennes Forest (pronounced "ar-DENN") in southeastern Belgium. The Ardennes was a weak spot in the American line, left largely unprotected by ground troops.

"The U.S. Army in retreat was a sad spectacle. When the 101st Airborne got to Bastogne on December 19, the columns marched down both sides of the road, toward the front. Down the middle of the road came the defeated American troops, fleeing the front in disarray…"

Using *blitzkrieg* (pronounced "BLITS-kreeg," meaning "lightning war" in German) tactics, the Germans caught the Americans by surprise, bombarding the enemy troops under the cover of a thick early morning fog. The Germany army pushed about 40 miles into the American line, producing a "bulge" in the line. (See map on p. 189.) For Americans, the Battle of the Bulge would become the costliest battle of the war.

Things to remember while reading the excerpt from *Citizen Soldiers*:

- In his book *Citizen Soldiers,* Stephen E. Ambrose examines how successful the U.S. Army was in its efforts to "creat[e] an army of citizen soldiers from scratch."

- The Battle of the Bulge is considered the last great German offensive in World War II.

- The following excerpt is set in the Ardennes at the height of the surprise attack on American troops.

- Note the importance of the airborne divisions in the Ardennes campaign, especially the U.S. 101st, whose members were veterans of combat in Normandy and Holland. (The 101st was a division of General George S. Patton's Third Army.)

Citizen Soldiers

December 16-19, 1944

The U.S. Army in retreat was a sad spectacle. When the 101st Airborne got to **Bastogne** *on December 19, the columns marched down both sides of the road, toward the front. Down the middle of the road came the defeated American troops, fleeing the front in* **disarray,** *moblike. Many had thrown away their rifles, their coats, all* **encumbrances.** *Some were in a panic, staggering, exhausted. . . .*

Bastogne: (Pronounced "bass-TONE") Town in southeastern Belgium where German forces surrounded Americans in December of 1944.

Disarray: Disorder.

Encumbrances: Impediments; things that slow or hinder.

Mourmelon: A military post in northeastern France.

The 101st had packed and left **Mourmelon** in a hurry. The troopers were short of everything, including ammunition. "Where's the ammo? We can't fight without ammo," the men were calling out as they marched through Bastogne to the sound of guns. The retreating **horde** supplied some. "Got any ammo?" the paratroopers would ask those who were not victims of panic.

"Sure, buddy, glad to let you have it."

Corp. Walter Gordon noted **sardonically** that by giving away their ammo, the retreating men relieved themselves of any further obligation to stand and fight (originally quoted in Walter Gordon interview, Eisenhower Center, University of New Orleans). They had long since left behind partly damaged or perfectly good artillery pieces, tanks, **half-tracks**, trucks, jeeps, food, rations, and more.

Abandonment of equipment was sometimes unavoidable, but often it was inexcusable. Panic was the cause. Guns that should have been towed out of danger were not. When a convoy stalled, drivers and passengers jumped out of their vehicles and headed west on foot. . . .

But by no means was everything abandoned. Reporter Jack Belden . . . described the retreat as he saw it in the Ardennes on December 17, 1944. There were long convoys of trucks, carrying gasoline, portable bridges, and other equipment headed west, with tanks and other armed vehicles mixed in. "I noticed in myself . . . the feeling of guilt that seems to come over you whenever you retreat. You don't like to look anyone in the eyes. It seems as if you have done something wrong. I perceived this feeling in others, too."

Belden went on, "The road was jammed with every conceivable kind of vehicle. An enemy plane came down and bombed and **strafed** the column, knocking three trucks off the road, shattering trees and causing everyone to flee to ditches. . . . It went on all night. There must have been a buzz bomb or a piloted plane raid somewhere every five minutes" (originally quoted in Jack Belden's "Retreat in Belgium," Reporting World War II, pp. 596-99).

- - - Front line, Dec. 15, 1944
— ■ ■ Limit of German advance by Dec. 25, 1944

NETHERLANDS

Antwerp

Brussels

BELGIUM

GERMANY

Meuse R.

Rhine R.

ARDENNES

Malmédy

Bastogne

Limit of German Advance

FRANCE

LUXEMBOURG

0   20   40 mi
0   20   40 km

The German counteroffensive in the Ardennes Forest of Belgium created a bulge in the front line, earning it the name Battle of the Bulge.

Horde: Swarm; crowd.

Sardonically: Sarcastically; mockingly.

Half-tracks: Military vehicles with wheels in the front and tanklike tracks in the back.

Strafed: Fired at (with machine guns) in a long line and at close range.

German soldiers take cover in a ditch beside a disabled American tank during the Battle of the Bulge.
(Reproduced by permission of the Corbis Corporation [Bellevue])

Belden was right in his perception that others . . . fleeing the fight felt guilty. . . . Pvt. Kurt Vonnegut [who later became an acclaimed novelist] was a recently arrived replacement in the 106th Division. He was caught up in the retreat before he could be assigned. To his eyes, it was just **rout**, pure and simple.

His unit surrendered. Vonnegut decided he would take his chances and bolted into the woods, without a rifle or rations, or proper winter clothing. He hooked up with three others who wouldn't

Rout: Disastrous defeat and disorderly retreat.

An American GI captured by Germans in the Battle of the Bulge. *(Reproduced by permission of the National Archives and Records Administration)*

surrender and set off hoping to find American lines (originally quoted in Kurt Vonnegut interview, Eisenhower Center, University of New Orleans).

     . . . **In May 1940, when German armor drove through the Ardennes, the French high command had thrown up its hands and surrendered.** . . . In December 1944, when German armor drove through the Ardennes, [American General Dwight D.] Eisenhower saw his chance.

In May . . . and surrendered: Ambrose is referring to the ease with which the Germans captured and occupied France at the beginning of the war.

Verdun: City in northeastern France, occupied by Germans during World War II. It was also the site of a major World War I (1914-18) battle in which the French fought off the advancing German army.

Dispirited: Having low morale; lacking enthusiasm.

Supreme Commander: Ambrose is referring to Eisenhower, who served as supreme commander of the Allied forces in Europe.

SHAEF: Supreme Headquarters Allied Expeditionary Forces.

GIs: Reference to U.S. soldiers, taken from the abbreviation for "government issue."

Unprecedented: Without example or model.

Tenacity: Strength; toughness; persistence; courage.

*At dawn on December 19, as German tanks prepared to surround Bastogne and the 101st marched into the town, Eisenhower met with his senior commanders in a cold, damp squad room in a barracks at **Verdun,** the site of the greatest battle ever fought. There was but one lone potbellied stove to ease the bitter cold. Eisenhower's lieutenants entered the room glum, depressed, embarrassed. . . .*

Eisenhower walked in, looked disapprovingly at the downcast generals, and boldly declared, "The present situation is to be regarded as one of opportunity for us and not of disaster. There will be only cheerful faces at this conference table."

[General George S.] Patton quickly picked up the theme. "Hell, let's have the guts to let the bastards go all the way to Paris," he said. "Then, we'll really cut 'em off and chew 'em up." . . .

*Eisenhower's decisiveness and Patton's boldness were electrifying. Their mood quickly spread through the system. **Dispirited** men were energized. For those who most needed help, the men on the front line, help was coming. . . .*

*From the **Supreme Commander** down to the lowliest private, men pulled up their socks and went forth to do their duty. It simplifies, but not by much, to say that here, there, everywhere, from top to bottom, the men of the U.S. Army in Northwest Europe shook themselves and made this a defining moment in their own lives, and in the history of the Army. They didn't like retreating, they didn't like getting kicked around, and as individuals, squads, and companies as well as at **SHAEF,** they decided they were going to make the enemy pay.*

*That they had time to readjust and prepare to pound the Germans was thanks to a relatively small number of front-line **GIs.** The first days of the Battle of the Bulge were a triumph of the soldiers of democracy, marked by innumerable examples of men seizing the initiative, making decisions, leading. Captain [Charles] Roland of the 99th [U.S. Army Division] put it best: "Our accomplishments in this action were largely the result of small, virtually independent and isolated units fighting desperately for survival. They present an almost-**unprecedented** example of courage, resourcefulness, and **tenacity**..."* (originally quoted in an interview with Stephen Ambrose, January 17, 1995). (Ambrose, pp. 205-09)

What happened next . . .

The Allied forces rallied and fought back. Their mission was to close the 40-mile-deep bulge in the Ardennes—all the while facing bad weather, rough terrain, and the unbelievable power of German "Tiger" tank warfare. Belgian citizens aided the Allied effort in small but invaluable ways–repairing blown truck tires, housing soldiers, even donating family linens for troops to drape over equipment as winter camouflage.

In the struggle for the key city of Bastogne in the Ardennes, German forces sought the surrender of American General Anthony McAuliffe of the 101st Airborne Division. His response to the proposal for surrender was just one word: "Nuts!" With the rest of General Patton's American force fighting in the South and General Bernard Montgomery's British force in the North, the Allies joined together and succeeded in driving the Germans out of Belgium by the end of December.

The "bulge" in the Ardennes was eliminated by mid-January 1945. About sixteen thousand Americans died in the

Two U.S. soldiers look at dead crewmen on a snow-covered German tank.
(Reproduced by permission of the Corbis Corporation [Bellevue])

The Massacre at Malmédy

Aggressive and brutal Lieutenant Colonel Jochen Peiper, commander of the First SS (*Schutzstaffel*) Panzer Division (an elite German tank division), directed a ruthless campaign westward through the Ardennes. On its way, his division overran a less-heavily armed American unit at Malmédy, a town in eastern Belgium. Somewhere between 125 and 150 Americans surrendered to the Germans. Rather than wasting time taking the prisoners to a camp, the German troops gathered the Americans together and shot them. It remains unclear whether Peiper issued a direct order for the shooting. Eighty-five of the captured Americans died in the mass execution; the rest escaped into the woods or "played dead" until the Germans moved on.

battle, and another sixty thousand were injured or captured. The Germans sustained even heavier losses.

The First American army crossed the all-important Rhine River—Germany's biggest and best natural line of defense–on March 7, 1945. Meanwhile, Soviet forces were moving in on Germany from the east. The German surrender was only two months away.

Did you know . . .

- General Dwight D. Eisenhower, the commander of Allied forces in Europe, was attending the wedding reception of one of his men in Versailles, France, on December 16, 1944. He did not learn of the German counterattack in the Ardennes until that night.

- Frostbite and trench foot (a painful foot ailment caused by exposure to cold and wetness) put more than fifteen thousand American soldiers out of commission during the Battle of the Bulge.

- Referring to the major role played by the Americans in the Allied campaign in the Ardennes, British prime minister Winston Churchill called the Battle of the Bulge "the greatest American battle of the War and . . . an ever-famous American victory."

Where to Learn More
Books

Astor, Gerald. *A Blood-Dimmed Tide: The Battle of the Bulge by the Men Who Fought It.* New York: Dell, 1994.

Blumenson, Martin. *Patton: The Man Behind the Legend.* New York: Morrow, 1994.

U.S. soldiers on their way to stop the German advance in the Ardennes. *(Reproduced by permission of the Corbis Corporation [Bellevue])*

Devaney, John. *Blood and Guts: The True Story of General George S. Patton.* New York: J. Messner, 1982.

Goldstein, Donald M., and others. *Nuts: The Battle of the Bulge.* Washington: Brassey's, 1994.

MacDonald, Charles B. *A Time for Trumpets: The Untold Story of the Battle of the Bulge.* New York: Morrow, 1985. Reprinted, 1997.

Orfalea, Gregory. *Messengers of the Lost Battalion: The Heroic 551st and the Turning of the Tide at the Battle of the Bulge.* New York: The Free Press, 1997.

Ryan, Cornelius. *A Bridge Too Far.* New York: Simon & Schuster, 1974.

Van Houten, Robert, ed. *Veterans of the Battle of the Bulge.* Paducah, KY: Turner Publishing, 1991.

Videos

Guts and Glory. "The American Experience." PBS/WGBH, 1998.

The War Chronicles: World War II. Volume 3: *Pursuit to the Rhine.* Volume 4: *The Battle of the Bulge* and *The Battle of Germany.* Produced by Lou Reda Productions. A&E Home Video Presents History Channel Video/New Video, 1995.

Web Sites

Battle of the Bulge. [Online] http://users.skynet.be/bulgecriba/battlebul. html (accessed on September 7, 1999).

Veterans of the Battle of the Bulge. [Online] http://www.battleofbulge.com/ (accessed on September 7, 1999).

Sources

Ambrose, Stephen E. *Citizen Soldiers: The U.S. Army from the Normandy Beaches to the Bulge to the Surrender of Germany.* Originally published in 1997. New York: Touchstone, 1998.

Black, Wallace B., and Jean F. Blashfield. *Battle of the Bulge.* "World War II 50th Anniversary Series." New York: Crestwood House, 1993.

Dolan, Edward F. *America in World War II: 1944.* Brookfield, CT: Millbrook Press, 1993.

Goolrick, William K., Ogden Tanner, and the editors of Time-Life Books. *The Battle of the Bulge.* "Time-Life Books World War II Series." Alexandria, VA: Time-Life Books, 1979.

E. B. Sledge

Excerpt from With the Old Breed at Peleliu and Okinawa
First published in 1981

On September 15, 1944, U.S. Marines invaded Peleliu (pronounced "PELL-eh-loo" or "PEH-lell-you"), one of the Palau Islands in the western Pacific Ocean. The Palau Islands campaign was viewed originally as a crucial stepping-stone in the liberation of the Philippines from Japan. (See box on Douglas MacArthur on p. 218–219.) The entire area was heavily defended by Japanese troops.

Peleliu was only 6 miles long and 2 miles wide, but its rugged terrain and unbearably hot climate made for a slow and miserable battle. Approximately twenty-eight thousand Americans—a combined force of marine and army divisions—participated in the brutal, bloody struggle for the island. More than eleven hundred marines were killed or wounded on the first day of fighting alone.

U.S. forces captured the island of Peleliu on October 21, 1944. The casualties suffered on both sides were staggering. When the fighting was all over, more than sixty-five hundred marines and thirty-two hundred army soldiers were dead or wounded. About eleven thousand Japanese soldiers were killed.

"Our company commander represented stability and direction in a world of violence, death, and destruction. Now his life had been snuffed out. We felt forlorn and lost. It was the worst grief I endured during the entire war."

E.B. Sledge

Eugene Bondurant Sledge (1923–), who acquired the nickname "Sledgehammer" while in the Marine Corps, was born in Mobile, Alabama, and raised in a strict household. He joined the marines at the age of nineteen and by the time he was twenty-three had witnessed many horrible things during the war. After World War II's end, following brief stints in the business world, Sledge found his niche in the fields of biology and zoology. He later became a professor of biology—with special concentration in ornithology, the study of birds—at Alabama's University of Montevallo.

Things to remember while reading excerpts from *With the Old Breed at Peleliu and Okinawa*:

- *With the Old Breed at Peleliu and Okinawa* began as a series of notes E.B. Sledge took while he was serving in the Pacific. He later pieced together his memoir to help his family understand his World War II experiences. It was Sledge's wife, Jeanne, who convinced him that his work should be published.

- Sledge was a member of Company K, Third Battalion, Fifth Regiment of the First Marine Division-K/3/5 for short. The Fifth Marine Regiment is known as the "Old Breed" because it fought in all of the nation's major wars in the twentieth century.

- In the preface to *With the Old Breed*, Sledge noted that the marines "suffered and . . . did their duty so a sheltered homeland [could] enjoy the peace that was purchased at such a high cost." The following excerpt is taken from Part I of Sledge's book, subtitled "Peleliu: A Neglected Battle" because it remains "one of the lesser known and poorly understood battles of World War II."

- Throughout *With the Old Breed,* Sledge repeatedly refers to war in general (and, in particular, fighting on the front lines) as a terrible waste—a waste of time, of effort, of human life. His moving account of the death of Company K's commander, Captain A.A. Haldane, exemplifies this theme. For his own part, Sledge feels that he beat "the law of averages" by never getting wounded.

- Note the horrible conditions the marines were forced to endure in the Pacific. Sledge enumerates with stunning clarity the physical and psychological stresses that reduced the men to virtual savages.

- Sledge's memoir shows how difficult it was to maintain faith, decency, honor, and compassion in the midst of a vicious war.

Excerpt from With the Old Breed at Peleliu and Okinawa

*[Sergeant] Johnny Marmet came striding down the incline of the valley to meet us as we started up. Even before I could see his face clearly, I knew from the way he was walking that something was dreadfully **amiss**. He lurched up to us, nervously clutching the web strap of the submachine gun slung over his shoulder. I had never seen Johnny nervous before, even under the thickest fire, which he seemed to regard as a nuisance that interfered with his carrying out his job. . . .*

*My first thought was that the Japanese had slipped in thousands of troops from the northern **Palaus** and that we would never get off the island. . . . My imagination went wild, but none of us was prepared for what we were about to hear.*

"Howdy, Johnny," someone said as he came up to us.

*. . . "OK, you guys, OK, you guys," he repeated, obviously flustered. A couple of men exchanged quizzical glances. "The **skipper** is dead. **Ack Ack** has been killed," Johnny finally blurted out. . . .*

*I was stunned and sickened. Throwing my **ammo** bag down, I turned away from the others, sat on my helmet, and sobbed quietly . . .*

*Never in my wildest imagination had I contemplated Captain [Andrew A.] Haldane's death. We had a steady stream of killed and wounded leaving us, but somehow I assumed Ack Ack was **immortal**. Our **company** commander represented stability and direction in a world of violence, death, and destruction. Now his life had been snuffed out. We felt **forlorn** and lost. It was the worst grief I endured during the entire war. The intervening years have not lessened it any.*

. . . Johnny pulled himself together and said, "OK, you guys, let's move out." We picked up mortars and ammo bags. Feeling as though our crazy world had fallen apart completely, we trudged slowly and silently in single file up the rubble-strewn valley to rejoin Company K. . . .

Amiss: Wrong.

Palaus: The name given to a group of 100 or so islands and islets (little islands) located about 500 miles east of the Philippines in the western Pacific Ocean. Peleliu is one of the southern Palau Islands.

Skipper: A master of a ship, a captain, or a leader; Johnny Marmet is referring to the commander of the unit, Captain Haldane.

Ack Ack: Usually used to refer to "antiaircraft" fire; in this case, Ack Ack is a nickname for Haldane, whose initials were A. A. (for Andrew Allison)."

Ammo: Ammunition—rifle and machine-gun bullets, high explosive shells, grenades, bombs, etc.

Immortal: Freed from death; able to live forever.

Company: A unit of soldiers.

Forlorn: Sad, alone, and hopeless.

U.S. troops make their way across a Peleliu beach.
(Reproduced by permission of AP/Wide World Photos, Inc.)

The Stench of Battle

Johnny led us on up through a jumble of rocks on Hill 140. . . . From the rim of [the hill] the rock contours dropped away in a sheer cliff to a canyon below. No one could raise his head above the rim rock without immediately drawing heavy rifle and machine-gun fire.

The fighting around the pocket was as deadly as ever, but of a different type from the early days of the campaign. The Japanese fired few **artillery or mortar barrages,** just a few rounds at a time when assured of inflicting maximum casualties. That they usually did, and then secured the guns to escape detection. Sometimes there was an eerie quiet. We knew they were everywhere in the caves and **pillboxes.** But there was no firing in our area, only the sound of firing elsewhere. The silence added an element of unreality to the valleys. . . .

The sun bore down on us like a giant heat lamp. Once I saw a misplaced phosphorous grenade explode on the coral from the sun's intense heat. We always shaded our stacked **mortar shells** with a piece of ammo box to prevent this.

Occasional rains that fell on the hot coral merely evaporated like steam off hot pavement. The air hung heavy and muggy. Everywhere we went on the ridges the hot humid air reeked with the stench of death. A strong wind was no relief; it simply brought the horrid odor from an **adjacent** area. Japanese corpses lay where they fell among the rocks and on the slopes. It was impossible to cover them. Usually there was no soil that could be spaded over them, just the hard, jagged coral. The enemy dead simply rotted where they had fallen. . . .

It is difficult to convey to anyone who has not experienced it the ghastly horror of having your sense of smell saturated constantly with the putrid odor of rotting human flesh day after day, night after night. This was something the men of an **infantry battalion** got a horrifying dose of during a long, **protracted** battle such as Peleliu. In the tropics the dead became bloated and gave off a terrific stench within a few hours after death. . . .

Each time we moved into a different position I could determine the areas occupied by each rifle company. . . . Behind each company position lay a pile of ammo and supplies and the inevitable rows of dead under their **ponchos.** We could determine how bad that sector of the line was by the number of dead. To see them so always filled me with anger at the war and the realization of senseless waste. It depressed me far more than my own fear.

Added to the awful stench of the dead of both sides was the repulsive odor of human excrement everywhere. It was all but impossible to practice simple, elemental field sanitation on most areas of Peleliu because of the rocky surface. . . . Under normal conditions, [each man] covered his own waste with a scoop of soil. At night when he didn't dare venture out of his foxhole, he simply used an empty grenade canister or ration can, threw it out of his hole, and scooped dirt over it [the] next day if he wasn't under heavy enemy fire.

Artillery or mortar barrages: Heavy, rapid fire from assorted missiles and cannonlike weapons.

Pillboxes: A roofed concrete compartment for machine guns and antitank weapons.

Mortar shells: Missiles; hollow tubes containing explosives.

Adjacent: Nearby; lying next to.

Infantry battalion: A unit of soldiers fighting together on foot.

Protracted: Extended; prolonged.

Ponchos: A sleeveless waterproof garment shaped like a blanket with a slit in the middle for the wearer's head.

Marines on Peleliu watch as a flame thrower fires into a cave thought to be hiding Japanese soldiers. *(Reproduced by permission of the Corbis Corporation [Bellevue])*

But on Peleliu, except along the beach areas and in the swamps, digging into the coral rock was nearly impossible. Consequently, thousands of men— . . . fighting for weeks on an island two miles by six miles—couldn't practice basic field sanitation. This fundamental neglect caused an already putrid tropical atmosphere to become **inconceivably vile**. . . .

With human corpses, . . . excrement, and rotting rations scattered across Peleliu's ridges, [the blowflies on the island] were so large, so **glutted,** and so lazy that some could scarcely fly. . . . Frequently they tumbled off the side of my canteen cup into my coffee. We actually had to shake the food to dislodge the flies, and even then they sometimes refused to move. I usually had to balance my can of stew on my knee, spooning it up with my right hand while I picked the sluggish creatures off the stew with my left. . . . It was revolting, to say the least, to watch big fat blowflies leave a corpse and swarm into our **C rations.**

Even though none of us had much appetite, we still had to eat. A way to solve the fly problem was to eat after sunset or before sunrise when the insects were inactive. Chow had to be unheated then, because no **sterno tablets** or other form of light could be used after dark. It was sure to draw enemy sniper fire. . . .

I still see clearly the landscape around one particular position we occupied for several days. It was a scene of destruction and **desolation** that no fiction could invent. The area was along the southwestern border of the pocket where ferocious fighting had gone on since the second day of battle (16 September). The 1st Marines, the 7th Marines, and now the 5th Marines, all in their turn, had fought against this same section of ridges. Our exhausted battalion, **3/5,** moved into the line to relieve another slightly more exhausted battalion. It was the same old weary shuffling of one tired, **depleted** outfit into the line to relieve another whose sweating men trudged out of their positions, hollow-eyed, stooped, grimy, bearded zombies.

The Company K riflemen and machine gunners climbed up the steep ridge and into the crevices and holes of the company we relieved. Orders were given that no one must look over the crest of the ridge, because enemy rifle and machine-gun fire would kill instantly anyone who did.

As usual the troops pulling out gave our men **"the dope"** on the local conditions: what type fire to expect, particular danger spots and possible **infiltration routes** at night.

. . . When . . . we came closer to the gun pit to set up our mortar, I saw [that the pit's] white coral sides and bottom were spattered and smeared with the dark red blood of . . . two comrades.

After we got our gun **emplaced,** I collected up some large scraps of cardboard from ration and ammo boxes and used them to cover the bottom of the pit as well as I could. Fat, lazy blowflies were reluctant to leave the blood-smeared rock.

Inconceivably vile: Incredibly disgusting; repulsive beyond belief.

Glutted: Filled with more than enough food.

C rations: Canned food consumed by American soldiers in the field.

Sterno tablets: Pellets used for heating up food.

Desolation: Misery; sorrow; loneliness.

3/5: 3d Battalion, 5th Regiment.

Depleted: Reduced in number; drained; exhausted.

The dope: Inside information; "the scoop."

Infiltration routes: Gaps in the American line through which Japanese troops could enter to launch a surprise attack.

Emplaced: Put in position.

Peleliu was only 6 miles long and 2 miles wide, but its rugged terrain and unbearably hot climate made for a slow and miserable battle. More than eleven hundred marines were killed or wounded on the first day of fighting alone. *(Photograph by Cpl. H. H. Clements. Reproduced by permission of the Corbis Corporation [Bellevue])*

*I had long since become used to the sight of blood, but the idea of sitting in that bloodstained gun pit was a bit too much for me. It seemed almost like leaving our dead unburied to sit on the blood of a fellow Marine spilled out on the coral. . . . As I looked at the stains . . . I recalled some of the **eloquent** phrases of politicians and newsmen about how "**gallant**" it is for a man to "shed his blood for his country," and "to give his life's blood as a sacrifice," and so on. The words seemed so ridiculous. Only the flies benefited. (Sledge, pp. 140-46)*

What happened next . . .

U.S. troops landed on Iwo Jima on February 19, 1945, and on Okinawa on April 1, 1945. Both islands were seen as critical locations that would serve as key launching points for

Eloquent: Artfully expressed.

Gallant: Brave and self-sacrificing.

the Allied invasion of the Japanese home islands. (The Allies were the countries fighting against Germany, Italy and Japan. They included the United States, Great Britain, Canada, France, the Soviet Union, and China.)

Sledge and the rest of K/3/5 fought in the costly battle for Okinawa, the largest of the Ryukyu (pronounced "ree-YOU-kyew") Islands, located about 350 miles south of the Japanese main islands. All together, about 186,000 U.S. troops engaged in the 82 days of fighting, which was heaviest on the southern part of the island. To Sledge, Okinawa was "the most ghastly corner of hell" he had ever seen. More than one hundred thousand Japanese were determined to defend it to the death.

U.S. naval ships shelled a long stretch of beach on the southwestern part of the island in preparation for the landing of marine and army troops on April 1. Japanese forces remained hidden for days before beginning their counterattack. Then, thousands of heavily armed troops emerged from

Medics prepare wounded soldiers for evacuation from Peleliu. *(Reproduced by permission of the Corbis Corporation [Bellevue])*

E.B. Sledge in Okinawa.
(© 1990 Oxford University Press. Originally published by Presidio Press © 1981)

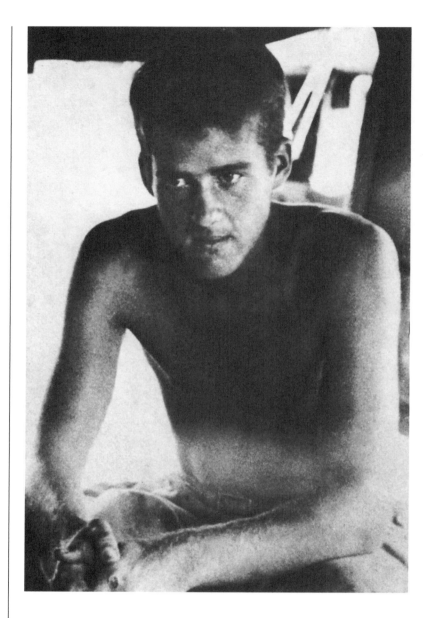

their underground hiding places to fight off the advancing Americans. Later, kamikazes (pronounced "kahm-ih-KAH-zeez"; translated as "divine winds") blasted the U.S. fleet in Okinawa's coastal waters. (Kamikazes were suicide bombers—Japanese pilots who purposely crashed their planes into Allied ships, knowing that the planes would explode in the attack and they would surely die.)

The battle continued for almost three months. One in three marines who fought on Okinawa died or was wounded. Nearly seventy-seven hundred men of the First Marine Division were killed, wounded, or listed as missing. Thousands of soldiers suffered psychological as well as physical wounds. The fighting continued until the third week in June, when Japanese troops began to surrender.

U.S. landings on Kyushu (one of the four main Japanese islands) were scheduled for November of 1945, but the war ended in September after atomic bombs were dropped on the Japanese cities of Hiroshima and Nagasaki. (See Harry S. Truman excerpt concerning the Manhattan Project and the Rodney Barker excerpt from *The Hiroshima Maidens: A Story of Courage, Compassion, and Survival* in chapter three for more information concerning the atomic bomb.)

Germany surrendered to the Allies on May 8, 1945. Sledge was still on Okinawa at the time. "We were told this momentous news, but considering our own peril and misery, no one cared much," admitted Sledge in *With the Old Breed*. "Nazi Germany might as well have been on the moon."

Japan followed suit, surrendering on August 14, 1945. This move, according to Sledge, made "the seizure of Peleliu . . . of questionable necessity."

Did you know . . .

- Of the 235 marines of K/3/5 who fought on Peleliu, only 85 made it through the battle without physical injury.

- The battle for Peleliu marked a turning point for the Japanese military. Japanese fighting tactics changed radically during this campaign. Instead of concentrating all their power on the defense of Peleliu's beaches, the soldiers spread out and fought from fortified positions in caves throughout the island. The Japanese would use—and refine—these same methods in the fights for Iwo Jima and Okinawa.

- Between March 26 and June 22, 1945, approximately fifteen hundred kamikaze attacks were launched against American ships around Okinawa.

American ships and supplies pour into Okinawa after U.S. troops captured the island. (*Reproduced by permission of AP/Wide World Photos, Inc.*)

For More Information

Books

Astor, Gerald. *Operation Iceberg: The Invasion and Conquest of Okinawa in World War II.* New York: Dell, 1996.

Fahey, James J. *Pacific War Diary: 1942-1945.* New York: Macmillan, 1993.

Videos

Okinawa. Columbia, 1952.

The War Chronicles: World War II. Volume 6: *Air War in the Pacific* and *The Bloody Ridges of Peleliu.* Volume 7: *Okinawa . . . The Last Battle.* Produced by Lou Reda Productions. A&E Home Video Presents History Channel Video/New Video, 1995.

Web Sites

World War II in the Pacific. [Online] http://www.cybertours.com/~awriter/wwii.htm (accessed on September 7, 1999).

Sources

Black, Wallace B., and Jean F. Blashfield. *Iwo Jima and Okinawa.* "World War II 50th Anniversary Series." New York: Crestwood House, 1993.

Dolan, Edward F. *America in World War II: 1945.* Brookfield, CT: Millbrook Press, 1994.

Sledge, E.B. *With the Old Breed at Peleliu and Okinawa..* Novato, CA: Presidio Press, 1981. Reprinted with a new introduction by Paul Fussell. New York: Oxford University Press, 1990.

Harry S. Truman

*Statements on the Surrender of Germany
and the Surrender of Japan*

**Transcribed and published in the *New York Times*,
May 9, 1945 and September 2, 1945
Both speeches reprinted in *Memoirs by Harry S. Truman*,
Volume 1: *Year of Decisions*, 1955**

Franklin D. Roosevelt, who was president of the United States through most of the war, died on April 12, 1945 and vice president Harry S. Truman took office. At the time, Germany was quickly retreating from Allied forces on both the western and eastern fronts. The Allies on the western front consisted of troops from the United States, Great Britain, France, and Canada. After the Normandy invasion the Allies made their way across France and Belgium, pushing the Germans eastward. (See the Veterans of D-Day and Stephen E. Ambrose entries in chapter four for more information on the Normandy invasion and the Battle of Normandy.)

On the eastern front the armies of the Soviet Union were pushing the Germans westward. Germany and the Soviet Union had been fighting for control of Soviet territory since June 1941, when Germany invaded its former ally. (See Adolf Hitler entry in chapter one for more information on the German invasion of the Soviet Union.) Germany was being squeezed between the Allied forces on the two fronts and being pushed back into its own territory. By the end of April 1945, Soviet troops were within the city limits of Germany's capital city, Berlin. On April 30, unable to face defeat, German

"Our rejoicing is sobered and subdued by a supreme consciousness of the terrible price we have paid to rid the world of [German leader Adolf] Hitler and his evil band."

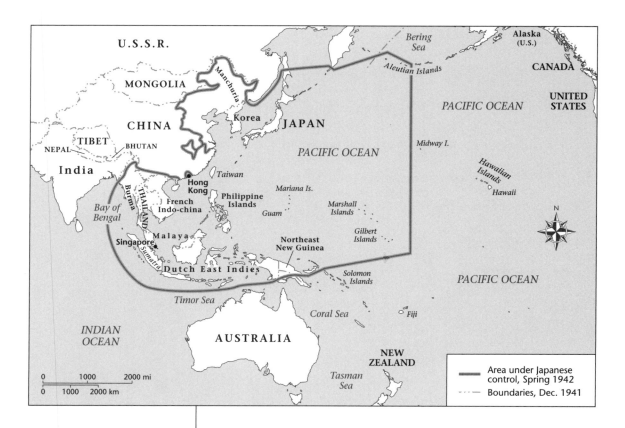

Territory under Japanese control in spring 1942.

leader Adolf Hitler committed suicide in an underground bunker in Berlin. On May 8, 1945, Germany surrendered to the Allied forces.

But World War II was far from over. The Allies were still fighting the Japanese in the Pacific. Japan had conquered a vast territory in the islands of the Pacific Ocean, beginning with Japan's invasion of an American naval base in Pearl Harbor, Hawaii, in December 1941. By the summer of 1942 American troops were pushing the Japanese back, working their way from Australia northward and from the Hawaiian Islands westward. For three years American troops landed on island after tiny island in the Pacific, slowly making their way toward Japan. When the war in Europe ended in May 1945, American forces were in the middle of the largest of these island battles, on Okinawa. They captured Okinawa at the end of June and were then only 400 miles from Japan. (See Franklin D. Roosevelt entry in chapter one and E. B. Sledge entry in chapter four for more information about the war with the Japanese.)

America's next move was to invade Japan's home islands. American war planners believed the invasion would be very difficult and many lives would be lost. Japanese troops had fought very hard in the Pacific and the planners felt that Japanese troops would fight even harder for their home islands. If Allied forces took casualties at the same rate during an invasion of the main Japanese islands as they had on Okinawa, hundreds of thousands would be killed or wounded.

Rather than send America's troops into another vicious battle, President Harry S. Truman decided to use the newly developed atomic bombs to try to force the Japanese to surrender. (See Harry S. Truman entry concerning the Manhattan Project in chapter three for more information about the atomic bomb project.) On August 6, 1945, the American bomber the *Enola Gay* dropped an atomic bomb on Hiroshima, utterly destroying the city and killing approximately seventy-eight thousand people. When on August 9 the Japanese still had not surrendered the United States dropped another bomb on the Japanese city of Nagasaki. The top Japanese and military leaders still did not want to surrender. The Japanese government argued over the matter until August 15, when the emperor made the difficult decision, and announced that Japan would surrender unconditionally to the Allies.

Things to remember while reading Truman's statements on the surrender of Germany and Japan:

- In late July 1943, shortly after the Allied invasion of Sicily, Italian leader Benito Mussolini was forced to resign. (Marshal Pietro Badoglio then became premier of Italy and governed the nation in conjunction with its king, Victor Emmanuel III, until 1946.) For about a year and a half Mussolini led a German-backed "puppet" government that operated out of northern Italy. On April 28, 1945 he was captured by his enemies in Italy and killed. Two days later German leader Adolf Hitler reportedly committed suicide in his underground bunker as Soviet forces moved into the German capital of Berlin.

- Soviet troops fought their way through Poland, Hungary, Austria, and finally all the way to Berlin. On May 2, 1945 the German troops in Italy surrendered. That same day the capital city of Berlin surrendered to the Soviets. Germany surrendered to the Allies on May 8. When the fighting in Europe was over, the Soviet Union joined in the war against Japan, hoping to claim territory in postwar Asia.

- U.S. general Douglas MacArthur was appointed Supreme Allied Commander and received the Japanese surrender on September 2, 1945. The proceedings took place on board the battleship USS *Missouri* as it floated in Tokyo Bay. Representing the conquered nation were Mamoru Shigemitsu, the Japanese foreign minister, and Yoshijiro Umeza, the chief of the Japanese imperial staff. Both men signed the surrender documents. Then, representatives of the Allied nations added their signatures. MacArthur was the last to sign his name.

Truman's Statement on the German Surrender, May 8, 1945

Excerpted from Memoirs by Harry S. Truman, *Volume 1:* Year of Decisions

*This is a **solemn** but glorious hour. General [Dwight D.] Eisenhower informs me that the forces of Germany have surrendered to the **United Nations**. The flags of freedom fly all over Europe.*

*For this victory, we join in offering our thanks to the **Providence** which has guided and sustained us through the dark days of adversity. Our rejoicing is **sobered** and **subdued** by a **supreme consciousness** of the terrible price we have paid to rid the world of [German leader Adolf] Hitler and his evil **band**. Let us not forget, my fellow Americans, the sorrow and the heartache which today abide in the homes of so many of our neighbors—neighbors whose most **priceless possession** has been **rendered** as a sacrifice to **redeem** our liberty.*

*We can repay the debt which we owe our God, to our dead, and to our children, only by work, by ceaseless devotion to the responsibilities which lie ahead of us. If I could give you a single **watchword** for the coming months, that word is work, work and more work. We must work to finish the war. Our victory is only half over. (Truman, pp. 206-8)*

Solemn: Serious.

United Nations: Also referred to as the U.N.; an international peacekeeping organization formed in the spring of 1945 by representatives of fifty countries.

Providence: God; or an all-powerful force that guides human destiny.

Sobered: Made serious or thoughtful.

Subdued: Reduced in intensity.

Supreme consciousness: Final realization or knowledge.

Band: Group; followers.

Priceless possession: Truman is referring to the lives of loved ones who died fighting the war.

Rendered: Given.

Redeem: Get or win back.

Watchword: Motto or guiding principle.

Truman's Statement on the Japanese Surrender, September 2, 1945

Excerpted from Memoirs by Harry S. Truman, *Volume 1:* Year of Decisions

My fellow Americans, the thoughts and hopes of all America—indeed of all the civilized world—are centered tonight on the battleship Missouri. *There on that small piece of American soil anchored in Tokyo Harbor the Japanese have just officially laid down their arms. They have signed terms of an unconditional surrender.*

Four years ago the thoughts and fears of the whole civilized world were centered on another piece of American soil—Pearl Harbor. The mighty threat to **civilization** *which began there is now laid to rest. It was a long road to Tokyo—and a bloody one.*

We shall not forget Pearl Harbor.

The Japanese **militarists** *will not forget the U.S.S.* Missouri.

General Douglas MacArthur signs the Japanese surrender documents aboard the USS *Missouri.* *(Reproduced by permission of the National Archives and Records Administration)*

Civilization: A world of order and cultural development.

Militarists: Those who advocate the use of aggressive warfare or combat to reach their goals.

GIs in a prisoner of war camp celebrate Japan's surrender. *(Reproduced by permission of the National Archives and Records Administration)*

War lords: Supreme military leaders.

Impotent: Lacking power or strength.

Tyranny: Oppressive power; a cruel and unjust government.

The evil done by the Japanese **war lords** can never be repaired or forgotten. But their power to destroy and kill has been taken from them. Their armies and what is left of their navy are now **impotent**.

To all of us there comes first a sense of gratitude to Almighty God who sustained us and our Allies in the dark days of grave danger, who made us . . . grow from weakness into the strongest fighting force in history, and who now has seen us overcome the forces of **tyranny** that sought to destroy His civilization. . . .

Our first thoughts, of course—thoughts of gratefulness and deep obligation—go out to those of our loved ones who have been killed or maimed in this terrible war. On land and sea and in the air, American men and women have given their lives so that this day of ultimate victory might come and assure the survival of a civilized world. . . .

We think of those whom death in this war has hurt, taking from them husbands, sons, brothers and sisters whom they loved. No victory can bring back the faces they longed to see.

Only the knowledge that the victory, which these sacrifices made possible, will be wisely used can give them any comfort. It is our responsibility—ours, the living—to see to it that this victory shall be a monument worthy of the dead who died to win it.

*We think of all the millions of men and women in our armed forces and merchant marine all over the world who, after years of sacrifice and hardship and **peril**, have been spared by Providence from harm.*

We think of all the men and women and children who during these years have carried on at home, in lonesomeness and anxiety.

Our thoughts go out to the millions of American workers and businessmen, to our farmers and miners—to all who have built up this country's fighting strength, and who have shipped to our Allies the means to resist and overcome the enemy. . . .

*And our thoughts go out to our **gallant** Allies in this war; to those who resisted the invaders; to those who were not strong enough to hold out, but who nevertheless kept the fires of resistance alive within the souls of their people; to those who stood up against great odds and held the line, until the United Nations together were able to supply the arms and the men with which to overcome the forces of evil.*

This is a victory of more than arms alone. This is a victory of liberty over tyranny.

From our war plants rolled the tanks and planes which blasted their way to the heart of our enemies; from our shipyards sprang the ships which bridged all the oceans of the world for our weapons and supplies; from our farms came the food and fibre for our armies and navies and for our Allies in all the corners of the earth; from our mines and factories came the raw materials and the finished products which gave us the equipment to overcome our enemies.

But back of it all were the will and spirit and determination of a free people—who know what freedom is, and who know that it is worth whatever price they had to pay to preserve it.

Peril: Danger.

Gallant: Brave; self-sacrificing.

Douglas MacArthur

Douglas MacArthur (1880-1964), the son of Captain Arthur MacArthur and Mary Pinkney MacArthur, was born January 26, 1880, in Little Rock, Arkansas. His family believed in the importance of a strong national military, and these beliefs rubbed off on young Douglas. Douglas's older brother, Arthur, attended the U.S. Naval Academy in Annapolis, Maryland. Douglas himself graduated from the Texas Military Academy in 1897, then went on to attend the prestigious U.S. Military Academy at West Point, New York. Gifted with an almost photographic memory, he excelled in his studies and ranked first in the academy's class of 1903.

During World War I (1914-18) MacArthur served as chief of staff of the 42nd "Rainbow" Division, which fought with the French against the Germans in France. After the war, he accepted the post of superintendent of West Point. He was promoted to the rank of brigadier general in 1920.

MacArthur served in the Philippines as a military adviser in the mid-1930s. Then, in 1941—the year the United States entered World War II—he commanded U.S. Army Forces in the Far East, leading both American and Filipino soldiers in the fight for the Philippine Islands. In March 1942 U.S. president Franklin D. Roosevelt ordered MacArthur to leave the Philippines and establish headquarters in Australia, prompting the general make his often-quoted promise to the Philippine people: "I shall return."

As commander of the Allied forces in the Southwest Pacific, MacArthur oversaw the capture of a series of Pacific islands north of Australia for the rest of 1942 and all of 1943. He was able to return to the Philippines in October of 1944, thus fulfilling his pledge to return and liberate the Philippines from the Japanese.

The U.S. Army landed on Leyte, in the central Philippines, on October 20, 1944. Americans defeated the Japanese Fleet in the

Invincible: Unconquerable.

V-J Day: Victory over Japan Day, celebrated on September 2.

Consecration: Being dedicated to a sacred purpose.

*It was the spirit of liberty which gave us our armed strength and which made our men **invincible** in battle. We now know that that spirit of liberty, the freedom of the individual, and the personal dignity of man are the strongest and toughest and most enduring forces in the world.*

*And so on **V-J Day**, we take renewed faith and pride in our own way of life. We have had our day of rejoicing over this victory. We have had our day of prayer and devotion. Now let us set aside V-J Day as one of renewed **consecration** to the principles which have made us*

Battle for Leyte Gulf, which raged between October 23 and October 26. By January, U.S. troops were landing at Luzon, the largest of the Philippine Islands, where fighting continued for six more months. The Allies were victorious, and the Philippines were finally freed from Japanese control. MacArthur, by this time a five-star general, won the Congressional Medal of Honor for his role in the defense of the Philippines.

On September 2, 1945, on board the battleship *Missouri*, MacArthur accepted the surrender of the Japanese nation. World War II had reached its official end. MacArthur then served as supreme commander overseeing postwar Japan and ruling its eighty-three million citizens.

When the Korean War (1950-53) broke out in 1950, MacArthur commanded the United Nations troops defending South Korea. (The civil war in Korea began when Communist North Korean troops crossed the 38th Parallel—a predetermined dividing line separating the nation's northern and southern sections—and entered non-Communist South Korea. Communism is a system of government in which the state controls the means of production and the distribution of goods. It clashes with the American ideal of capitalism, which is based on private ownership and a free market system.) MacArthur was fired by President Harry S. Truman in April 1951 after organizing an unauthorized move into China from Korea.

Throughout a military career that spanned fifty years, Douglas MacArthur earned a reputation as a difficult man. An unquestionably bold and gutsy military leader, he was also arrogant, temperamental, and even a bit eccentric: he reportedly had a fifteen-foot-long mirror installed in his office so he could be seen from all angles of the room. MacArthur, one of the most controversial and compelling American figures of the World War II era, died April 5, 1964, at the age of eighty-four.

the strongest nation on earth and which, in this war, we have striven so mightily to preserve.

. . . . Liberty . . . has provided more solid progress and happiness and decency for more people than any other philosophy of government in history. And this day has shown again that it provides the greatest strength and the greatest power which man has ever reached.

. . . We face the future and all its dangers with great confidence and great hope. America can build for itself a future of

employment and security. Together with the United Nations, it can build a world of peace founded on justice and fair dealing and tolerance. . . .

From this day we move forward. We move toward a new era of security at home. With the other United Nations we move toward a new and better world of peace and international goodwill and cooperation.

God's help has brought us to this day of victory. With His help we will attain that peace and prosperity for ourselves and all the world in the years ahead. (Truman, pp.460-63)

What happened next . . .

Germany and Japan were occupied by Allied armies, and key decisions were made about the territorial division of postwar Europe. General MacArthur oversaw the occupation of Japan. Its military was disarmed and work began on the formation of a new constitution.

Did you know . . .

- The Japanese lived and fought by a code of honor. Members of Japan's military considered dying in war a glorious end; they dedicated their lives—and deaths—to their emperor, Hirohito (1901-1989).

- In August 1945 Emperor Hirohito proclaimed that Japan was ready to stop the fighting and accept the terms of the Potsdam Declaration, provided the Allies allowed him to remain as sovereign ruler. Japan's military leaders wanted to continue the fight, but Hirohito felt that surrender was the only way to save the Japanese nation from complete destruction. In his radio broadcast to the Japanese regarding the surrender, he urged his people to "unite" their "total strength to be devoted to the construction for the future." Prior to this broadcast, the citizens of Japan had never heard Hirohito's voice.

✦ Major Conferences of World War II

CONFERENCE NAME	DATE HELD	AGREEMENTS MADE
Casablanca	January 1943	Set date for invasion of Sicily (1943) but put off invasion of France (the Normandy invasion) until 1944; announced policy of "unconditional surrender" for Axis nations.
Teheran	November 1943	Set tentative date of Western European invasion (the Normandy invasion; Operation Overlord) for May of 1944.
Yalta	February 1945	Scheduled first United Nations conference. Established postwar goals regarding future forms of government in Germany and the rest of Europe.
Potsdam	July 1945	Finalized the Potsdam Declaration and the policy on German reparations. The Soviet Union agreed to enter the war against Japan.

- An estimated fifty million people—fourteen million of them in the military—died during the course of World War II.

For More Information
Books

Mee, Charles L., Jr. *Meeting at Potsdam*. New York: M. Evans & Co., 1975.

Wheeler, Keith, and the editors of Time-Life Books. *The Fall of Japan*. "Time-Life Books World War II Series." Alexandria, VA: Time-Life Books, 1983.

Videos

MacArthur. Parts I and II. Narrated by David Ogden Stiers. "The American Experience." PBS/WGBH, 1999.

The War Chronicles: World War II. Volume 7: *The Return to the Philippines*. Produced by Lou Reda Productions. A&E Home Video Presents History Channel Video/New Video, 1995.

Web Sites

The Avalon Project. *German Act of Military Surrender; May 8, 1945.* [Online] http://www.yale.edu/lawweb/avalon/wwii/gs7.htm (accessed on September 7, 1999).

Sources

Darby, Jean. *Douglas MacArthur.* Minneapolis: Lerner Publications, 1989.

Dolan, Edward F. *America in World War II: 1944.* Brookfield, CT: Millbrook Press, 1993.

Dolan, Edward F. *America in World War II: 1945.* Brookfield, CT: Millbrook Press, 1994.

Dunnahoo, Terry. *Pearl Harbor: America Enters the War.* New York: F. Watts, 1991.

Feinberg, Barbara Silberdick. *Hiroshima and Nagasaki.* "Cornerstones of Freedom Series." Chicago: Children's Press, 1995.

Feis, Herbert. *The Atomic Bomb and the End of World War II.* Princeton, NJ: Princeton University Press, 1966. Originally published as *Japan Subdued,* 1961.

Freedmen, Russell. *Franklin Delano Roosevelt.* New York: Clarion Books, 1990.

Newsweek, March 8, 1999, p. 53.

New York Times, May 9, 1945, pp. 1, 6; June 2, 1945, p. 4; August 15, 1945, p. 3; September 2, 1945, p. 4.

Ross, Stewart. *World Leaders.* New York: Thomson Learning, 1993.

Sandberg, Peter Lars. *World Leaders Past and Present: Dwight D. Eisenhower.* New York: Chelsea House, 1986.

Sweeney, James B. *Army Leaders of World War II.* New York: F. Watts, 1984.

Truman, Harry S. *Memoirs by Harry S. Truman* Volume 1: *Year of Decisions.* Garden City, NY: Doubleday, 1955.

Text Credits

The editors wish to thank the copyright holders of the excerpted documents included in this volume and the permissions managers of many book and magazine publishing companies for assisting us in securing reproduction rights. What follows is a list of the copyright holders who have granted us permission to reproduce material for *World War II: Primary Sources*. Every effort has been made to trace copyright; if omissions have been made please contact the publisher.

Ambrose Stephen E. From *Citizen Soldiers.* Simon and Schuster, Inc. Copyright © 1997 by Ambrose-Tubbs, Inc. Reproduced by permission of Simon and Schuster.

Barker, Rodney. From *Hiroshima Maidens: A Story of Courage, Compassion, and Survival.* Copyright © Rodney Barker, 1985. All rights reserved. Robin Straus Agency, Inc. Reproduced by permission.

Churchill, Winston. From *Blood, Toil, Tears and Sweat: The Speeches of Winston Churchill.* Edited by David Cannadine. Copyright © 1989 by Winston S. Churchill. Reproduced by permission of Curtis Brown Ltd., London, on behalf of the Estate of Sir Winston S. Churchill.

Drez, Ronald K. From *Voices of D-Day: The Story of the Allied Invasion.* Copyright © 1994 Louisiana State University Press. Reproduced by permission.

Fessler, Diane Burke. From *No Time For Fear: Voices of American Military Nurses in World War II.* Copyright © 1996 Diane Burke Fessler. Michigan State University Press. Reproduced by permission.

From *Since You Went Away: World War II Letters from American Women on the Home Front.* Edited by Judy Barnett Litoff and David C. Smith. Copyright © 1991 by Judy Barnett Litoff and David C. Smith. Reproduced by permission of Oxford University Press, Inc.

Pyle, Ernie. From *Ernie's War.* Copyright © 1986 by David Nichols. All rights reserved. Reproduced by permission of Random House, Inc.

Sender, Ruth Minsky. From *The Cage.* Copyright © 1986 by Ruth Minsky Sender. Aladdin Paperbacks. An imprint of Simon & Schuster. All right reserved. Reproduced by permission of Simon & Schuster Books for Young Readers, an imprint of Simon & Schuster Children's Publishing Division.

Sledge, Eugene B. From *With the Old Breed: At Peleliu and Okinawa.* Copyright © 1990 Oxford University Press. Originally published by Presidio Press © 1981. Reproduced by permission.

Stanley, Jerry. From *I Am An American: A True Story of Japanese Internment.* Copyright © 1994 by Jerry Stanley. Crown Publishers, Inc. All rights reserved. Reproduced by permission.

The New York Times, October 10, 1941. Copyright © 1941 by The New York Times Co. Reproduced by permission.

Werner, Herbert A. From *Iron Coffins: A Personal Account of the German U-boat Battles of World War II.* Copyright © 1969 by Herbert A. Werner. Reproduced by permission of Henry Holt and Company. LLC.

Index

A

Allied Powers 6, 22, 45, 47, 66,
  81, 119, 123, 125, 129, 130,
  138, 140, 143, 144, 156,
  173–75, 184, 187, 193, 205,
  211, 212, 220
Ambrose, Stephen E. **187-96**
Anti-Semitism 35, 101, 102
Antwerp 187
Appeasement 5, 15
Ardennes 187–96, 189 (ill.),
  190 (ill.), 191 (ill.), 193 (ill.),
  195 (ill.)
Arizona, USS 60 (ill.), 61, 67
Army Nurse Corps (ANC) 159,
  168, 169
Athenia, 43, 44 (ill.)
Atlantic Charter 22, 23, **26–27**, 29
Atlantic Ocean 51 (map)
Atomic bomb 117–28, 121 (ill.),
  129–142, 213
Auschwitz 108, 109, 111, 112
Axis Powers 6, 60, 61, 67, 87, 143

B

Badoglio, Pietro 213
Barker, Rodney **129–42**
Bastogne, Belgium 193
Bataan 65
Battle of Midway 65, 66
Battle of Stalingrad 37, 39
Battle of the Atlantic 43–58,
  54 (ill.)
Battle of the Bulge 187–194,
  189 (ill.), 190 (ill.), 191 (ill.),
  193 (ill.), 195 (ill.)
"Be Ye Men of Valour" **11–13**
Bismarck 48, 49 (ill.)
Blitzkrieg 8, 188
"Blood, Toil, Tears and Sweat"
  10–11
Bock's Car 138
Bolshevism 38
Brokaw, Tom 87, 95
Bush, George 94

C

The Cage **104–12**
Casablanca Conference 221

Bold type indicates
main documents and
speaker profiles.

**Illustrations are marked
by (ill).**

Chamberlain, Neville 5, 15
Churchill, Winston **5–19**, 9 (ill.),
    18 (ill.), **21–30**, 26 (ill.), 44,
    55, 56 (ill.), 78, 119, 120,
    123, 140, 194
Citizen Soldiers **188–92**
Communism 38, 39, 123, 219
Concentration camps 103, 112,
    113 (ill.), 114
Convoys 44–46, 48
Cousins, Norman 139
Czechoslovakia 31, 102

D

Danzig 32
"A Date Which Will Live in
    Infamy" **62–64**
D-Day 173–86, 178 (ill.),
    180 (ill.), 184 (ill.)
"The Death of Captain Waskow"
    147–51
Death camps 103, 112
Deportation, of Jews 102–12,
    106 (ill.)
Desert Fox *see* Erwin Rommel
Discrimination 85–95, 86 (ill.)
Donitz, Karl 45

E

Einstein, Albert 124 (ill.), 126
Eisenhower, Dwight David 174,
    181 (ill.),182, 183, 185, 194
Enola Gay 130, 131, 131 (ill.), 213
*Ernie's War: The Best of Ernie Pyle's
    World War II Dispatches*
    147–155
Europe, borders before WWII
    8 (map)
Executive Order 8802 81
Executive Order 9066 86, 87

F

Fair Employment Practices Act 82
Fairall, Evangeline Bakke 164–66
"Fat Man" 118, 121 (ill.),
    126, 138
Federation of American
    Scientists 141
Fermi, Enrico 118, 126

Fifth Marine Regiment 198
Final Solution 102, 103
First Marine Division 198
First SS Panzer Division 194
442nd Regimental Combat Team
    94, 94 (ill.)

G

Gas chambers 103, 105 (ill.)
Gold Beach 174
Grafenort 112
Great Depression 6, 25, 71
Groves, General Leslie R. 118
Guadalcanal 66
Guam 61, 65

H

Hibakusha 132, 135 (ill.), 136,
    137 (ill.), 138
Hiroshima, Japan 123, 125,
    130–142, 137 (ill.), 213
*The Hiroshima Maidens: A Story of
    Courage, Compassion, and
    Survival* 131 (ill.) **133–38**
Hiroshima Peace Memorial 141
Hitler, Adolf 5, 6, 21, 25, 28 (ill.),
    31–41, 32 (ill.), 101, 102,
    140, 213
"Hitler's Order of the Day to the
    German Troops on the
    Eastern Front" **34–37**
Hoftiezer, Myrtle Brethouwer
    166–67
Holocaust 35, 101–16, 105 (ill.),
    106 (ill.), 113 (ill.)
The Holocaust Lady 109
Home front 69–85
Hood 46, 46 (ill.), 48
Hoover, Herbert 24, 25
Hull, Cordell 62, 64

I

*I Am an American: A True Story of
    Japanese Internment* **89–92**
"I Thought It Was the End"
    151–52
Ie Shima 146, 149
Inouye, Daniel 94
Internment camps 85–95, 93 (ill.)

Iron Coffins: A Personal Account of the German U-Boat Battles of World War II **48–55**
Isolationism 21
Italy 144, 147–52, 150 (ill.), 156
Iwo Jima 119–20, 144–45, 145 (ill.), 204

J

Japan 119, 129–32, 130 (map), 144–46, 54 (map)
Japanese Americans 85–95, 86 (ill.), 88 (ill.), 90 (ill.)
Juno Beach 174

K

Kamikaze 119, 140, 146, 206
Korean War (1950–53) 123, 219
Kretschmer, Otto 55
Kriegsmarine 44, 45

L

Lend–Lease Act (March 1941) 23, 24
Lenin, Vladimir 38
"Little Boy" 118, 121 (ill.), 126, 131, 138
London, evacuation 16 (ill.)
Los Alamos, New Mexico 118
Luftwaffe 144, 173

M

MacArthur, Douglas 214, 215 (ill.) 218–220
Manhattan Project 117–28
Manzanar (California internment camp) 89–93, 93 (ill.)
Marx, Karl 38
Marxism 38, 39
Massacre at Malmédy 194
McAuliffe, Anthony 193
Memoirs by Harry S. Truman Volume 1: Year of Decisions **120–25, 214–20**
Missouri, USS 214
Montgomery, Bernard 146, 174, 193
Mount Suribachi 145, 145 (ill.)
Mussolini, Benito 21, 28 (ill.), 213

N

Nagasaki, Japan 123, 125, 126, 130, 136, 138, 139 (ill.), 140, 213
National Socialist German Workers' Party 5, 27
Nationalism 5, 35
Nazi Party 5–6, 27, 35, 37, 101–02
Nazi-Soviet Nonaggression Pact (1939) 6, 17, 22, 32
Nevada, USS 61
New Deal 25
Newfoundland 22
Niimoto, Shigeko 133, 136–38, 139
No Time for Fear: Voices of American Military Nurses in World War II **161–67**
Nomuri, Shiro 89–92
Normandy, France 156, 173–86, 176 (map), 180 (ill.), 184 (ill.), 188
North Africa 143
"Notes from a Battered Country" **147**
Nuclear energy 117, 126
Nurses **159–69**, 160 (ill.), 163 (ill.), 167 (ill.), 168 (ill.)

O

Office of Price Administration (OPA) 72
Okinawa 119, 120, 145, 146, 153 (ill.), 156 (map), 204–07, 208 (ill.), 212
Omaha Beach 174, 176, 184, 184 (ill.), 185
"On Victory in Europe" **155**
101st Airborne Division 188, 193
116th Infantry Regiment of the 29th Division 174, 176
Operation Barbarossa 33, 36 (ill.)
Operation Overlord 174–85, 178 (ill.), 180 (ill.), 184 (ill.)
Oppenheimer, J. Robert 118
"Order of the Day to the German Troops on the Eastern Front" **34–37**

P

Pacific Theater 212 (map)
Palau 197
Paris, France 187
Patton, George S. 146, 174, 188
Pearl Harbor 26, 37, 59–68, 63 (ill.)
    78, 85, 94, 118, 140, 212
Peiper, Jochen 194
Peleliu 197–204, 200 (ill.),
    205 (ill.), 207
Perkins, Frances 28
Philippines 61, 65, 218, 219
Pike, Catherine "Renee" Young
    71–84
Poland 7, 7 (ill.), 31–32
Poliomyelitis, Franklin D.
    Roosevelt contracts 24
Potsdam Conference 119, 123,
    140, 221
Potsdam Declaration 125,
    130, 221
Prien, Günther 44, 55
Prisoners of war (POWs) 161, 168,
    191 (ill.), 216 (ill.)
Pyle, Ernie **143–57**, 148 (ill.)

R

Racism 82, 85, 87, 91, 94, 169
Radiation sickness 136
Raffa, Margaret Richey 162–64
Rationing 72–74, 73 (ill.)
Recycling 76 (ill.)
Relocation 85–95, 86 (ill.),
    88 (ill.), 90 (ill.)
Rhine River 194
Rommel, Erwin 173, 176
Roosevelt, (Anna) Eleanor 24, 78
Roosevelt, Franklin D. **21–30**,
    23 (ill.), 26 (ill.), 46, **59–68**,
    65 (ill.), 71, 78, 82, 86,
    122, 126
Royal Air Force (RAF) 17, 173
Royal Canadian Air Force 56 (ill.)
Russian Revolution of 1917 38
Ryukyu Islands 205

S

Saving Private Ryan 185
Schutzstaffel 112, 114
Segregation in the armed forces

91, 94, 169
Sender, Ruth Minsky **101–16**
Shurr, Agnes 161–62
Sicily 144
*Since You Went Away: World War II
    Letters from American Women
    on the Home Front* **74–81**
Sledge, E. B. **197–209**, 206 (ill.)
Solomon Islands 66
SS 112, 114
Stalin, Joseph 10, 33, 38–39,
    39 (ill.), 119, 120, 123, 140
Stanley, Jerry **85–95**
Submarines 43–58, 52 (ill.)
Sudetenland 31, 102
Suribachi, Mount 145, 145 (ill.)
Surrender, of Germany 214–15
Surrender, of Japan 215–20,
    215 (ill.), 216 (ill.)
Sword Beach 174
Szilard, Leo 126

T

Tasaka, Hiroko 133–36, 138, 139
Teheran Conference 221
"Their Finest Hour" **13–17**
Tibbets, Lieutenant Colonel Paul
    W. 131, 131 (ill.)
To Life 109
Tojo, Hideki 66, 67 (ill.)
Topp, Erich 55
Tripartite Pact (1940) 17, 28, 61
Truman Doctrine 123
Truman, Harry S. **117–28**,
    118 (ill.), 140, **211–22**
Tuskegee Airmen 91

U

U–boats 43, 45, 47, 55, 56, 61
United Kingdom 175 (map)
United Nations 23, 214, 221
United States Holocaust
    Memorial Museum
    (USHMM) 114
U.S. Pacific Fleet 61, 64
Uranium–235 118
USS *Arizona* 60 (ill.), 61, 67
USS *Missouri* 214
USS *Nevada* 61
USS *West Virginia* 61, 63 (ill.)
Utah Beach 174

V

Veterans of D-Day **173–86**
"V-for-victory" 10
Victor Emmanuel III 213
"Victory gardens" 81
"Victory tax" 72
Voices of D-Day: The Story of the Allied Invasion Told By Those Who Were There **177–84**

W

"Waiting for Tomorrow" **152–54**
Wake Island 61, 65
War bonds 72

War Relocation Authority (WRA) 87, 91
Werner, Herbert A. **43–58**
West Virginia, USS 61, 63 (ill.)
Wilson, Woodrow 24
With the Old Breed at Peleliu and Okinawa **199–204**
Wolf packs 45
Women, in U.S. workforce 72, 72 (ill.), 82, 82 (ill.)
World War I (1914–18) 6, 14, 21, 35, 122, 156

Y

Yamamoto, Isoroku 61, 68